Since the early nineteenth century, African-Americans have turned to black newspapers to monitor the mainstream media and to develop alternative interpretations of public events. Ronald Jacobs tells the stories of these newspapers, showing how they increased black visibility within white civil society and helped to form separate black public spheres in New York, Chicago and Los Angeles. Comparing African-American and "mainstream" media coverage of some of the most memorable racial crises of the last forty years such as the Watts riot, the beating of Rodney King, the Los Angeles uprising and the O. J. Simpson Trial, Jacobs shows why a strong African-American press is still needed today. *Race, Media, and the Crisis of Civil Society* challenges us to rethink our common understandings of communication, solidarity and democracy. Its engaging style and thorough scholarship will ensure its appeal to students, academics and the general reader interested in the mass media, race and politics.

RONALD N. JACOBS is Assistant Professor of Sociology at the University at Albany, State University of New York. Before moving to Albany he was an Annenberg Scholar at the Annenberg School for Communication, University of Pennsylvania. He has published extensively on the relationship between news media, culture, and democracy in *American Journal of Sociology*, *International Sociology*, *Sociological Theory*, *Media, Culture & Society*, *Real Civil Societies* and *Media, Ritual and Identity*.

DATE DUE
SUBJECT TO RECALL
AFTER 2 WEEKS

MAY 1 6 2001	
NOV 2 9 2001	
JAN 0 7 2002	
DEC 1 2 2002	
MAR 0 3 2004	
NOV 1 1 2004	
FEB 1 6 2007	

Race, Media, and the Crisis of Civil Society

Cambridge Cultural Social Studies

Series editors: JEFFREY C. ALEXANDER, *Department of Sociology, University of California, Los Angeles, and* STEVEN SEIDMAN, *Department of Sociology, University at Albany, State University of New York.*

Titles in the series

CHANDRA MUKERJI, *Territorial Ambitions and the Gardens of Versailles*
0 521 49675 6 Hardback 0 521 59959 8 Paperback

LEON H. MAYHEW, *The New Public* 0 521 48146 5 Hardback
0 521 48493 6 Paperback

VERA L. ZOLBERG AND JONI M. CHERBO (eds.), *Outsider Art*
0 521 58111 7 Hardback 0 521 58921 5 Paperback

SCOTT BRAVMANN, *Queer Fictions of the Past* 0 521 59101 5 Hardback
0 521 59907 5 Paperback

STEVEN SEIDMAN, *Difference Troubles* 0 521 59043 4 Hardback
0 521 59970 9 Paperback

RON EYERMAN AND ANDREW JAMISON, *Music and Social Movements*
0 521 62045 7 Hardback 0 521 62966 7 Paperback

MEYDA YEGENOGLU, *Colonial Fantasies* 0 521 48233 X Hardback
0 521 62658 7 Paperback

LAURA DESFOR EDLES, *Symbol and Ritual in the New Spain*
0 521 62140 2 Hardback 0 521 62885 7 Paperback

NINA ELIASOPH, *Avoiding Politics* 0 521 58293 8 Hardback
0 521 58759 X Paperback

BERNHARD GIESEN, *Intellectuals and the German Nation*
0 521 62161 5 Hardback 0 521 63996 4 Paperback

PHILIP SMITH (ed.), *The New American Cultural Sociology*
0 521 58415 9 Hardback 0 521 58634 8 Paperback

S. N. EISENSTADT, *Fundamentalism, Sectarianism and Revolution*
0 521 64184 5 Hardback 0 521 64586 7 Paperback

MARIAM FRASER, *Identity without Selfhood* 0 521 62357 X Hardback
0 521 62579 3 Paperback

LUC BOLTANSKI, *Distant Suffering* 0 521 57389 0 Hardback
0 521 65953 1 Paperback

PYOTR SZTOMPKA, *Trust* 0 521 59144 9 Hardback
0 521 59850 8 Paperback

SIMON J. CHARLESWORTH, *A Phenomenology of Working Class
Culture* 0 521 65066 6 Hardback 0 521 65915 9 Paperback

ROBIN WAGNER-PACIFICI, *Theorizing the Standoff* (2)
0 521 65244 8 Hardback 0 521 65915 9 Paperback

Race, Media, and the Crisis of Civil Society

From Watts to Rodney King

Ronald N. Jacobs

CAMBRIDGE
UNIVERSITY PRESS

PUBLISHED BY THE PRESS SYNDICATE OF THE UNIVERSITY OF CAMBRIDGE
The Pitt Building, Trumpington Street, Cambridge, United Kingdom

CAMBRIDGE UNIVERSITY PRESS
The Edinburgh Building, Cambridge CB2 2RU, UK   http://www.cup.cam.ac.uk
40 West 20th Street, New York, NY 10011–4211, USA   http://www.cup.org
10 Stamford Road, Oakleigh, Melbourne 3166, Australia

First published 2000

Printed in the United Kingdom at the University Press, Cambridge

Typeset in 10/12.5 pt Times New Roman in QuarkXPress™   [SE]

A catalogue record for this book is available from the British Library

Library of Congress cataloging in publication data

Jacobs, Ronald N.
Race, media, and the Crisis of Civil Society : from Watts to Rodney King /
Ronald N. Jacobs.
    p.   cm. – (Cambridge cultural social studies)
Includes bibliographical references and index.
ISBN 0 521 62360 X (hardback) – ISBN 0 521 62578 5 (paperback)
1. Afro-Americans and mass media – United States.   2. Mass
media and race relations – United States.   3. Afro-Americans in
mass media.   4. Afro-American press.   5. Mass Media – Social
aspects – United States.   6. United States – Race relations.   I. Title.
II. Series.
P94.5.A372   U557   2000
302.23′089′96073–dc21   00–047914

ISBN 0 521 62360 X hardback
ISBN 0 521 62578 5 paperback

Contents

Acknowledgments

I have been fortunate to have enjoyed an unusual amount of academic support and advice throughout this project. I began working on the book during my years as a graduate student at UCLA, continued it as a visiting scholar at Rice University and University of Pennsylvania, and finished it at the University at Albany, State University of New York. To all of my colleagues, I owe a tremendous debt of gratitude.

During my years at UCLA, Jeff Alexander was extraordinary as my teacher, mentor, and dissertation chair. He gave me thousands of hours of his time, discussing ideas and offering useful advice. He read every word of every draft from this project as well as others, always providing penetrating commentary and luminous critique. His exemplary embodiment of intellectual scholarship continues to serve as a model of practice for me today, as I interact with my own graduate students. Other UCLA faculty also helped me during the early stages of this project, the most important of whom were Walter Allen, Steve Clayman, and Rogers Brubaker. Finally, members of the "Culture Club" reading group at UCLA offered a supportive forum and a critical audience for thinking through new ideas and refining old ones; particular thanks are owed to Phil Smith, Steve Sherwood, Anne Kane, and Andy Roth.

My colleagues at Rice University offered a wonderfully supportive environment while I finished my dissertation. Elizabeth Long, Chandler Davidson, Steve Klineberg, and Chad Gordon made special efforts to make me feel like a member of their Sociology Department, and made funds available for travel and research.

I was most fortunate to have had the opportunity to spend a year as an Annenberg Scholar at the Annenberg School for Communication, University of Pennsylvania. Special thanks are due to Elihu Katz, the director of the program, for creating a climate of intellectual dialogue and critique. Ravina Aggarwal, Hannah Kliger, Tali Mendelberg, Jeffrey Strange, and Itzhak Roeh, the other Annenberg scholars, were stimulating colleagues who contributed mightily to the creative intellectual climate. I also thank Barbie Zelizer and Carolyn Marvin, at the Annenberg School, and Diana Crane in the Sociology Department, for helping to make Penn such a welcoming and engaging place.

My colleagues at the University at Albany have been extremely generous with their time and advice. Richard Alba, Nancy Denton, Hayward Horton, Richard Lachmann, John Logan, and Steve Messner have all discussed some of the ideas in the book with me. Steve Seidman read several chapters of the book, offering sage advice and helping me to work through some theoretical uncertainties I had been struggling with for far too long. Students who took my graduate course in Civil Society and the Public Sphere asked sharp and stimulating questions, helping me to develop a clearer sense of the project as a whole. Dan Glass and Dalia Abdel-Hady provided crucial research assistance, allowing me to complete Chapter 5 much more quickly than would have otherwise been possible.

Other colleagues have also been very generous with their time. Craig Calhoun, Margaret Cerullo, Patricia Clough, Bruce Haynes, Jim McKay, Steven Pfohl, Vincent Price, Lyn Spillman, Ken Tucker, Michael Traugott, Robin Wagner-Pacifici, and Craig Watkins have all spent time reading or discussing my analysis of race, media, and civil society. Susan Douglas and Charles Lemert read the entire book manuscript during a crucial stage in its development, offering important and valuable suggestions.

Financial assistance for this project came from a UCLA Communication Studies Fellowship, the Walter Hall Fund at Rice University, the Annenberg Scholars Program at the University of Pennsylvania, and the Faculty Research Awards Program at the University at Albany, State University of New York.

Finally, I thank Eleanor Townsley, whose contributions to this project are surpassed only by her more general impact on my happiness and well-being. Interrupting her own research more often than I deserved, she provided thoughtful criticisms at every stage of the project, coaxed me off the floor during moments of depression and frustration, and kept my life in balance.

Introduction

Los Angeles is wonderful. Nowhere in the United States is the Negro so well and beautifully housed. Out here in this matchless Southern California there would seem to be no limit to your opportunities.
(W. E. B. DuBois, 1913)

Stop your protest or we will use Los Angeles measures against you.
(Tadzhikistan police, 1992)

This book is about three disturbing events in the history of Los Angeles, and the ways in which those events were made meaningful in African-American and mainstream news media. The 1965 uprisings in Watts, the 1991 videotaped police beating of Rodney King, and the post-verdict events of 1992 have transformed the image of racial Los Angeles from one of a Utopian Oz,[1] extolled by DuBois in 1913 and named by the Urban League in 1964 as the best city for blacks to live; to a dystopian *Blade Runner*, with Los Angeles the setting for a tale of moral decay, despair, and the loss of authenticity.[2] Images of racial violence and police brutality hang heavily, casting a dark shadow over glitzy images produced in the dream factories of the City of Angels. Tourists no longer have to wonder what lies on the other side of the Hollywood sign; it is the haunting specter of racial fragmentation.

While most research on Los Angeles has focused on economic change, population shifts, and public space, this book focuses on civil society, culture, and the spaces of representation. The Watts and Rodney King crises were certainly indicative of significant structural strains which heightened racial tensions in Los Angeles and the nation. But they also provided key moments of public debate and public reflection about such heady matters as the meaning of the American dream, the promise of the civil rights movement, and the rights and responsibilities of citizenship. These crises offered social drama of the highest order to the American public. Would they end with unity or fragmentation? Trust or suspicion? An opening of social boundaries, or an increase in tribalism and other hyperactive forms of social closure? People who were otherwise disengaged from public life turned on their television sets and opened their newspapers, in the process having often heated arguments about what each crisis meant, and what should be done to resolve it. By exposing racial representations in their rawest form, the Watts and Rodney King crises changed public discussions about matters of common concern in ways which were far from trivial.

Mass media and civil society

In the social sciences, the study of public communication and democracy is coming increasingly to be framed through the twin concepts of *civil society* and *public sphere*. Civil society refers to the entire web of associational and public spaces in which citizens can have conversations with one another, discover common interests, act in concert, assert new rights, and try to influence public opinion and public policy.[3] This rather expansive definition includes the activities of social movements, voluntary associations, public relations specialists, media personalities, reading groups, and any other individuals or groups who gather together to discuss matters of common concern. It includes the pursuit of common political agendas as well as common cultural identities and solidarities. It understands that a vibrant civil society is supposed to prevent the state from dominating and atomizing the rest of society, allowing groups and communities simultaneously to resist subordination and to demand inclusion.[4] Finally, and most importantly, it binds the normative ideals of democracy to the arena of the public sphere.

The concept of the public sphere refers to a particular type of practice which takes place in civil society: the practice of open discussion about matters of common public concern. The concept owes much of its academic popularity to Habermas, and the publication of his now-classic *Structural Transformation of the Public Sphere*. Habermas wanted to explain why the normative model of politics changed, during the seventeenth and eighteenth centuries (particularly in the Anglo-American world), so that the principle of open public discussion came to replace that of parliamentary secrecy.[5] He explained this change in politics as being caused by the development of a bourgeois public sphere, which he defined as the sphere of private people come together as a public, who claimed the space of public discourse from state regulation, and demanded that the state engage them in debate about matters of political legitimacy and common concern. Envisioning the public sphere primarily as a political space that could help challenge, engage, and regulate public authorities, Habermas emphasized face-to-face communication, rational-critical discourse, and a single public arena.

More recent scholars, however, have begun to question the historical, empirical, and normative validity of a single public sphere grounded in rational-critical discourse. Instead, contemporary theorists argue that civil society consists of multiple, frequently nonrational, and often contestatory public spheres, which are oriented just as often to cultural issues as to political ones.[6] Established and maintained by communication media, these public spheres support many different (but overlapping) communities of discourse.[7] The new model of civil society that is emerging is one of a multiplicity of public spheres, communities, and associations nested within one another, most of which are also oriented (in differing degrees) to a putative larger "national sphere".[8]

In this portrait of overlapping, interconnected, and competing public spheres, which are likely to remain always fractured and disconnected in some degree or another, the mass media – and in particular, the news media – take on an ever increasing significance.[9] News media provide a common stock of information and culture, which private citizens rely on in their everyday conversations with others. Indeed, sixty-eight percent of the American public watches at least one television news program in a typical day, for an average duration of fifty-eight minutes.[10] Fifty-four percent of adults read a newspaper every day, and eighty-eight percent read the paper at least once a week.[11] This common stock of information makes intersubjectivity possible, even among those who may never come into contact with one another. By creating an open-ended space where ideas can be expressed and received by a potentially limitless and universal audience of present and non-present others, modern communications media – contrary to theories of "mass society" – have actually expanded the public sphere.[12]

If mass media have expanded the public sphere, however, they have done so in rather unexpected ways. On the one hand, they have expanded the spatial and temporal limits of public communication, creating a "global civil society" that has the potential to impact any public discussion about matters of common concern. International media events today are addressed to a fictional world audience that is believed to be an important source of international public opinion.[13] On the other hand, mass media have multiplied the number of publics immeasurably, stretching the beliefs about shared communication, so important to democracies, to the limit. Mass media serve simultaneously as forces of inclusion and exclusion, universalism and particularism, globalization and localization, integration and fragmentation, freedom and constraint. To understand their impact, they need to be located within a communicative geography of civil society.

In Chapter 1, I offer a theory about the role of news media in a civil society consisting of multiple public spheres. Recognizing that news media do not offer perfect public forums for open dialogue about matters of common concern, I argue that there are, nevertheless, many instances where news media do act as public spheres: during press conferences, interview shows, call-in shows, live broadcasts of public events, and the like. In addition, news media shape most other publics in significant ways, by defining the public agenda – a fact which leaders of social movements, voluntary associations, and other civil society organizations ignore at their peril. In order to gain a voice in the larger, more politically-consequential public spheres, these leaders must develop successful strategies for gaining media access.

In a civil society consisting of multiple publics, the media strategies of citizens, associations, and communities can be accommodated most effectively when there are both large and small news organizations. Access to large news media such as *ABC News*, the *New York Times*, and the *Los Angeles Times* is crucial for those who want to try to influence public opinion and public policy. Indeed, the lure of this kind of publicity leads many people to adapt their media strategies to the preferences and practical routines of mainstream journalism. But there are risks involved when people try to participate in large public spheres over which they have little or no control. There is no guarantee of gaining a larger public voice, and there is a danger of too much accommodation and too little cultural autonomy. Because of these risks, there is still a powerful need for smaller, more local spaces of discussion and news which offer greater autonomy and more control. This suggests that alternative media such as the African-American press have an important role to play in the creation of a more open and inclusive civil society.

If Chapter 1 provides a theoretical justification for multiple publics and multiple news media, Chapter 2 offers a more historical one, by describing the development of the African-American and mainstream press and public spheres over the last 200 years. Separate public spaces and communicative institutions formed among Northern free blacks in the 1700s; the black press was established in 1827. At least forty different black newspapers were published before the Civil War, and the establishment of a national black press was generally agreed upon as the second most pressing issue among African-American leaders. The historical need for a strong black press was three-fold: (1) to provide a forum for debate and self-improvement; (2) to monitor the mainstream press; and (3) to increase black visibility in white civil society. African-Americans could not count on the mainstream press of the time to publicize black voices or to represent black issues in a non-patronizing manner. By establishing an independent black press, African-Americans were able to secure a space of self-representation: not only to craft common identities and solidarities, but also to develop arguments which might effectively engage white civil society.

The African-American press was never intended to substitute for participation in the majority media. Rather, it was designed to encourage continuous discussion about matters of common concern, to develop arguments for later engagement in the majority public spheres, and to correct the prejudices and misrepresentations which resulted from engagement in those other public spheres. The point was to continue discussion and conversation, and to keep open the possibility of expanding the conversation to include new participants and new venues. This, after all, is the ultimate value of civil society, regardless of how many different publics compose it: to keep a conversation going, to open up ongoing dialogue to new narratives and new points of difference, and to expand the substantive content of existing solidarities.

The normative vision of the black public sphere does not map perfectly, however, onto its history. The African-American press was strongest between 1900 and 1950, during the period of forced residential segregation and mainstream press neglect. During this time the black press provided an important and powerful space for forming arguments about integration and civil rights which would later find their way into the public spaces of communication in white civil society. Thurgood Marshall summed up the power of the black press in 1954, when he remarked that "without the Negro press, the NAACP would get nowhere."[14] In a certain sense, though, it was easier for African-Americans to prioritize the black press during the first half of the twentieth century, given their near-total exclusion from the mainstream press and public spheres. Before the 1960s, fewer than one percent of journalists were African-American, and it was rare for race news to account for more than one percent of total news space in the mainstream press.[15] Quite simply, the only publicity African-American leaders could count on was that which came from the black press.

Since 1960, however, most black newspapers have seen their circulation decrease rapidly, by some fifty to seventy-five percent. This decline has a number of reasons: a more general decline in newspaper use resulting from the rise of television news; an inability of black newspapers to publish a successful daily edition (with the notable exception of the *Chicago Defender*), which became more of a problem with the fast pace of life characteristic of the modern media age; and the increased distribution costs arising from a more residentially dispersed black middle class. But in addition to these structural factors, there was another, more subjective one. Between 1950 and 1970, the attention to African-Americans and African-American issues increased dramatically in the mainstream press, as a result of the civil rights movement and the 1960s urban uprisings. With this increased visibility came an increase in participation and voice for African-American leaders desiring to speak in the mainstream media. This increased participation was limited and, as Chapter 2 shows, it has stagnated or declined ever since the early 1970s. Regardless, however, a significant minority of African-American intellectuals during the 1950s and early 1960s were beginning to believe that racial integration would remove the need for a separate black newspaper, and began arguing that the black press should fight for its own disappearance.[16]

There are new forms of black media, of course – such as talk radio, Black Entertainment Television, and Internet discussion groups – just as there are more black journalists and more black voices in the mainstream news media. But even if these new public forums were able to support a vibrant black public sphere without African-American newspapers, the loss of a vital black press would still constitute a crisis, just as the disappearance of multi-newspaper cities has been interpreted as a crisis for the mainstream press and mainstream civil society. A diversity of news media helps to guarantee a diversity of public voices, and increases the likelihood that there will be vital public debate about matters of common concern. The crisis of the black press, then, is a crisis for American civil society.

While the current crisis of the black press is largely the result of declining circulation, the actual power of the black press is not only tied directly to the number of people who read it. In addition to circulation, the potential power of the African-American press resides in the fact that people know it is there, available to be read should the need be perceived. Indeed, during periods of racial crisis, such as the Watts and Rodney King uprisings, sales of black newspapers surged, as African-Americans sought out the "black perspective," compared it with the news stories in the *New York Times*, *Los Angeles Times*, or *ABC News*, and then proceeded to have conversations. Put simply, the existence of the black press adds diversity to civil society, and offers the possibility of new forms of discussion to emerge. Alternative news media provide public forums for subordinate groups to develop arguments free of the hegemonic gaze of the dominant group. They also provide public spaces for repairing the symbolic damage which inevitably occurs with participation in the larger, mainstream media. Chapters 3, 4, and 5 support this claim about symbolic repair conclusively, as would any empirical analysis comparing African-American and mainstream media coverage of racial crises.

Comparing racial discourses in the news

Because news media are plural, the study of media discourse is best accomplished through comparative research. How does news coverage of racial crisis differ in Chicago, Los Angeles, or New York? How is race news in the mainstream press different from the African-American press? How has it changed over time? Does it matter if the events being reported took place in the geographic "home" of a newspaper and its readers? These are some of the empirical questions this book addresses, by comparing news accounts of the Watts and Rodney King crises in the African-American and mainstream news media of New York, Chicago, and Los Angeles.

Three goals motivated my selection of news sources: (1) to use the same news sources for all three racial crises; (2) to compare news coverage in different cities; and (3) to compare African-American and mainstream news coverage. Ultimately, these goals led to the selection of six newspapers as primary source material. The *Chicago Tribune, Los Angeles Times*, and *New York Times*, as the largest daily newspapers in their respective cities, were obvious choices to represent the mainstream news media. For the African-American press the choices were slightly more difficult, because circulation sizes for many African-American papers are not audited. In addition, there are very few black newspapers which are published daily. Only the *Chicago Defender,* in fact, has published a daily edition continuously between 1965 and 1992.[17] To try to equalize the comparisons of the African-American newspapers, I chose the weekly edition of the *Chicago Defender* (published Thursdays), as well as the two African-American papers regarded as the most important in New York and Los Angeles: the *New York Amsterdam News* and *Los Angeles Sentinel*, respectively. Data collection involved extensive microfilm research, as well as the use of electronic databases such as Lexis-Nexis and Ethnic Newswatch, and included the collection and analysis of every news article from the first twelve weeks of each crisis. All told, there were a total of 2269 news articles in the six newspapers.

News reports from *ABC News* were also collected, but only for the two Rodney King crises. Because transcripts of its news broadcasts are stored on the Lexis-Nexis news database, *ABC News* was the obvious choice among the television news organizations. Unfortunately, this collection of transcripts dates back only to 1990. In fact, systematic collection of television news broadcasts did not begin until 1968, with the establishment of the

Vanderbilt Television Archive. The Museum of Radio and Television only had a single television program about Watts, a one-hour news special from *NBC News*. Attempts to find complete holdings of television news about Watts proved unsuccessful, mirroring Gitlin's experiences of nearly twenty years ago.[18] Fortunately, my study of the Rodney King crises led me to the same conclusion that Gitlin had reached: namely, that the *New York Times* and network television news were similar enough to be analyzed together. This should not be surprising, of course. The *New York Times* is the only paper which can legitimately make a claim to be *the* national newspaper. It is virtually mandatory reading for the political, intellectual, and journalistic elite, and has a tremendous influence over the network television news broadcasts.[19] For these reasons, I treated the *New York Times* and *ABC News* together, as representatives of a more national news public.

In order to compare how the racial crises were reported and made meaningful in the different news media, I relied primarily on the methods of narrative analysis. As Abbott and Sewell have noted recently, narrative analysis has become an important analytical tool in the social sciences.[20] There are two main reasons for this. The first has to do with the role narrative plays in constructing identities and enabling social action. As Alexander and Smith have argued, narratives help individuals, groups, and communities to "understand their progress in time in terms of stories, plots which have beginnings, middles, and ends, heroes and anti-heroes, epiphanies and denouements, dramatic, comic, and tragic forms."[21] As studies of class formation, collective mobilization, and mass communication have demonstrated, social actions and identities are guided by narrative understandings.[22] Furthermore, by connecting their self-narratives to collective narratives, individuals can identify with such "imagined communities" as class, gender, race, ethnicity, and nation.[23] As Steinmetz has noted, these collective narratives can be extremely important for how individuals evaluate their lives, even if they did not participate in the key historical events of the collective narrative.[24]

A second useful feature of narrative for studying public communication is that it enables the analyst to consider the significance of events. Theories of civil society too often fail to consider how events have cultural significance "on their own terms."[25] Depending on how they are defined, how they are linked together in a story or plot, and what determines their selection or exclusion into a particular narrative, events can have important consequences for social identities and social actions. Some events "demand" narration and therefore have the power to disrupt prevailing systems of belief and to change understandings about other events in the past, present, and future.[26] Other events get called up from the past, pointing to a foundational point of origin for a newly mobilizing community. The point is that events do not have a unitary causal meaning; they contain multiple plot structures, multiple narrative antecedents, and multiple narrative consequences. The same event can be narrated in a number of different ways and within a number of different public spheres. These competing narratives influence not only how individuals will understand an event, but also how they will evaluate different communities, including the idealized "societal community" described by Parsons.[27]

Today, when global media collapse the space and time in which people experience their lives, events that "demand narration" are absolutely essential for the possibility of a public sphere in which people can aspire to participate. Most people do not have the time to retire at the end of the day to the salon or coffeehouse, in order to discuss matters of common concern. In this sense, the bourgeois public sphere idealized by Habermas is a contemporary impossibility. But there are certain events which encourage a break from the quotidian, the instrumental, the self-focused, and orient public attention to questions of society and morality. This is not an original point, of course. Durkheim recognized that all societies needed ritual events that provoked extended periods of collective moral reflection.[28] It is during these times, transcending the mundane moments of everyday life, that the affective bonds of sociality are mobilized, participation in the public arena is maximized, and past, present, and future are fused together in an ongoing, mythic, mystical collective story about "who we are." While "narrating the social" is an ongoing process, occurring at multiple moments that confound temporal and spatial assumptions of linearity, the process of narration does tend to slow down, to "linger" on certain events.[29]

Of those types of events that "demand narration," crisis is one of the most important. Crisis develops when a particular event gets narratively linked to a central cleavage in society and demands the attention of citizens as well as political elites.[30] In the modern media age, a crisis becomes a "media event," announced through an interruption of normal broadcast schedules, repeated analysis by "experts," and opinion polling about the central characters involved in the crisis.[31] Events such as Watergate, Watts, and Rodney King become important plot elements for the different narratives of civil society and nation. Crisis produces a particular kind of narrative lingering, which emphasizes not only the tragic distance between is and ought but also the possibility of heroic overcoming. Indeed, it is the tension between romantic overcoming and tragic failure which provides crisis with its dramatic power. Because the end of crisis is never known in advance, the temporal lingering associated with it is charged with collective anticipation and tension; in certain respects, then, crisis is even more of a "moment out of time" than other forms of ritual.[32]

My approach to studying public sphere communication during times of crisis focuses on three different structural components of narratives. The first is *plot*, which is concerned with the selection, evaluation, and attribution of differential status to events. A narrative's plot is fluid and complex in its relationship to events; as Eco has shown, it can "linger" on a particular event, flash back to past events, or flash forward to future events.[33] Plot is the best way to study what Abbott has called the "time-horizon problem," where events can differ in their speed and duration.[34] A focus on which events are selected for narration (and which events are not selected) provides important clues about how a given individual, group, or collectivity understands the past, present, and future. For example, as Chapter 3 demonstrates, the *Chicago Tribune* and *Los Angeles Times* narrated the 1965 Watts uprisings in a way that linked it to a larger Cold War narrative. In this form of emplotment, all criticism of the American government was deemed illegitimate, and any discussion about the possible causes of the uprisings was criticized as Communist propaganda. In such a plot, considerations of the historical deprivations suffered by African-American urban residents were unlikely to be incorporated into the news narrative. Furthermore, within this type of plot, African-American leaders were unlikely to shift public opinion about matters of urban policy, because they would end up spending most of their time explaining why they were not Communist propagandists. Faced with such an environment, it is quite possible that their efforts would be better rewarded by participating in other large news media, such as the *New York Times*, where the plot was much more open to historical discussions about race and urban policy. In addition, participation in the smaller, more specialized African-American press would help to counter the forms of plots found within the more hostile publics.

In addition to plot, I also examine the *characters* portrayed in the narratives and their relationship to one another. The analysis of characters is particularly important for nonfictional narratives, because the narrators are often the same as the characters in the plot.[35] I analyze the characters in terms of the opposition between heroes and anti-heroes, using Alexander and Smith's recent work on the analytic code of American civil discourse to provide clues about how the characters are evaluated in various narrations.[36] This research has demonstrated how public actors make use of the binary structure of civil discourse to "purify" themselves and their allies, and to "pollute" their enemies. In order to portray themselves as powerful and heroic, public actors must describe others as dangerous, foolish, weak, or anti-heroic in some other way. They describe their enemies as irrational, out of control, secretive, or deceitful; by contrast, they describe themselves and their allies as rational, reasoned, and straightforward. They describe the projects and policies of their enemies as perverse, futile, and jeopardizing, while those of their friends are synergistic, mutually supportive, and progressive.[37] Over time, these identifications of similarity and difference develop into a cultural structure based on sets of homologies and antipathies, resulting in a semiotic system of civil society discourse. This "common code" allows for a degree of intersubjectivity among public speakers as well as a relatively stable system for evaluating persons. Members of a civil society know when they are being "symbolically polluted," and must spend a great deal of their time trying to repair the symbolic damage. Groups and associations who find themselves continually polluted in a given newspaper's narrative, to the extent that they wish to engage in that news public, must continually operate from a defensive and reactive position.

The final analytical tool of my narrative analysis is that of *genre*. Genre provides a temporal and spatial link between the characters and events of a narrative, and also influences the relationship between a story's characters, audience, and narrator. We can see how genre affects narrative by considering Frye's discussion of the four narrative "archetypes" of Western literature.[38] In *comedy*, the protagonists, or heroes, are viewed from the perspective of their common humanity, and the general theme is the integration of society. The movement in comedy is usually from one kind of society, where the protagonist's wishes are blocked, to another society that crystallizes around the hero. Comic heroes have average or below-average power, and typically fall into three general types: the imposter, the buffoon, and the self-deprecator. In *romance*, the hero has great powers, the enemy is clearly articulated and often has great powers as well, and the movement takes the form of an adventure with the ultimate triumph of hero over enemy. Romantic genres are viewed by the audience from a perspective of wish fulfillment, where heroes represent ideals and villains represent threats. In *tragedy*, the hero typically possesses great powers, but is isolated from society and ultimately falls to an omnipotent and external fate or to the violation of a moral law. Because the reader expects catastrophe as its inevitable end, tragedy is a particularly dangerous form of discourse if one values civic engagement because, as Frye describes, tragedy "eludes the antithesis between moral responsibility and arbitrary fate."[39] Finally, in *irony* the protagonist is viewed from an attitude of detachment and through the negative characterization of parody and satire. As I have argued elsewhere, irony encourages reflexivity, difference, tolerance, and healthy forms of critique in civil society.[40]

The literary texts described by Frye differ in some important respects from the news texts which form the object of study in this book. Most importantly, there are many competing narratives (and narrative creators) in news, all battling for interpretive authority over an event. Nevertheless, the genre used to narrate an event provides important clues about the relative openness of a particular news narrative. For example, narratives about social movements which are told through a comic genre tend to be relatively inflexible and conservative, characterizing the social movement as a "buffoon" or imposter, with the ultimate message serving to reinforce the status quo. Crisis narratives which are composed through the genre of tragedy tend to encourage an attitude of resignation, and often prevent the agenda of public discussion from moving toward a concern with solutions.

Using tools of narrative analysis, this book shows how the black press has provided communicative spaces which encouraged the monitoring of the mainstream media in order to counter negative racial stereotypes and interpretations, the development of alternative interpretations of public events, and the creation of arguments which could prove more effective in engaging those in the hegemonic public spheres. It also shows how certain cultural forms of representation – together with the racially stratified geography of public sphere communication – have prevented the black press from having a more significant impact on American civil society. These forms of representation are not neutral carriers of pre-existing interests and dispositions toward public engagement; rather, cultural forms constitute interests and dispositions at the same time as they help to express them.[41] Some cultural forms of representation are more likely to turn civil society into a discursive arena supportive of new narratives, new points of difference, and an expanded substantive content of social solidarity; other cultural forms are less likely to do so. Chapters 3, 4, and 5 of this book seek to demonstrate this in detail, focusing on the cultural geography of civil society during times of racial crisis. Chapters 1 and 2, through a theoretical and historical account of race, news media, and multiple publics, provide a more general context for these discussions. The remainder of the introduction provides some historical background about the city of Los Angeles, and some general description of the three crises which form the empirical foundation for the book.

Los Angeles, race, and urban America

While this book is not really a work on urban sociology, I want nevertheless to provide some historical background about Los Angeles, for those who may be unfamiliar with the city's history. To tell the story of racial crisis in Los Angeles over the past thirty years is to tell the story of urban America, only in a more distilled, concentrated, and visible form. As Edward Soja has argued, "whereas Watts marked the first major rebellion against the late modernism of postwar America, the civil disturbances of 1992 may represent the first explosion of resistance to neoconservative American postmodernism and post-Fordism."[42] Los Angeles, it would seem, has provided some of the most dramatic events in the recent history of race relations in American cities. While the Watts uprising was one of 194 racial disorders between 1965 and 1968, it was the most costly and the most memorable.[43] While the videotaped police beating of Rodney King was one of countless instances of police brutality, and certainly not the first videotaped instance of brutality, it was the most memorable. And while the not-guilty verdicts handed down in the trial of Los Angeles police officers Briseno, Koon, Powell, and Wind were simply the latest instance in a long history of racial injustice, they were, again, among the most memorable. If the problem of the color line has provided the greatest challenge to twentieth-century America, as DuBois predicted, the spotlight has shone as brightly in Los Angeles as it has anywhere else.

One of the most intriguing things about Los Angeles is that it took an unusually short historical path to become one of the world's most significant cities. In 1870, Los Angeles contained only 15,000 residents.[44] By 1920, its population exceeded 900,000, and by 1930 it had surpassed two million. By 1950 Los Angeles contained more than four million inhabitants, making it the third-largest city in the country, and by 1960 it had become the second-largest city, with over six million inhabitants. The 1990 census counted 8,863,000 residents in Los Angeles County, and 14,531,000 in the metropolitan statistical area. Metropolitan Los Angeles now contains the largest Asian (1,339,990) and Hispanic (4,714,405) populations in the United States, and the third-largest African-American population (1,226,477). It has perhaps the largest concentration of engineers, scientists, mathematicians, computer technicians, and military weapons specialists in the world; its garment industry is the largest in the country, and its financial sector is beginning to emerge as a legitimate challenger to London, Tokyo, and New York.[45] It has been the center of the film industry since the 1920s and the center for the television industry since the 1950s.[46] Its largest newspaper, the *Los Angeles Times*, has the third-largest daily circulation in the country, and the largest of any city-identified newspaper, trailing only *USA Today* and *Wall Street Journal*. The speed with which this growth has occurred belies the fact that, in the early years of the twentieth century, it was assumed that San Francisco would be the largest and most important city in the western United States, and that San Diego would be the most significant city in Southern California.[47]

Recently, a number of scholars have begun to argue that Los Angeles offers an indicator of things to come for other metropolitan cities, in terms of its spatial form, its economic restructuring, and its police-minority relations. Spatially, modern Los Angeles has provided the paradigmatic case of decentralization and urban sprawl. Among the residents streaming into the city during the early decades of the twentieth century, many were midwesterners fleeing the population densities and cultural differences they had encountered in cities such as Chicago and St. Louis; their vision of Los Angeles was one of open space and homogeneity – in other words, a metropolis self-consciously designed to be the mirror opposite of New York or Chicago.[48] It was no accident that Los Angeles took the shape it did; its spatial form was built into the dreamscapes of these new migrants. By 1920, the city of Los Angeles had incorporated more than forty different cities into a sprawling, decentered urban space. What held everything together was the highest automobile ownership rate in the country (one automobile for every nine residents in 1920), as well as a mass-transit rail system offering service which extended well over 1,000 miles.[49] Real estate developers were the principal stockholders in the rail lines, and they tended to build new lines in anticipation of residential development, into the tracts of land they owned. In this way, mass-transit in Los Angeles was a force of decentralization, exactly the opposite of the northern and eastern cities. Edward Soja has described this spatial distinctiveness, noting that, while there was an identifiable downtown, Los Angeles provided a different vision of urban form from the very beginning:

From its first major urban boom in the late nineteenth century, Los Angeles seemed to have a morphological mind of its own. The classic urban forms were never entirely absent, and glimmerings of them are discoverable even today, but from the beginning the Los Angeles urban fabric took on a very different texture. Although the centrality of downtown Los Angeles has been recognizable for more than two hundred years, the surrounding urban region grew as a fragmented and decentered metropolis, a patchwork quilt of low-density suburban communities stretching over an extraordinarily irregular terrain of mountains, valleys, beaches, and deserts.[50]

The region's industrial growth has been characterized by a similarly decentralized pattern. This has been true since the late 1890s, when San Pedro was chosen over Santa Monica as the city's major seaport.[51] By 1930, fifty-two oil refineries stretched from Venice Beach southward to Huntington Beach, accounting for some five percent of the world's petroleum.[52] Goodyear built its Pacific coast branch facilities in south Los Angeles, while Ford Motor Company built its assembly plant in Long Beach.[53] Today, most high-wage, skilled labor is located in various "technopoles" located near the airport, Irvine, Canoga Park, Ventura County, the San Gabriel Valley, and the Eastern San Fernando Valley; low-skilled, low-wage labor, by contrast, is concentrated in the inner-city garment industry and service sector.[54]

While Los Angeles has indeed been exceptional in many respects, its history of racial and ethnic relations is more typical of the American urban experience. Already by 1940, African-Americans were nearly as segregated in Los Angeles as they were in New York and Chicago.[55] The active enforcement of restrictive housing covenants, combined with the refusal to build new public housing, led to dramatic increases in population densities for African-Americans between 1940 and 1965.[56] This trend has continued, so that today many sections of inner-city Los Angeles have higher population densities than in Chicago or St. Louis.[57] Guaranteeing the restricted movements of the city's racial minority populations was the paramilitary-style Los Angeles Police Department, revamped by police chief William Parker into the most technologically-advanced police force in the country. Abandoning foot patrols in favor of auto and air surveillance, this group of police officers, most of whom did not live in the communities they patrolled, operated more as an occupying force than a community institution. Harassment and violence against racial minorities became increasingly frequent after Parker took over the police department, and more than sixty African-Americans were killed by Los Angeles police between 1963 and 1965. During the same period that White America was growing increasingly captivated by the conflicts between civil rights protesters and southern police, they remained largely unaware of the daily harassment of racial minorities by police in major urban centers such as Los Angeles.

It was within this context that the Watts events resonated so strongly throughout the country. What the 1965 Watts uprising did was to show how serious the problems of race still were, and how the public's understanding of racial issues had thus far ignored the problems existing in the urban centers of the north and west. Efforts to overturn racial apartheid in the South had done nothing for urban residents in the North and West, who already possessed formal civil liberties such as the freedom of expression and the right of association. In addition, while efforts to open up the economy to greater African-American participation had created a nascent black middle class, they had left behind an increasingly isolated black urban "underclass."[58] Los Angeles provided a paradigmatic example of the costs of the urban transformation. Despite the fact that the opening up of the war industries had brought nearly 600,000 new African-Americans into Los Angeles county between 1942 and 1965, and despite a "tantalizing proximity to one of the largest pools of high-wage, unionized, blue-collar jobs in the country," nearly one-third of African-Americans in Los Angeles were unemployed in 1965, and nearly sixty percent were on welfare.[59] To make matters worse, public housing construction had come to a virtual halt in Los Angeles after 1950, and police paramilitary tactics which antagonized African-Americans were receiving national awards, were being emulated by other police departments, and were receiving symbolic acclamation in the television program *Dragnet.*[60]

The combination of police swaggering and African-American resentment helped to transform the arrest of Marquette Frye into a five-day period of urban revolt, totalling thirty-four deaths, 1,032 injuries, over 4,000 arrests, and an estimated $40 million in property damage.[61] The Watts uprisings precipitated an emotional and intense period of public discussion about race, poverty, and police relations in American cities. As Chapter 3 demonstrates, this public debate and commentary took various local, regional, national, and racial forms, and was filtered through competing interpretive lenses, including those of the Cold War, the federal anti-poverty program, the racism of Los Angeles police and Los Angeles politicians, and the problem of black invisibility in the mainstream media. The uprisings in Watts also led to the public realization that not all African-Americans felt adequately represented by a middle-class black leadership and its civil rights agenda, as well as a growing fear that new African-American leaders might not be as accommodating as the older ones. When Martin Luther King, Jr. came to Los Angeles several days after the uprisings, he was criticized by the Los Angeles political establishment as well as the African-American "underclass."[62] The known contours of the civil rights debate, it seemed, were inadequate to speak the problems uncovered by Watts.

Twenty-six years later, the videotaped beating of Rodney King by members of the Los Angeles Police Department showed that little had changed regarding police-minority relations. As the end of the twentieth century drew near, the problem of the color line still appeared to be drawn sharply in Los Angeles, and forums for discussing the problem publicly seemed to be hauntingly elusive. Reflections about social and economic conditions in black inner-city ghettos tended to spring up during every five-year anniversary of the release of the Kerner Commission's 1968 report on civil disorders; what tended to be left out of the discussions, however, were the Kerner report's warnings about the crisis of police-minority relations. The Rodney King beating changed all of that. Transmitted worldwide on television news screens, the Rodney King beating galvanized the public and encouraged a new discussion about police practices and police tactics. As Chapter 4 shows, criticism of the Los Angeles Police Department was nearly universal in the media in 1991, a criticism which ultimately was symbolized by a new report: the Report of the Independent Commission of the Los Angeles Police Department, headed by Warren Christopher. The report uncovered systemic racism and sexism within the police department, and a lack of punishment for even the most egregious offenders of the department's use-of-force policies. With the release of the report, Los Angeles and the nation hoped that police departments would reform themselves and end the toleration of excessive force by their officers. Hopeful that the Rodney King crisis had been resolved, the public turned to the trial of officers Briseno, Koon, Wind, and Powell. The end of the Rodney King story had already been forecast in most public forums, particularly those of mainstream civil society; it would come with the conviction of the four indicted police officers, a reinforced belief in the effectiveness of regulative institutions, and the moral rejuvenation of American citizens. Discussions about racial fragmentation seemed to disappear into the background, as the Rodney King crisis turned into a matter of legal redress and institutional supervision.

Social dramas do not always end as forecasted, however. As the public was beginning to heal from the wounds which an extended discussion of race so often produces,[63] the sense of calm and normality exploded again in May 1992, when a jury found the police officers not guilty of beating Rodney King. Public outrage at the verdicts was widespread, and was complicated further by the most costly and destructive civil disturbances in the nation's history: fifty-two deaths, 2,383 injuries, 16,291 arrests, over 500 fires, and property damage estimated in the range of $785 million–$1 billion.[64] More people followed the events of the uprisings in the news media than followed the Gulf War. This new event re-introduced the issues brought forth in the 1991 Rodney King beating crisis, and extended the discussion back toward those problems which had been brought forth by the urban crises of the 1960s. "Rodney King" now symbolized two different events: the police brutality of 1991, and the urban upheaval of 1992. And the "event" of Rodney King is certain to occupy a special place in the ongoing collective mythology of American civil society. Public narratives about the 1992 verdicts established a new master framework for talking about racial crisis; this new framework, as Chapter 5 demonstrates, emphasized tragedy, resignation, fragmentation, and the loss of hope. This new framework for discussing racial crisis was clearly evident during the Reginald Denny beating trial and the O. J. Simpson trial. But the new framework for talking about race found its origins in the unfolding drama of the Rodney King affair.

1

Race, media, and multiple publics

On May 28, 1997, John Sengstakke died at the age of eighty-four. For six decades Sengstakke had been owner and editor of the *Chicago Defender*, the most important and most famous of all African-American newspapers. Sengstakke's death was a noticeable event in the world of American journalism; Brent Staples wrote a 1400-word obituary in the *New York Times*, calling Sengstakke the "Charles Foster Kane of the black press." But Sengstakke's death was only the beginning of the story. Northern Trust Co., acting as executor of Sengstakke's estate, put the *Defender* up for sale in December 1997, in order to pay for a four-million-dollar estate tax bill. Contacting both African-American and white investors, the bank would only commit to seeking "fair value for the shareholders." A crisis ensued within the black journalism community, with most insisting that the paper remain in African-American hands. In a front-page editorial, the *Chicago Defender* wrote that there were no plans to sell the paper, that the Sengstakke family was committed to maintaining the *Defender*, and that the reports about its sale were an "outright fabrication." Several months later the family removed Northern Trust from its financial control of the estate, ending worries that the paper could fall into white hands.

Why did it matter that the *Chicago Defender* remain in African-American control? This question, I think, goes to the heart of current debates about civil society and the public sphere, particularly those which have emphasized that civil society consists of multiple, frequently non-rational, and often contestatory public spheres, which are oriented just as often to cultural issues as to political ones. This understanding of the public sphere differs substantially from how it was introduced nearly forty years ago by Habermas. For Habermas the public sphere represented the space of private people come together as a public, who claimed the space of public discourse from State regulation, and demanded that the State engage them in debate about matters of political legitimacy and common concern. The result of this development of the bourgeois public sphere, which took place during the seventeenth and eighteenth centuries, was that the principle of open public discussion came to replace that of parliamentary secrecy. Envisioning the public sphere primarily as a political space that could help challenge, engage, and regulate public authorities, Habermas emphasized face-to-face communication, rational-critical discourse, and a single public arena.

If it was only that Habermas had neglected to consider the non-bourgeois, non-dominant, and more identity-oriented public spheres, the argument for multiple publics would not present such a fundamental challenge, because recognition of these other publics would simply provide a more detailed picture of a more differentiated civil society. But the challenge of multiple publics is more fundamental than this, because it suggests that civil society has a fractured quality which is not being overcome by some trend toward an integrated public sphere.[1] Habermas admitted as much in a 1989 conference, writing that "a different picture emerges if *from the beginning* one admits the coexistence of competing public spheres and takes account of the dynamics of those processes of communication that are excluded from the dominant public sphere."[2]

If ever a case can be made for the existence of separate public spheres *from the beginning*, African-American history provides it. Separate public spaces and communicative institutions formed among Northern free blacks in the 1700s: prominent examples included the African Union Society of Newport, Rhode Island (1780), the Free African Society of Philadelphia (1787), the African Methodist Episcopal Church, the African Methodist Episcopal Zion Church, the Bethel Charity School, and the African Free School Number 2. From these separate spaces of public communication came the black press, which was established in 1827. At least forty different black newspapers were published before the Civil War, and the establishment of a national black press was generally agreed upon as the second most pressing issue among African-American leaders.

The history of the African-American public sphere and the black press is neither an isolated nor an exceptional case; numerous historical studies point to the existence of non-bourgeois, non-male, and otherwise non-official publics. As early as the eighteenth century, there were plebian publics, women's publics, and an entire set of public spheres which were organized more around "festive communication" than rational discourse.[3] During the women's suffrage movement of the nineteenth century, there developed national, regional and local women's papers simultaneously articulating the principles of women's rights and the vision of a new kind of media organization.[4] The working class press at the turn of the century consisted of hundreds of newspapers in dozens of languages.[5] What these alternative publics and alternative media point to, according to historians such as Geoff Eley, is the fact that Habermas's account of the rise of the bourgeois public sphere "is an extremely idealized abstraction from the political cultures that actually took shape at the end of the eighteenth and the start of the nineteenth century."[6] Real civil societies have always contained plural and partial publics.

The historical need for a strong black press was three-fold: (1) to provide a forum for debate and self-improvement; (2) to monitor the mainstream press; and (3) to increase black visibility in white civil society. As Chapter 2 will show, African-Americans could not count on the mainstream press of the time to publicize black voices or to represent black issues in a non-patronizing manner. Most of the Northern papers were against slavery and in favor of emancipation, but their positions were crafted through stories which favored the voices of white politicians over black abolitionists. Even in dealings with their white abolitionist allies, black leaders often found their voices excluded and marginalized, highlighting yet again the need for a separate black public sphere. The white abolitionist press, while receiving most of its early subscription support from African-Americans, eventually decreased its coverage of black news items in favor of reports about the activities of white abolitionists; in fact, William Lloyd Garrison actively discouraged the establishment of early black papers such as *Colored American* and *North Star*.[7] By establishing an independent black press, African-Americans were able to secure a space of self-representation: not only to craft common identities and solidarities, but also to develop arguments which might effectively engage white civil society.

It is because there are overlapping and competing publics in civil society, that the news media take on a special significance. Tocqueville recognized this in his description of nineteenth-century American civil society, arguing that the number of newspapers was closely tied to the number of associations and, by implication, that they were not, in fact, oriented to a single public sphere.[8] The multiplication of news publics continues today, with forty percent of the total newspaper circulation in America being that of papers with circulation of less than 100,000.[9] The rise of cable television and the introduction of new communication technologies have brought in new forces which have contributed to the pluralization of media publics – by narrowing and sharpening their focus – which divides the news public into increasingly smaller and specialized market segments. If anything, the figures on market segmentation actually undercount the significance of "small" media. Almost every voluntary association publishes its own newsletter, and an increasing proportion of them now maintain their own websites. These smaller media spaces, which Habermas ignored entirely in his mass culture critique, provide sites in which new experiences are invented and crafted, in which new meanings get discussed and popularized, in which new forms of political engagement are tried out; in other words, they are potential sources of social change, simultaneously increasing the likelihood of inter-public engagement and intra-public autonomy.

News media and the public sphere

While news media and the public sphere have always been intricately intertwined, it is important to maintain an analytical distinction between them. The concept of the public sphere refers to a particular type of practice which takes place in civil society: the practice of open discussion about matters of common public concern. These discussions can take place in public spaces such as meeting halls and universities, in the private spaces of someone's home, or in the "virtual" spaces of print, television, or the Internet. What turns a discussion into a public sphere is the fact that it is composed of private citizens, engaged in free public debate about matters of common concern, and free of worries about state censorship or coercion. The news media, on the other hand, consist of any space in which information of some public interest is circulated to some portion of the public.[10] Like public spheres, news media can circulate in private, public, or virtual spaces, and they involve matters of common concern. But whereas public spheres are oriented primarily toward the circulation of discussion, news media deal in the circulation of information, broadly construed. Certainly the information being disseminated includes public sphere discussions; but it includes other things as well.

There are clearly many instances in which news media operate as something other than a public sphere. While public spheres must contain actual dialogue between specific individuals, news media can include other forms of communication as well. For example, news media often produce selective reports about actual dialogues. This is the case with television soundbites, in which the public is deprived of the full sequence of events which preceded the reported statement. Journalists frequently write stories in which they contact a number of sources independently, and then juxtapose the comments of these sources into virtual dialogues that never actually took place. Many news stories are never intended as dialogues, but instead appear as declarative descriptions or reports of an event. None of these examples of news can properly be thought of as public sphere discussions.

Nevertheless, there are many instances in which news media *do* operate as public spheres. In the pages of the newspaper and on the digital images of television, real individuals engage in description, discussion, and commentary about important public matters. In press conferences, for example, politicians as well as representatives of voluntary associations make statements, challenge public statements which have been made by others, and respond to questions. These represent examples of public spheres organized for the benefit of the media. In other instances, news media organize public spheres of their own, usually consisting of a media personality, a few politicians, some representatives from voluntary associations, and other private citizens. Television programs like ABC's *Nightline* and CNN's *Larry King Live* do this on a daily basis. Their topics change nightly, and are typically shaped by what is currently of public concern. For example, during the 1992 civil uprisings in Los Angeles, Ted Koppel organized one episode of *Nightline* as a discussion with gang members in Los Angeles; another episode was filmed on location at the First African Methodist Episcopal Church, as a discussion with black politicians, community leaders, and citizens. In these instances, the news media provided a forum for private individuals to discuss matters of common concern, and broadcast these discussions to between ten and twenty million viewers.

Without doubt these news media form imperfect public spheres, because they tend to provide only partial access, which is organized in structurally-predictable ways.[11] But this criticism should not be overstated. Empirically, *all* public spheres provide limited access, and as such all public spheres are imperfect. But the news media are *in principle* open to anyone. News editors are continuously trying to expand the space of media participation, through letters to the editor, man-on-the-street interviews, and the like.[12] The introduction of phone-in segments to television and radio news programs represents a further attempt at expanding participatory access.[13] Even talk shows can be seen as a method of expanding participation in media spaces of deliberation, despite the fact that they do not look anything like the processes of rational consensus formation idealized by Habermas.[14] Try as they might, politicians are unable to maintain anything approaching total control of media publicity.[15] The reason for this is that journalistic routines are known well enough so that citizens, associations, and leaders of social movements can package their activities in ways which will be more likely to be seen as news. The same is true of the increasingly numerous bands of roving videographers, ensuring that the news will be sufficiently open and porous so as to constitute a public sphere in which many can aspire to participate.[16]

In addition to creating public spaces for discussing matters of common concern, news media shape other publics in significant ways. News media provide a common stock of information and culture, which private citizens rely on in their everyday conversations with others. The possibility of conversation requires a common stock of knowledge among participants, and the news media are the best candidates for providing it.[17] As I mentioned in the introduction, sixty-eight percent of the American public watches at least one television news program in a typical day, for an average duration of fifty-eight minutes.[18] Fifty-four percent of adults read a newspaper every day, and eighty-eight percent read the paper at least once a week.[19] By creating an open-ended space where ideas can be expressed and received by a potentially limitless and universal audience of present and non-present others, modern communication media have actually expanded the public sphere.

For many citizens, then, there is a strong empirical connection between news media and public sphere discussions. Habermas himself recognized the importance of this connection when discussing the historical genesis of the bourgeois public sphere, noting how articles written in eighteenth-century periodicals were made an integral part of discussions taking place in coffee houses and other public spaces.[20] Today, there is general agreement that media information is one of the most important tools people use when talking about matters of common concern.[21] The research establishing this relationship has pointed to the ways in which media texts provide a flow of cultural material from producers to audiences, who in turn use the media texts to construct a meaningful world and to maintain a common cultural framework through which intersubjectivity becomes possible. Mass media do not produce a one-way flow from text to putatively passive audience but, rather, a "two-step flow" where individuals incorporate media texts into their existing social networks and social environment.[22] And while they may not be successful in telling people what to think, the news media have been remarkably successful in shaping what people think about and what they talk about.[23] More often than not, then, news media find their way into the discussions between citizens about matters of common concern.

Given the strong presence of news media in contemporary civil society, associations and communities are faced with a dilemma: namely, that they must try to strike a balance between protecting their cultural autonomy and engaging other publics in discussion and deliberation. In order to protect cultural autonomy, they need to develop smaller, more local spaces of discussion over which they have a lot of control. This suggests that smaller, more targeted news media, such as the African-American press, have an important role to play in the creation of a more open and inclusive civil society. On the other hand, in order to influence public opinion and public policy, associations need to participate in large public spheres over which they have little or no control. For this, they need to establish strategies for gaining publicity in larger news media such as *ABC News*, the *Los Angeles Times*, or the *New York Times*. In other words, a civil society consisting of multiple publics requires a media system consisting of multiple media. Without smaller media over which they have a high degree of control, associations become too dependent on the preferences and practical routines of mainstream journalists. Without access to larger media, they lose the ability to influence the larger public agenda.

Media access and participatory inequality

It is not difficult to understand why access to mainstream news media is an important issue. Large media offer a powerful forum for changing public opinion, by defining what issues people are most likely to talk about. Access to these kinds of media is crucial if an association hopes to garner widespread publicity, and to have even the chance of influencing public opinion. Through processes of agenda-setting and priming, the issues and stories reported in the mainstream news media are the ones that people tend to think about and to talk about. In societies obsessed by opinion polling, the mainstream media agenda also shapes the polling agenda, the results of which, when reported back to the public, reinforces even further the stories and the topics appearing in the news.[24] These agenda-setting effects tend to be even stronger for new issues that have not been widely discussed.[25] For associations who desire to influence public policy and public opinion, and particularly for small associations trying to bring new issues into debate in the majority public sphere, these agenda-setting effects make the appeal of mainstream media exposure virtually irresistible.

Gaining publicity in large news media is also a good way for associations to gain access to the sites of political power and public policy formation. More than any other type of public space, the large media organizations have replaced political parties as the best link between politicians and the people. In a typical day more than one million people will read the *New York Times*, *Los Angeles Times*, and *USA Today*. Somewhere between ten and twenty million viewers nightly will watch *ABC News*, *CBS News*, or *NBC News*.[26] These news organizations, recognizing their political power, have responded by devoting somewhere between one-fifth and one-half of their available news space to political news.[27] This has resulted in a cycle of mutual need, whereby politicians and journalists pay closer and closer attention to one another. Skill in dealing with the media has become a crucial talent for politicians, who actively try to win the favor of important political journalists: by being accessible, by supplying scores of press releases, and by staging newsworthy events during news-gathering times of the day and week.[28] To the extent that an association can get its issues onto *ABC News* or into the *New York Times*, it is more likely to get those issues onto the agenda of congressional debate.

The problem is that access to the dominant media is stratified. Indeed, the stratification of access is inherent to the very process of news work, because the everyday practical routines of journalists tend to favor dominant over subordinate groups. This stratification of access operates on many different levels. For example, because events are more likely to be newsworthy if they occur during the working day of the journalist, non-professional and resource-poor associations begin from a position of temporal disadvantage. Since their members must work in full-time jobs, these associations are typically forced to meet at night and on weekends, placing them outside the journalist's working day and temporally more distant from the news production process.[29] More generally, journalists tend to see events as newsworthy when those events can be fit into regularly-used news codes (called "slugs" in the newsroom), or when they can fit the event into an ongoing story. Public relations agents are adept at knowing how to frame their events appropriately, and are more likely to gain media access for their associations. Associations which do not have public relations resources are at an obvious disadvantage here. Finally, a journalist's status is often parasitic upon the status of his or her sources.[30] Ambitious journalists therefore have a career motivation to cultivate high-status sources. Factors such as these continue to make it difficult for minority associations to gain access to the majority media.

Another problem associated with the goal of equal access to mainstream news media is that the very thing being sought after, access, is porous and ever-changing. News work is not shaped by the desire to include the greatest number of voices or the most compelling argument; rather, journalists are motivated by the desire to tell the best story.[31] This means that news media (and, as a consequence, public spheres) are shaped more by narrative than by the dictates of "rational-critical discourse." News workers understand events by placing them into stories, composed of actors and events, and having a beginning, middle, and end. Indeed, the narrative style allows news workers to do much of the work of producing the news in the very act of discovering it. Events are perceived as newsworthy when they are recognized as plot elements in a story. They become legitimate and newsworthy through stories told to editors and news directors. They are written and/or enacted according to their received and narrative genre elements, such as romance, tragedy, comedy, and irony.

The narrative contingency of media access is not always a bad thing for marginalized groups, of course. When events get transformed into particular types of stories, they can open up media possibilities to individuals and groups who usually have a very difficult time gaining publicity. As Chapter 5 will show, this type of expansion of mainstream media access occurred during the initial days after the 1992 uprisings in Los Angeles. After the return of not-guilty verdicts in the trial of the police officers charged in the videotaped beating of Rodney King, the initial reaction in the majority news media was one of disbelief and shock about the verdict, combined with anger and criticism of "racist Simi Valley jurors." As long as the media focus remained on the Simi Valley jurors, it remained open to the voices of individuals who almost never got to speak for themselves in the dominant public sphere; gang members, residents of inner-city Los Angeles, and community activists were all granted voice on ABC's evening news program, *Nightline*, and described by host Ted Koppel as "eloquent," "impressive," and "passionate." Needless to say, this voice came in a very specific and delimited context, and it was not going to increase their likelihood of gaining access to *ABC News* in the future. The mainstream media access of these individuals was tied directly to the Rodney King story, and it would disappear as soon as the story ended.

While access to mainstream news media is certainly a necessary precondition for associations desiring publicity, it is by no means a sufficient one, and its importance should not be overstated. As legal scholar Monroe Price has argued, access doctrines only provide the "surface architecture of free speech that combines the trappings of government non-interference with the illusion that narratives – the stories of the good life – are fairly distributed among its tellers."[32] The problem is that media access does not guarantee a more pluralistic collection of media narratives which reflect historically-excluded groups. The public narratives which circulate in the dominant public spheres tend to reserve the heroic character positions for the dominant groups in a society, creating public environments which favor those dominant groups at the expense of minorities.

Out of a desire to create "active consent," dominant groups establish public spheres in which they include the subordinate groups, but do so under discursive rules which favor the dominant group. Historically, the establishment of "rational, critical discourse" and "objectivity" as the organizing tropes of the bourgeois public sphere and the mainstream news media was accomplished through a binarism intended to delegitimize excluded groups. These exclusions were created through discourse which criticized the "undisciplined" and "mob-like" activity of the working class, the "natural" sexuality and desire of women, and the "natural" passivity and indolence of non-whites.[33] In other words, as Alexander has demonstrated so convincingly, the discourse of civil society has developed through a semiotic binary in which criteria of inclusion were intertwined with criteria of exclusion, and where the ideal of civic virtue required an anti-ideal of civic vice.[34] As a form of social closure, this binary discourse advantages dominant groups by being formally open yet informally closed; while in principle anyone can enter a dominant public sphere, "insiders" and "outsiders" are defined and identified by the tacit categories of the binary code, the practical mastery of which is unequally distributed among the participants.[35] Thus, while the bourgeois public sphere was organized according to the open and democratic principles of rationality and publicity, it was at the same time – as Nancy Fraser has argued so convincingly – "the arena, the training ground, and eventually the power base of a stratum of bourgeois men who were coming to see themselves as a 'universal class' and preparing to assert their fitness to govern."[36] In short, problems of cultural hegemony are inherent to dominant public spheres, regardless of how formally open they may be.

The counter-hegemonic function of multiple publics

Exclusion, inequality, and symbolic disadvantage are not things that can be eradicated from the public sphere. They are, as Alexander rightly notes, anti-civil intrusions which form an important part of any empirical civil society.[37] For this reason, subordinate groups need to develop what Fraser has called "subaltern counterpublics" in order to "invent and circulate counterdiscourses to formulate oppositional interpretations of their identities, interests, and needs."[38] Put simply, the publicity strategies of marginalized groups cannot concentrate solely on mainstream media and dominant publics, but must also include active participation in, and cultivation of alternative public spheres. These alternative publics offer a place for counteracting the effects of hegemony, by constructing alternative narratives which contain different heroes and different plots.

Historically, minority groups have turned to alternative publics and alternative media as a way to compensate for their exclusion from the dominant publics. In these alternative communicative spaces, groups are able to discover common interests, to develop arguments which could more effectively engage white civil society, and to provide deliberative spaces which could nurture the development of new public leaders. Motivations to participate in these alternative publics were not only reinforced by the experiences of exclusion, but also by the hope that new arguments and new rhetoric would be able to capture mainstream public attention and shift public opinion. In this hope, minority groups were no different than any other voluntary associations; after all, as Tocqueville observed, all associations "entertain hopes of drawing the majority over to their side, and then controlling the supreme power in its name."[39]

As Chapter 2 will document, the early history of the black press was shaped precisely by the experience of exclusion and the hope of future engagement. As the fight for inclusion intensified throughout the twentieth century, the black press thrived. Chicago and New York both had black newspapers with circulations exceeding 100,000 during the first half of the century; nationally, the total weekly circulation in the black press was in excess of 2,000,000 by 1945, and new black newspapers were appearing at the rate of three a month.[40] It was quite clear, as Thurgood Marshall claimed in 1954, that the African-American press was an indispensable part of the early civil rights movement, because of the way that it allowed for debate about matters of racial concern to circulate among black elites as well as ordinary black citizens.

But what of the argument that in a fully integrated society the African-American press would be unnecessary? After all, the African-American press was never intended to substitute for participation in the majority media. Rather, it was designed to encourage continuous discussion about matters of common concern, to develop arguments for later engagement in the majority public spheres, and to correct the prejudices and misrepresentations which resulted from engagement in those other public spheres. The point was to continue discussion and conversation, and to keep open the possibility of expanding the conversation to include new participants and new venues. This, after all, is the ultimate value of civil society, regardless of how many different publics compose it: to keep a conversation going, to open up ongoing conversations to new narratives and new points of difference, and to expand the substantive content of social solidarity. It is not necessary that participants reach an agreement about all matters of common concern. In a multicultural society, this may in fact be impossible. What is essential is that they continue the discussion. As Benhabib has argued:

when we shift the burden of the moral test in communicative ethics from consensus to the idea of an ongoing moral conversation, we begin to ask not what all would or could agree to as a result of practical discourses to be morally permissible or impermissible, but what would be allowed and perhaps even necessary from the standpoint of continuing and sustaining the practice of the moral conversation among us. The emphasis is now less on *rational agreement*, but more on sustaining those normative practices and moral relationships within which reasoned agreement *as a way of life* can flourish and continue.[41]

The point is that if civil society is to be a space organized around the ideal of "universalistic solidarity," as Alexander suggests, then it requires a communicative geography which can open up ongoing conversations to new narratives and to new points of difference.[42] Because of the problems of cultural hegemony and unequal access, this is most likely to happen if there is a differentiated and diverse set of communication media – both large and small, universalistic and particularistic.

It is not a new argument, of course, to claim that both large and small publics have their place. But it is important not to conflate small publics and direct, face-to-face interaction. Certainly, direct interaction in small public spheres of physical co-presence has been important in the past for forming common identities and solidarities. But today, the power of this kind of solidarity increases in direct relation to its latency. In other words, the power of something like the black press is not tied directly to the number of people who read it. Rather, its potential power resides in the fact that people know it is there, available to be read should the need be perceived. Indeed, during periods of racial crisis, such as the Watts and Rodney King uprisings, sales of black newspapers surged, as African-Americans sought out the "black perspective," compared it with the stories they were reading in newspapers like the *New York Times*, and then proceeded to have conversations. Such a thing would be far less likely to occur if a paper like the *Chicago Defender* was owned by Rupert Murdoch or some other magnate of the mainstream media. And it was this recognition that led to the sense of crisis which surrounded John Sengstakke's death. As the publisher of the *Michigan Citizen* commented, "these papers . . . have to remain in the hands of someone within the same ethnicity, because we've seen from history that if we're not around to record our stories, they will either be manipulated or ignored."[43]

2

Historicizing the public spheres: New York, Los Angeles, Chicago

In the last chapter, I argued that multiple publics and alternative news media helped to expand the scope of participation and to broaden the substantive content of social solidarity in civil society. By helping to counter the forces of participatory inequality and cultural hegemony in the dominant communicative spaces of mainstream civil society, multiple publics enable minority groups simultaneously to maintain cultural autonomy and to engage other publics in discussion and deliberation. In a civil society consisting of multiple publics, voluntary associations need to develop strategies for participating in both large and small media spaces. Without smaller media over which they have a high degree of control, associations become too dependent on the preferences and practical routines of mainstream journalists. Without access to larger media, they lose the ability to influence the larger public agenda.

This chapter offers historical evidence for the value of multiple publics and alternative media, by describing the development of the African-American and mainstream press and public spheres in New York, Chicago, and Los Angeles. The need for alternative publics developed early in American history, as the exclusion of African-Americans encouraged the formation of separate publics and the desire to build a national black press. The first black newspaper was established in 1827, and more than forty separate black papers were started before the Civil War. By establishing an independent black press, African-Americans were able to secure a space of self-representation: not only to craft common identities and solidarities, but also to develop arguments which might effectively engage white civil society. However, most black newspapers existed in a rather tenuous state before the twentieth century due to the lack of economic support and the absence of large urban communities of African-Americans.

With the migration of large numbers of African-Americans to the met-ropolitan cities of the north and west, the black press and public spheres experienced a golden age of growth and vitality, lasting roughly from 1910 to 1950. New York, Chicago, and Los Angeles all developed vibrant insti-tutions of African-American public and civic life during the first half of the twentieth century. The black public sphere during this period provided a forum for cultural expression, for the forging of strongly-held shared iden-tities, and for the articulation of a common plan of collective action to end discrimination. By the 1950s and 1960s, leaders of the civil rights move-ment were beginning to participate more fully in both the African-American and the mainstream press, attempting simultaneously to increase black visibility and to end white discrimination.

The irony is that increased participation by middle-class blacks in main-stream civil society created a subsequent crisis for the black press. As the goal of integration was articulated more and more forcefully, some African-American leaders began to believe that the African-American press would become unnecessary in an integrated society. As a nationaliz-ing mainstream press incorporated more black voices and more race news, the African-American press struggled to maintain circulation. Many black newspapers have seen their circulation decrease rapidly, by some fifty to seventy-five percent; as a result, the African-American public sphere has become more dependent on mainstream news media. Integration into the mainstream press has been incomplete at best, however. For this empirical reason, as well as the issues of cultural hegemony raised in the previous chapter, the existence of the black press is still vitally important for American civil society and American democracy.

An early history of the press and public spheres

While African-American and mainstream newspapers looked much different in the nineteenth century than they do today, there were develop-ments during the period which were significant for both. It was during the nineteenth century that the seeds of the mass-circulation press were planted. It was also during this time that African-Americans established black-owned newspapers to create a national public forum for discussing African-American concerns. Both of these developments have had far-reaching consequences for American journalism.

For the mainstream press, newspapers were chiefly political tracts during the early days of the American Republic, interested primarily with advanc-ing party doctrine. During the 1830s, however, changes in the newspaper began to appear, which encouraged an emphasis on news over editorial, advertising over subscription revenue, and a strong rhetoric of impartiality. The chief agent of change was the penny press, so named because it reduced subscription costs from six cents to a single cent; those who established the penny press discovered that the reporting of information was a way to increase readership.[1] During the decade of the 1830s, spurred largely by the popularity of the penny press, the number of daily newspapers increased from sixty-five to 138, and average newspaper circulation increased from 1,200 to 2,200.[2]

The transition to informational reporting was gradual, and included a significant period of mixed reporting and continued political party influence over the press.[3] Indeed, many newspaper publishers associated with the penny press were intimately involved in politics during this transition period. For example, Henry Raymond, who established the *New York Times* in 1851, gave the keynote speech at the Republican Party's national convention in 1856, and was elected to Congress in 1862.[4] Joseph Medill, who took over the struggling *Chicago Tribune* in 1855 and transformed it into a paper with a daily circulation of over 100,000 by the time of his death in 1899, was also one of the founders of the Republican Party, and served as Mayor of Chicago from 1871 to 1873. In fact, only five percent of newspapers were registered as neutral or independent in 1850.[5] Still, it was the urban, locally-oriented, avowedly impartial penny press which was the most consequential for mainstream American journalism. As Michael Schudson has described the situation:

There were rural papers, hundreds of them, but the papers which set the standard for journalism then and passed on their legacy to the present were urban. There were party papers, there were socialist papers and labor papers, there were business papers, but, again, the papers to which modern journalism clearly traces its roots were the middle-class penny papers. These papers, whatever their political preferences, were spokesmen for egalitarian ideals in politics, economic life, and social life through their organization of sales, their solicitation of advertising, their emphasis on news, their catering to large audiences, their decreasing concern with the editorial.[6]

The story of the *New York Times* during the nineteenth century is illustrative. During its early years, it was somewhat of a hybrid paper. On the one hand it began as "effectively a party paper, in favor of business, commerce, growth and against slavery and the South."[7] On the other hand, the *New York Times* was a direct descendant of the penny press, competing with the *New York Herald* and *New York Tribune* for news, and frequently emphasizing the news-gathering process itself over political doctrine.[8] In the area of financial reporting, the *New York Times* was the penny paper *par excellence*. Selected by the State Banking Department in Albany as the official paper in which metropolitan banks should publish their weekly statements, it was the only New York paper *paid* – at regular advertising rates, no less – to publish these statements.[9] This market focus and emphasis on informational reporting was emphasized even further when the paper was purchased in 1896 by Adolph Ochs, who reduced the price of the paper from three cents to one cent per copy, added a separate financial section to the paper, began to report on real estate transactions, and published a daily list of out-of-town buyers.[10]

With the rise of informational reporting, the mainstream press during the nineteenth century focused less and less on editorial opinion, and more and more on quick and accurate reportage. By the end of the nineteenth century, both the *New York Times* and *New York Herald* had considered dropping the editorial column altogether, ultimately deciding to keep it as a way of reinforcing the value and distinctiveness of the news which was printed in the rest of the paper.[11] The *New York Times*, which had an average daily circulation of only 9,000 in 1892, used the informational mode of reporting to increase its daily circulation to 487,000 by the end of the First World War.[12] Adopting its now-famous motto of "All the News That's Fit to Print" in 1897, the *New York Times* emphasized news scoops and exhaustive coverage, and was the first to report such events as the 1909 Peary expedition to the North Pole, the sinking of the *Titanic* in 1912, the British and German versions of the outbreak of the First World War, and the full text of the 1919 Versailles Treaty.

Even though the shift toward informational reporting developed in the context of the Civil War – which, in turn, helped reinforce the value of news-gathering[13] – the "information" being reported had some significant gaps. One of the most glaring of these, particularly given the Civil War context, was a tendency to ignore black voices and black discussions. Reportage tended to mean, as it still does to a large degree, a reliance on "official sources."[14] Most of the Northern papers were against slavery and in favor of emancipation, but their position was crafted through stories which favored the voices of white politicians over black abolitionists. While editorial discussion of slavery first began to appear during the Administration of Andrew Jackson, most newspapers only reported or discussed the matter in the context of statements made by Washington politicians.[15] Even Frederick Douglass was heard only occasionally in the mainstream press. Despite the fact that his 1845 autobiographical slave narrative sold over 5,000 copies in the first four months of its publication (and more than 30,000 copies by 1860), and the fact that he toured the country continuously giving abolitionist speeches, Douglass was mentioned only twelve times in the *New York Times* between 1851 and 1864.[16] Of these twelve articles, three reported rumors of Douglass's involvement in the Harper's Ferry Raid of 1859, and helped to create the climate which forced Douglass to leave the country for about a year, waging his campaign against slavery from England. Douglass, like most other black writers and orators of the period, found that he had to establish his own newspaper if he wanted to secure a voice in the public sphere.

It was within this context of mainstream press invisibility that the African-American press developed its mission. Samuel Cornish, co-editor of the first African-American newspaper, *Freedom's Journal*, gave four reasons for establishing a black newspaper: (1) to speak out against slavery in the South and prejudice in the North; (2) to provide a forum for dialogue and communication between African-Americans in the free states; (3) to mobilize national public opinion on behalf of African-Americans and African-American issues; and (4) to correct the many misconceptions about African-Americans which were being communicated in the mainstream press.[17]

The seeds of the African-American press developed in the common spaces carved out by freedmen in the northern states. For a short period after the American Revolution, free blacks were allowed to vote in Maryland, New York, and Pennsylvania. In addition, those in the northern states enjoyed a freedom of association and communication that was unknown in the South, where slaves could not leave the plantation without authorization, possess firearms, entertain free blacks in their homes, assemble without the presence of a white person, or possess "incendiary literature."[18]

While the right of association enabled the formation of African-American communicative spaces, however, it was the experience of exclusion that made them specifically African-American. The tightening of voting restrictions, the exclusion from public education, the segregation experienced in church, and the restrictions in work opportunities – together with the fact that a large and ever-increasing number of freedmen were escaped slaves – all combined to help develop a sense of race consciousness among African-Americans in the urban North.[19] Those living in the Northern states tended to concentrate in certain areas,[20] and quickly perceived the need for creating common black public spaces, where members of the community could interact with one another within a setting of mutual support and respect. These common spaces developed as early as the 1780s, with the formation of the African Union Society of Newport, Rhode Island (1780) and the Free African Society of Philadelphia (1787). The African Union Society was founded for the "moral improvement" of freedmen, and to serve "as a forum for debating and acting on issues of importance to the community."[21] The Free African Society of Philadelphia was also founded for moral improvement; after some of its members were removed from their seats to the perimeter walls during a church service at St. George Methodist Church, they formed the African Methodist Episcopal Church. Led by Richard Allen and Absolom Jones, the A. M. E. Church had expanded into New Jersey, Delaware, and Maryland by 1816. Similarly, the desire for an independent church among free blacks in New York City led to the formation of the African Methodist Episcopal Zion Church in 1796, the Bethel A. M. E. Church in 1819, and other churches spread across the lower east and west side of New York City.[22] These mutual aid societies and independent churches fostered a critical sensibility, placed a premium on education, and established their own schools.[23] In other words, they provided the institutional settings for the formation of African-American public spheres.

It was from these mutual aid societies, independent churches, and educational institutions of the African-American community in the North that the black press developed. *Freedom's Journal*, which was the first black newspaper, included among its founders Richard Allen, the co-founder of the A.M.E. Church; Alexander Crummell, founder of the Phoenix Society; Nathaniel Paul, a Baptist minister in Albany, New York; William Hamilton, chairman of the People of Colour of New York; and Samuel Cornish, Pastor of the first Negro Presbyterian Church in New York.[24] *Freedom's Journal* was neither isolated nor exceptional; at least forty different newspapers were published by blacks before the Civil War, with about one-third of them based in New York City; in addition to *Freedom's Journal*, this included such papers as *Colored American*, *Ram's Horn*, *North Star*, and *Anglo-African*.[25] While most of these publications were short-lived, and while their concern was almost exclusively with the antislavery movement, their existence demonstrated the formation of a public voice and the desire for self-representation within specifically African-American public spheres.

Even in dealings with their white abolitionist allies, black leaders often found their voices excluded and marginalized, highlighting yet again the need for separate black public spheres. The white abolitionist press, while receiving most of its early subscription support from African-Americans, eventually decreased its coverage of black news items in favor of reports about the activities of white abolitionists; in fact, William Lloyd Garrison actively discouraged the establishment of early black papers such as *Colored American* and *North Star*.[26] Faced with exclusion and marginalization in white abolitionist societies, African-American leaders established their own anti-slavery conventions, which began in 1830 and continued intermittently until 1893.[27] During these national conventions black leaders gathered to discuss strategies which would best suit the African-American vision of freedom in America. While there was much disagreement about what those strategies should be, even those leaders most opposed to the conventions attended, treating them as "a medium through which we may deliberately devise means to operate and cooperate with our white friends, against . . . slavery and prejudice."[28] One of the most important topics of these conventions was the need to establish a national press, from which the proceedings of the conventions could be communicated to the everyday world of the free black community. The point is that both the black press and the black public sphere were established for the purpose of self-repre-sentation and for the creation of autonomous, supportive spaces of public dialogue and deliberation.

Frederick Douglass, one of the leaders of the convention movement, was one of the most ardent supporters of the idea of a national black press. Douglass argued that if free blacks could build successful public institu-tions they would be better able to reach both whites and blacks who were "outside" of the African-American communicative spaces organized by the convention movement. What Douglass was pointing to was a dual role for the black press and public sphere: (1) to provide a forum for debate and self-improvement; and (2) to increase black visibility in white civil society. In other words, the black press was designed to protect cultural autonomy at the same time as it would allow for the possibility of more successful inter-public engagement. This dual role of the black press, which I identified in Chapter 1 as being characteristic of alternative counter-publics, was a standard feature in the self-representation of the black press. As John Russworm argued in an 1827 editorial of *Freedom's Journal*: "the dissemi-nation of useful knowledge among our brethren, and to their moral and religious improvement, must meet with the cordial approbation of every friend of humanity."[29] The point was that white society did not have a true knowledge of black affairs, and that the only way to correct this was to develop active, aggressive, public, and progressive black spaces of debate and opinion formation. Thus, the formation of a national black press was seen as the solution to the ills of black society, white society, and the nation as a whole.

Despite the fact that such a broad consensus existed among nineteenth-century African-American leaders regarding the importance of a national black press, no durable successful black papers developed until the late-nineteenth and early-twentieth century. Before that time, most of the papers were forced to rely for economic support on contributions from (mostly white) fraternal, religious, and abolitionist groups; advertising inserts and subscription revenues were simply too small to provide enough revenue.[30] This overwhelming reliance on private subsidies meant that the existence of a given newspaper was always uncertain, because of the relationship of dependence between subsidizer and publisher. Even Frederick Douglass's papers suffered from this precarious position of dependence; his *North Star*, which was renamed *Frederick Douglass' Paper* in 1851, failed in 1860; his *New National Era* failed in 1874.[31] The conditions for a more stable African-American press would not develop until the twentieth century.

The urban ghetto and the public sphere

The first part of the twentieth century was a period of rapid population growth for the cities of the north and west. Between 1900 and 1940, the population of New York and Chicago more than doubled; the population of Los Angeles increased by more than 1600 percent. As a percentage of total population, the African-American populations of these cities also increased dramatically, from between 1.7 and two percent of population in 1900 to well over ten percent of population in 1940; this surge was consistent with a more national trend, as the number of blacks in the north surged by over 316 percent between 1900 and 1940.[32] This demographic movement was caused by developments in the north and in the south. From the south, African-Americans were "pushed" northward by an increase in lynchings, which were made easier after the discontinuation of the Freedmen's Bureau. From the north, they were "pulled" by greater economic prospects, and by the publicity activities of black newspapers such as the *Chicago Defender*.

As African-American populations surged in the northern cities, so too did the number of restrictions and the nature of hostility against black residents. The result was a rapid rise in residential segregation between 1900 and 1940.[33] While there may have been an increase in the *regional* integration of African Americans, it was generally accompanied by the creation of urban ghettos and correspondingly higher levels of neighborhood-level segregation.[34] This occurred most rapidly in Chicago, and somewhat more slowly in New York and Los Angeles.[35] By 1940, however, segregation was extremely high in all three cities.[36] The rise in residential segregation was generally accompanied by a corresponding increase of physical hostility and exclusion against African-American residents. In the area of employment, blacks were largely excluded from skilled industrial labor, paid at much lower wage levels when allowed to work, excluded from union membership, and used by management as strikebreakers.[37] As

Wilson has noted, "the significance of black strikebreaking is not that it provided an early opportunity for Negroes to enter northern industries . . . but that it created incidents that dramatically revealed and directly contributed to a racially charged atmosphere."[38] The consequence of these increasing exclusions and hostilities was an increased threat for blacks living in northern cities.

These demographic and social changes had important consequences for the African-American and mainstream public spheres, as well as for their corresponding news media. In the African-American publics, the combination of increased population, segregation, and external threat had the effect of producing an institutional ghetto, where the community was forced to create separate social institutions: banks, hospitals, YMCAs, community centers, and other service organizations. On the one hand, many of these institutions faced continual economic pressures that threatened their ability to provide quality service. On the other hand, they helped to produce vibrant black public spheres. Although the specific character of black public life varied between cities, what all of them shared were strong social supports and civic institutions. Indeed, this vibrancy has provided an important context for many of today's social science narratives of black urban decay. At the beginning of *The Truly Disadvantaged*, to take one of the most famous examples, Wilson comments that "unlike the present period, inner-city communities prior to 1960 exhibited the features of social organization – including a sense of community, positive neighborhood identification, and explicit norms and sanctions against aberrant behavior."[39] Lonnie Bunch has made the same point with specific reference to Los Angeles:

Talk with any Black Angeleno over the age of fifty and he will wax poetic about the richness of life along Central Avenue, describing the plethora of homes, the wonderful atmosphere and music that flowed from the Club Alabam and The Apex Club, the economic promise of black business . . . the pride in self that sprang from the bookstores, literary guilds, and community organizations like the YMCA or Garvey's UNIA. Compare that passion with the spirit of resignation that accompanies his discussion about life along "the avenue" in 1989.[40]

The important thing to note in the comments of Wilson and Bunch is that the social disorganization of today's black urban community is not understood through a comparison with contemporary white urban communities, but rather, through comparisons with black urban communities of the past. New York, Chicago, and Los Angeles all claim a more supportive past for their black communities, corresponding with the golden age of the black press. It is worth examining the specific ways in which those cities developed vibrant civic spaces within a context of increased segregation, exclusion, and external threat.

New York

New York's black community during the first part of the twentieth century was associated most closely with Harlem, and with the cultural movement that came to be known as the Harlem Renaissance. Harlem was not always the residential center of New York's African-American community. In the early nineteenth century most African-Americans in New York lived in the Five Points district, on the site of the present City Hall and in the blocks surrounding it.[41] At the turn of the century most of the population lived between Twentieth and Sixty-Third Streets, in a scattering of neighborhoods, none of which was all-black. Harlem itself was largely an upper- and upper-middle-class residential suburb from the 1870s until the turn of the century, its attractiveness spurred largely by the building of the elevated railroad. The construction of new subway routes into the neighborhood in the late 1890s set off a boom in land speculation, which continued until the collapse of land values in 1904–1905. At the same time, many of the black residents in the Tenderloin district were being displaced to make way for the construction of Pennsylvania Station. This confluence of factors, together with the rapidly increasing African-American population in New York, led many landlords in Harlem to begin renting to blacks, charging the traditionally-higher rents associated with such practices at the time; other landlords used the threat to frighten neighbors into buying their property at higher than market prices; still others sold to African-Americans and bought the adjoining properties from white neighbors at a fraction of their price. By 1910, Harlem had become a distinctive and unusual setting for New York's African-American community. As Osofsky describes it, many "were willing to scrimp to live in beautiful apartments in an exclusive section of the city."[42]

For the "talented tenth" represented by the Harlem Renaissance, Harlem became the ideal spatial setting, a landscape which could nurture the creation of an African-American culture of world-historical significance. Many of the intellectual leaders of the Harlem Renaissance migrated from the Southern states to live in Harlem, causing DuBois to refer to a "migration of the talented tenth."[43] The migration was not composed exclusively, or even primarily, of intellectual, political, and cultural leaders; most, as DuBois recognized, were young, unskilled, and unmarried. But Harlem did benefit from the migration of a large pool of intellectual talent, and it came to take on an epic and utopian air during the first decades of the twentieth century. Alain Locke described the situation in the following way: "In

Harlem, Negro life is seizing upon its first chances for group expression and self determination . . . Harlem has the same role to play as Dublin had for the New Ireland or Prague for the New Czechoslovakia."[44]

The spatial location of the community in Harlem helped to shape the black public sphere there through a conflict or dialogue between DuBoisian elitists and Garveyite populists. For the intellectual and professional elite, who could afford to live in the large apartments designed for upper-middle-class lifestyles, Harlem provided a comfortable and exciting setting for fashioning a new program of African-American culture. Correspondingly, the reception class of the Harlem Renaissance was not the African-American masses, but rather "the physicians, dentists, educators, preachers, business people, lawyers, and morticians who comprised the bulk of the African-American affluent and influential – some ten thousand men and women out of a total population in 1920 of more than ten million.[45] The goal of this movement was to catalyse a new culture of racial assertiveness, and to establish institutions that could provide the strength of solidarity and identity as a base for fighting for the extension of social rights. The Renaissance produced an outpouring of cultural expression: the writings of Countee Cullen, Claude McKay, Langston Hughes, Alain Locke, and W. E. B. DuBois; the art of Winold Reiss and Aaron Douglas; the music of Ma Rainey. It also produced some of the first mass-circulation African-American political journals, including *The Crisis*, which DuBois edited from 1910 to 1934, and which had well over 100,000 subscribers at one point.

Reacting against the elitism of the DuBoisian program, other black politicians in New York argued that the African-American community could only reach its potential through a more populist movement and through the complete separation from white society.[46] The difficult circumstances of poor blacks living in Harlem led to a reaction by some against the elitism of Harlem's intellectual leaders, leading many of them to find an alternative worldview in the leadership of Marcus Garvey and his Universal Negro Improvement Association (UNIA). Garvey argued that "pseudo-leaders" such as DuBois, the National Association for the Advancement of Colored People (NAACP), and "others of the race aristocracy," were trying to construct for themselves a buffer class between whites and blacks, and to eventually "join the powerful race and crush the blood of their mothers."[47] Garvey did not want only to create a new and distinctive African-American culture, but rather wanted to create an entirely new civilization. He complained that the "professional Negro leader" felt that it was "easier to seize on to the civilization of the white man and under the guise of constitutional rights fight for those things that the white man has created."[48]

While the Garvey movement developed in opposition to DuBois and the

Harlem Renaissance, it participated in a parallel and often overlapping communicative space; as David Levering Lewis has described it, the Garvey movement was "a parallel but socially different force [from the Renaissance] related primarily through dialectical confrontation."[49] Garvey's weekly *Negro World* newspaper, which reached a circulation of nearly 200,000 in the 1920s,[50] counted among its frequent contributors such Harlem Renaissance luminaries as Claude McKay, Zora Neale Hurston, Eric Waldron, Arthur Schomburg, and Carter G. Woodson.[51]

By the 1920s, the African-American community in New York had articulated a strong vision of distinctiveness in the cultural and political realms. This dialogue and debate, if it did nothing else, encouraged active participation in the black public spheres and news media of New York. Despite the high circulation figures for Garvey's *Negro World* and DuBois's *Crisis*, by the mid-1930s the media organs of the Harlem Renaissance and the Garvey movement were in crisis. Garvey was deported to Jamaica in 1926, and his newspaper suspended publication in 1933. DuBois stopped editing *The Crisis* in 1934, leaving New York to become chair of the Sociology Department at Atlanta University. Into the newly-created media void stepped the *Amsterdam News*, which became the leading press organization of New York's African-American community. Established in 1909, the paper received stronger financial backing when it was purchased in 1936 by two doctors, Philip Savory and C. B. Powell, who combined sensationalism with the theme of racial equality to build the circulation of the paper.[52] A leading participant in the "Don't Buy Where You Can't Work" campaign of the 1920s and 1930s, the paper faced competition from the *New York Age* and from Adam Clayton Powell's *People's Voice* until about 1950, by which time it had clearly become the dominant African-American newspaper in New York. An heir to the discursive history of Black New York, the *Amsterdam News* has tended toward greater militancy in its reporting and editorials than either the *Chicago Defender* or *Los Angeles Sentinel*. While it never reached the circulation figures of *Negro World* or *The Crisis*, it did continue to build its readership base through the 1950s and 1960s, and in 1971 the paper had a circulation of more than 70,000.[53]

Chicago

While Chicago has for some time been the most segregated city in the country, it did not begin that way.[54] In 1870, when the number of African-Americans living in Chicago amounted to less than one percent of the city's population, there was no definable black ghetto. While discrimination in housing and employment certainly existed, most neighborhoods of

Chicago in which African-Americans lived were mixed; while most African-Americans lived on the South Side of Chicago, there were almost no all-black residential blocks.[55] The franchise was granted to blacks in Chicago in 1870, and the school system was desegregated in 1874. As Spear notes, most African-American leaders during this period had good reasons to be firmly committed to the ideal of a fully integrated community.[56]

With the influx of large numbers of African-Americans into Chicago, however, practices of exclusion, hostility, and violence increased dramatically. There were several strategies used by white residents of the city. One was the "neighborhood improvement association," in which real estate agents were directed to sell property only to whites in certain residential blocks.[57] These associations typically appointed committees to purchase property owned by blacks in "white" blocks, and they offered bonuses to black renters who would surrender their leases. In order to enforce this segregationist movement further, the associations also threatened to blacklist any real estate firm that defied them. There was also, during this time, a concerted and open movement to re-segregate the schools. The use of black skilled labor as strike-breakers exacerbated anti-black sentiments even further. As Spear has commented in his excellent history of black Chicago, "The use of Negro scab labor heightened anti-Negro feeling in the city and left a legacy of bitterness and distrust between white and black workers. In the 1904 stockyard strike and the 1905 teamsters strike, the importance of non-union Negro labor set off the most serious racial conflicts of the prewar period."[58] Between July 1917 and March 1921, there were fifty-eight racially-inspired bombings in Chicago, and a major race riot in 1919.[59]

While most African-American leaders in Chicago had been relentless crusaders against the biracial system, the increasing violence in Chicago forced many of them to reassess their goals, to shift toward Booker T. Washington's ideology of self-sufficiency and separate institutions, and to help create the "black metropolis" described in Drake and Cayton's ethnographic study of "Bronzeville."[60] Perhaps more than any other city, the experience of hostility, violence, and exclusion in Chicago encouraged the development of an "institutional ghetto," completely separate from the business and service organizations of the larger city. Between 1910 and 1920, the number of census tracts in Chicago which were more than fifty percent African-American increased from four to sixteen; by 1920, thirty-five percent of blacks in Chicago lived in areas which were more than seventy-five percent African-American.[61] In order to compensate for this increasing isolation, a myriad number of community organizations, institutions, and businesses helped to convert the dream of an integrated city into the vision of a "black metropolis." This separate community life extended into the realms of religion, healthcare, insurance, and even politics. By 1937, Chicago had more than 4,000 formal African-American associations, serving an African-American population of less than 275,000.[62]

Perhaps the best expression of the new self-understanding of Chicago's African-American community can be found in the leading African-American newspaper in Chicago, the *Defender*. Founded in 1905 by Robert Abbott, the *Defender* was always friendly towards Washington's ideology.[63] Abbott clearly disliked the "talented tenth" theory of DuBois, and argued strongly for race pride, self-help, and race solidarity. The *Defender* also waged a vigorous campaign against Garveyism, which was an important reason for the relative weakness of the movement in Chicago. Generally, the *Defender* supported self-sufficiency and self-help, but not separatism: cultivation of manners and civility, but not elitism.

The success of the *Chicago Defender* was unparalleled among African-American newspapers. Circulation figures for the newspaper reached as high as 230,000 in 1915.[64] During this period the *Defender* became the closest thing to a national newspaper the African-American press has ever produced, circulating in seventy-one cities; it also became the largest African-American business in Chicago, with sixty-eight employees and a physical plant worth about $500,000.[65] Drake and Cayton have argued, in fact, that the *Defender* became by far the most important forum for public opinion in the black community of Chicago, even more significant than the church.[66] This type of business success and communicative centralization, along with parallel developments in the areas of business, insurance, healthcare, and politics, helped to create the specific civic character of "Bronzeville" – a fictitious name actually created by the *Defender* as part of the promotion of race pride and race solidarity.[67] After the First World War the *Defender*'s circulation dropped to about 180,000, due to competition from the new *Chicago Whip*, and its editorial policy began to shift from its previous stance of sensationalism and "race-angling" to a more muted policy of patience in matters of racial conflict and social change.[68] After the Depression, circulation dropped even further, and by 1935 was down to 73,000. But the *Defender* has remained one of the leading African-American papers, and has been the only one to successfully maintain a daily edition.

Los Angeles

Although much smaller during the first part of the twentieth century, the African-American public sphere in Los Angeles benefited from the vitality of the nationalizing spheres in Chicago and New York. In 1900 there were only about 2,000 African-Americans in Los Angeles, and only about 102,000 residents in the entire city; even by 1920 the number of African-Americans living in Los Angeles was a relatively modest 15,579. Yet during this early period, the "California Dream" seemed attainable to white as well as to black migrants.[69] *The Liberator*, an African-American newspaper of the time, declared in 1913 that "the colored people in California are the best fixed in the United States."[70] W. E. B. DuBois, upon returning from a trip to Los Angeles in 1913, wrote: "Los Angeles is wonderful. Nowhere in the United States is the Negro so well and beautifully housed, nor the average efficiency and intelligence in the colored population so high. Out here in this matchless Southern California there would seem to be no limit to your opportunities, your possibilities."[71] One reason for optimism of this sort was the ability for African-Americans to purchase homes in Los Angeles. Housing subdivisions in Watts were advertised for as little as $10 down payment and $5 per month; by 1910, 36.1 percent of Black Angelenos owned their own home, as compared to 2.4 percent of African-Americans living in New York.[72] Segregation in Los Angeles was significantly lower during this period than it was in New York or Chicago.

The black community in Los Angeles was organized around the Central Avenue district, which housed the black-owned *California Eagle*, the Golden State Mutual Life Insurance Company, the Liberty Savings and Loan, the Dunbar Hospital, and the 28th Street YMCA.[73] Culturally and politically, the Central Avenue district looked like a miniature Harlem. The jazz clubs made Central Avenue one of the entertainment centers for the entire city, replete with the "slumming" practices of white youth; theatrical and literary productions also followed the pattern of the Harlem Renaissance. The Hotel Somerville, built by one of the early presidents of the Los Angeles branch of the NAACP, opened in 1928 and hosted the national convention of the NAACP in the very same year. In addition to the NAACP, Marcus Garvey's UNIA was also quite popular in Los Angeles during the 1920s.[74]

While segregation may have been lower in 1920 in Los Angeles than it was in Chicago or New York, this does not mean that racism was absent. In fact, while praising Los Angeles, DuBois also realized that "Los Angeles is not paradise . . . the color line is there and sharply drawn."[75] An increase in racial antagonisms began with the migration of southern whites after 1910, who brought their anti-black prejudices with them; hostilities also resulted from the narrow civic culture of eastern and midwestern migrants who were consciously striving to build a city free of the ethnic heterogeneity from where they had sought to escape.[76] Southern whites created a whites-only jitney bus system in Los Angeles in 1914, with the goal of creating separate public transportation facilities.[77] The Ku Klux Klan arrived in Los Angeles in 1915, and by 1920 racial housing covenants were common, public, and strictly enforced. As a 1922 article of the *Santa Monica Weekly Interpreter* exclaimed, "Negroes . . . we don't want you here; now and forever, this is to be a white man's town."[78] With the imposition of restrictive housing covenants, segregation in Los Angeles increased rapidly, and was almost as high as New York by 1940, and only slightly lower than Chicago.[79]

Because Los Angeles started with a much smaller African-American population than Chicago or New York, the black public sphere there was maintained almost exclusively, for some time, by an interactional public sphere, organized by the Los Angeles Forum. The Forum began in February 1903 at the First A. M. E. Church, as a "club of intelligent colored men from the various churches of the city."[80] In its weekly meetings, the Forum offered lectures, debates, and discussions of political affairs. It encouraged "even the humblest citizens" to attend the meetings and to participate in the discussions; its "committee on strangers" was designed to help new migrants to adjust to life in Los Angeles. By 1920, even though the population of African-Americans was relatively small in Los Angeles, local and state politicians actively sought the support of Forum leaders.[81] As the community began to expand rapidly in the 1930s and 1940s, however, the Forum began to lose its viability, and the group held its last meeting in 1942. As the interactional public sphere declined, it came to be replaced by a mass-mediated public sphere, and the city's black press grew accordingly.

As the press became the dominant communicative space for the black public sphere of Los Angeles, the *Los Angeles Sentinel* came to replace a number of older and smaller newspapers to become the community's dominant paper. Founded in 1934, the *Sentinel* did not suffer the economic calamities of the Depression, as had its main competitor the *California Eagle* (founded in 1879, ceased publication in 1967). Begun in 1934 by Leon Washington, who organized in that same year a "Don't Buy Where You Can't Work" campaign in Los Angeles, the *Sentinel* fought hard for integration. It continued to grow in circulation through the 1940s and 1950s, helped in part by the large number of African-Americans streaming into Southern California to work in the expanding war industries. The *Sentinel* has tended to be moderate rather than militant in its orientation, strongly outspoken on issues of civil rights, and generally supportive of the Democratic Party.[82]

In general, then, the first half of the twentieth century was a good time for the black press, even if, in other respects, it was a very difficult period for the urbanizing African-American population. Total circulation was at an all-time high, and new newspapers were appearing almost every week.[83] There was a strong link with the NAACP, which sent regular news releases to black papers, and whose leaders wrote regular columns for the leading black papers. The National Negro Press Association, which had been founded in 1909, was reorganized and revitalized in 1940 by John Sengstakke of the *Chicago Defender*.[84] It was in this context that African-American leaders such as Thurgood Marshall praised the black press, recognizing its importance for organizing African-American public discussions about matters of racial concern.

There were two meanings to Marshall's statement, "without the Negro press, the NAACP would get nowhere." Certainly the black press provided a space for forming arguments about integration and civil rights which would later find their way into the public spaces of communication in white civil society. This is the normative picture of counter-publics, which are supposed to simultaneously increase the likelihood of inter-public engagement and intra-public autonomy. But the NAACP had no other news media it could rely on *except* the black press. By 1940, the *New York Times*, *Chicago Tribune*, and *Los Angeles Times* had emerged clearly as the dominant newspapers of their respective cities, and could easily afford to ignore the growing African-American residents in their cities. Before the 1960s, it was rare for race news to account for more than one percent of total news space in the mainstream press.[85]

In general, the first half of the twentieth century was a period when the mainstream newspaper filtered its stories through wartime narratives that pushed racial concerns to the sidelines, or through the wartime tropes of patriotism and brotherhood. During the First World War, many mainstream journalists became directly involved in the efforts of wartime propaganda: James Keeley, managing editor of the *Chicago Tribune*, served on the Inter-Allied Board for Propaganda; Charles Merz, of the *New York Times*, served as a lieutenant in the intelligence service; President Wilson's Committee on Public Information, which employed many journalists, wrote some 6,000 press releases during the war.[86] As the imperatives of national security came increasingly to influence the practice of news work, and as the public relations activities of government flooded journalists with press releases and "pseudo-events," it became harder and harder for other public actors or public issues to find their way onto the stage of the mainstream public sphere. What race news did appear was likely to be stereotypical, prejudicial, and pejorative, and overcoded by the narrative imperatives of wartime patriotism. Within this context, the African-American press received significant and negative attention. During the First World War, the

American government believed that the black press was dangerous for morale, and attempted to control the editors of black newspapers.[87] During the Second World War, the *New York Times*, *Chicago Tribune*, and *Los Angeles Times* criticized the black press for "irresponsible," "misleading," and "inaccurate" coverage of the war.[88] All of these factors helped to ensure that the black press would remain an important communicative institution of the African-American public sphere.

General trends in the African-American and mainstream public spheres, 1950–1990

The second half of the twentieth century has been a trying time for the black press. Many African-American newspapers reached their highest circulation figures in the late-1940s, but since then most have suffered circulation declines. Between 1950 and 1969, many African-American papers lost between fifty and seventy-five percent of their circulation, and they have continued to lose circulation ever since.[89] For example, the *New York Amsterdam News* had a circulation of 74,213 in 1966, which decreased to 37,561 in 1986 and to 30,994 in 1994. The circulation of the *Chicago Defender* decreased from 36,541 in 1966 to 22,611 in 1986 and 23,498 in 1994. The *Los Angeles Sentinel*'s circulation decreased from 34,284 in 1966 to 25,225 in 1986 and 25,000 in 1994. These losses have weakened a set of communicative institutions which have been historically important for the African-American public sphere: not only as spaces for protecting cultural autonomy, but also as spaces where arguments could be crafted that would be used in the future to engage other publics in discussion and deliberation. Several factors have contributed to this decline.

One factor leading to the decline of the black press has been the nationalization of the news, precipitated by the rise of television and the extension of major metropolitan newspapers into increasingly nationalized markets. Journalism has increasingly become a national profession, dominated by the national television networks and the elite metropolitan newspapers. In 1962, each of the three national television networks offered fifteen minutes of news each day; by 1966 this had increased to ninety minutes, and by 1987 most television stations broadcast at least three hours of news every day.[90] The rise of television news encouraged an expectation that news delivery be immediate and convenient. As a result black newspapers, which are produced weekly and sold predominantly at urban newsstands, became far less convenient in relative terms.

The rise of television news also nationalized the scope of news coverage and the practice of journalism, forcing newspapers to nationalize their staff by opening regional bureaus and appointing correspondents all over the country. Between 1971 and 1992, the proportion of journalists who had a college degree in communication or journalism increased from 27.5 to 48.4 percent and newspapers were more likely than ever to recruit nationally for their writers and editors.[91] This has made the elite press more influential than ever; a recent survey found that twenty-six percent of journalists read the *New York Times* regularly.[92] As Schudson has argued in this regard, "the managers of small papers or television news shows around the country are aware, as never before, of what goes on the networks, in *USA Today*, in the *New York Times*. So are their employees."[93]

The more nationalized orientation of journalism has primarily benefited the strongest metropolitan dailies, who could profit from the formation of national news services. The *New York Times* news service, which in 1960 had only fifty clients (after fifty years of operation), had more than 500 clients by 1980; the *Los Angeles Times* was transformed from a provincial newspaper with only one foreign bureau and a reporting staff of two in its Washington bureau in 1960, to a "distinguished professional newspaper" less than ten years later.[94] The *Los Angeles Times* and *Washington Post* combined in 1961 to create their own separate news service, which had more than 350 clients by 1980.[95] The *Chicago Tribune* has made similar types of changes, establishing a Washington bureau of more than twenty reporters, and setting up its own news service.[96] By establishing successful national news services, these "elite newspapers" have created an additional source of revenue at the same time as they have seen their circulation increase rapidly. Papers which could not establish news services faced declining circulation and rising costs, paying for the new news services in order to maintain their readership. In this sense, the crisis of the black press was part of a larger crisis facing small and medium-sized newspapers.

Of all the factors leading to the decline of the black press, however, two stand out: the increasing isolation of the urban ghetto, and the residential mobility of an increasingly large black middle class. Historically, the black public sphere and the black press were spatially grounded in vibrant urban communities. After the Second World War, however, structural changes in the economy, together with improvements in transportation and communication, brought about a decentralization in American business that has decreased the number of jobs in the inner city. The proportion of manufacturing done in the central cities of the twelve largest metropolitan areas, to take an example, dropped from 66.1 percent in 1947 to less than forty percent in 1970, and has continued to decline ever since.[97] In Chicago, the number of manufacturing jobs located within the city limits decreased from 616,000 in 1954 to 172,000 in 1982.[98] The result of these structural changes

has been that much of the tax base for the cities has been eroded, leading
to chronic fiscal crises in the increasingly ghettoized inner cities. This has
hurt poor blacks disproportionately.[99] It has also encouraged middle-class
blacks to leave the inner city.

The residential mobility of a growing black middle class has led to the
increasing social isolation of the urban areas that have traditionally housed
civic institutions such as the black press. In the 1940s and 1950s, black
middle-class professionals lived in the ghetto communities, on higher-
income streets, and serviced those ghetto communities. As they began to
leave these communities in the 1960s, to live in higher-income parts of the
city and suburbs, their exodus removed an "important social buffer" which
would otherwise have been able to deflect some of the impact of poverty
and joblessness.[100] With the exodus of middle-class blacks the basic institutions of ghetto communities – such as churches, schools, newspapers, and
recreational facilities – have found it more difficult to remain viable as the
more stable and secure residents migrated out of the area. As middle-class
students have moved out of inner-city public schools, those schools have
become decoupled from a culture of academic success and the dominant
linguistic patterns of American society.[101] As the successes of the Civil
Rights movement allowed many middle-class blacks to shop at the better-
stocked and lower-priced white department stores, inner-city black retail
businesses lost many of their customers.[102] As middle-class blacks moved
further away from the newsstands which sold black newspapers, those
black papers were forced to deal with increased distribution costs. Finally,
as the mainstream press began to court the black middle class, African-
American newspapers lost many of their readers.

By the late 1960s, there was developing an urgent realization among
those in the mainstream press that they had excluded African-Americans
from the pages of the newspaper and from the spaces of the newsroom. The
1968 Kerner Commission report, trying to explain the causes of the 1960s
urban revolts and to suggest possible remedies, found that one of the most
significant problems was that the everyday lives of African-Americans were
largely invisible in the mainstream media, and that African-American journalists were severely under-represented in the mainstream newsroom.
During the 1965 Watts uprising, for example, the *Los Angeles Times* found
itself without a single African-American reporter, and had to rely on
someone from the advertising department to get reports from the streets.[103]
The Kerner Commission recommended a quick remedy to both of these
absences.

Efforts to recruit and develop African-American journalists for the mainstream daily press, begun after the urban uprisings of the 1960s, have had some success. The Kerner Commission report had found that fewer than one percent of journalists in the daily press were African-American, and strongly urged that the hiring of black journalists begin immediately.[104] By 1971, only three years later, there had been an increase to 3.9 percent. Most of these journalists joining the mainstream press came from the black press, leading *Chicago Defender* publisher John Sengstakke to comment that "over the years, we have been training them and they have been stealing them."[105] In other words, increased hiring of African-American journalists by mainstream news organizations has created problems for the African-American press, which has suffered a loss of participation by leading African-American journalists and guest columnists. Today, national African-American leaders are far more likely to write guest editorials in the mainstream press, whereas Martin Luther King, Jr., Roy Wilkins, Whitney Young, Langston Hughes, and even Jackie Robinson all wrote regularly for the African-American press during the 1960s, and only occasionally for the mainstream press. In 1970 James Williams, information director of the U. S. Commission on Civil Rights, and a former editor of a black newspaper, wrote that "in a fully integrated society, the black press would shrink and eventually vanish."[106] The problem is, however, that while the black press has been shrinking, the mainstream press is nowhere near to being fully integrated.

While the goal of eliminating the African-American press was predicated on a commitment to participate in an integrated mainstream press, in reality this never came to pass. The proportion of mainstream journalists who are African-American actually declined between 1971 and 1992, leaving blacks vastly under-represented in the news rooms of the major papers.[107] News about African-Americans and African-American issues has also stagnated or declined since 1970, never surpassing four percent of total column inches.[108] Exceptions occur, of course, during times of racial crisis, but here the forms of coverage show strong traces of white hegemony, such that heroic character positions are reserved almost exclusively for whites. Where no white heroes can be found to narrate a romantic conclusion to the crisis, mainstream news coverage tends overwhelmingly to favor the tragic genre, as Chapter 5 will show. Clearly, any integration into the mainstream press has been incomplete at best. In the meantime, the black press has continued to shrink, a fact which has discouraged black newspapers from investing in new communications technology. Thus, while the *New York Times*, *Chicago Tribune*, and *Los Angeles Times* all maintain extensive and regularly visited websites, the *New York Amsterdam News*,

Chicago Defender, and *Los Angeles Sentinel* have yet to set up websites of their own. While the mainstream press becomes easier and easier to access, the African-American press becomes comparatively more remote.

Still, this decline in circulation should not be taken to mean that the black press is completely unimportant. As I argued in Chapter 1, the power of something like the black press is not tied directly to the number of people who read it. Rather, its potential power resides in the fact that people know it is there, available to be read should the need be perceived. One important reason for this is that interest in the black press tends to increase during periods of racial crisis. This was particularly true during the 1960s, when the African-American press stood on the cusp of a past vitality and a future crisis. For example, the *Los Angeles Sentinel* distributed 61,000 issues of its August 19, 1965 issue (the first after the Watts uprisings), which sold out on the first day despite the fact that this was nearly twice as many copies as the average weekly circulation for that year. From 1966–1970, during the period after Watts, circulation figures for the *Sentinel* actually increased, from 34,384 to 41,482. A similar phenomenon occurred during the 1990s, where the *Sentinel* saw an increase in circulation during the two years after the Rodney King crises. The point is that the black press offers an autonomous voice which is "other" than mainstream civil society. During periods of crisis, the black press offers an additional resource for African-Americans to use in dialogue when discussing matters of common concern, as well as an autonomous source of public narratives about civil society and nation. The black press, to put matters simply, continues to secure the existence of an independent black public sphere. For all of these reasons, the decline of the African-American press should be viewed as a crisis for civil society.

The Watts crisis of 1965 occurred during an important transitional period in the history of race, press, and public sphere. Nationally, Watts was the event that served as the wake-up call for the mainstream press, which quickly moved to change its racial hiring and reporting practices. The 1965 crisis also occurred during a transitional stage of development for the black public sphere, particularly when compared to the crises of the 1990s. During the 1960s, circulation for the black press was still quite large, national leaders of the African-American community contributed regularly to the black press, and the successes of the civil rights movement encouraged an understanding of the future through a romantic "theme of ascent." By 1990, however, more black journalists wrote for the mainstream press, more national leaders of the African-American community participated primarily in the mainstream public sphere, circulation in the black press had declined severely, and the urban ghetto – the former space of the "golden age of the black public sphere" – had become markedly segregated by class. This question about the fragmentation of the black public spheres, as well as the question regarding the corresponding nationalization of news culture in the mainstream public spheres, offer a useful way to frame the particular case studies that follow. How much did African-American news narratives change as a result of contemporary circulation declines? How much did the nationalization of news culture influence news narratives of racial crisis in the *Chicago Tribune* and *Los Angeles Times*? And how did the greater dependence on the mainstream press influence the black public sphere?

3

The Watts uprisings of 1965

A good deal of ink has been spilt in an attempt to determine the causes, both short- and long-term, that were responsible for the five days of destruction and unrest in the Watts section of Los Angeles during August 1965.[1] A good deal less attention has been paid, however, to the cultural effects Watts had on the many different public spheres of civil society, both in Los Angeles and throughout the nation. At the national level Watts, along with the 1964 urban riots in Harlem, Rochester, and Philadelphia, not to mention Chicago in 1965 and Detroit in 1967, was important in re-directing some attention away from the civil rights struggles of the south and toward the different problems that existed in the urban centers of the north and west. In these cities, where African-Americans already were sup-posed to possess the rights being fought for in the south, the urban upris-ings led to the first recognition in the mainstream public of the existence of a frustrated and desperate "underclass." In Los Angeles, the riot shattered the indifference of the white population toward the activities and concerns of the African-American community. At the same time, the events of Watts were crucial in galvanizing African-American opposition against Los Angeles Mayor Samuel Yorty, and they were central to the biracial coali-tion through which Thomas Bradley was eventually able to defeat Yorty and become mayor.[2]

The uprisings of Watts should not have come as a total surprise; there were definite and identifiable factors contributing to racial tension in Los Angeles. The 1964 passage of Proposition 14, which was intended to repeal the Rumford Fair Housing Act, had been heavily supported in most pre-dominantly white districts in Los Angeles and strongly opposed in predomi-nantly black districts.[3] Mayor Samuel Yorty had refused to pursue federal anti-poverty funds, costing Los Angeles – and in particular the predomi-nantly African-American district of Watts – millions of dollars.[4] There was

54

also a general and persistent refusal on the part of conservative white members of the City Council to consider any investigations into police-minority relations, despite the fact that this issue was important to the African-American community and was introduced repeatedly by council members Thomas Bradley and Rosalind Wyman.[5]

These problematic signs were not noticed, however, for two important reasons: first, because African-American issues were generally invisible in the mainstream press, unless they were raised by Martin Luther King, Jr.; and second, because the national image of Los Angeles had historically been one where the African-American community was seen to be better situated than in most other American cities. The historical experience of the African-American community of Los Angeles was one of lower population density and higher rates of home ownership than in northern cities. In the area of employment, wartime industry had been tremendously beneficial to the African-American community in Los Angeles; in March 1965, only five months before the uprisings, *Ebony* magazine had listed Los Angeles as one of the top ten cities for African-American employment. Finally, black Los Angeles had historically suffered less discrimination than the adjacent Latino communities, a factor which created a sense of relative advantage.

This positive image of black Los Angeles was shattered, however, during the Watts uprisings and the period of crisis that ensued. On August 11, 1965, a white California highway patrolman arrested an African-American, Marquette Frye, on suspicion of drunk driving. While the details which followed this arrest are disputed, what is known is that tensions escalated as a crowd grew to some 250–300 persons, more police arrived, and subsequent arrests were made. Members of the crowd began throwing stones as the last police car left the area, setting off a period of rioting that continued for some five days. At the conclusion of these events on August 15, there were thirty-four deaths, 1,032 injuries, over 4,000 arrests, and an estimated $40 million in property damage.[6] Governor Brown appointed a commission headed by John McCone to make "an objective and dispassionate study of the Los Angeles riots."[7] The commission began its investigation on September 16; after hearing from seventy-nine witnesses, conducting an additional ninety interviews, and questioning some 10,000 persons, the commission released an eighty-six page report on December 2. The report identified a number of factors which contributed to the Watts crisis, including police-community relations, unemployment, discrimination in employment, disadvantages in education, poverty, and ineffective and irresponsible African-American leadership. This last point, as well as the report's general descriptions of the rioters, fell under heavy criticism by an

African-American member of the commission, by other African-American leaders, and by a number of academics.

Between August 12 and December 10, a total of 606 news articles were written about Watts in the *Los Angeles Times*, *Los Angeles Sentinel*, *New York Times*, *New York Amsterdam News*, *Chicago Tribune*, and *Chicago Defender*. Seventy-five percent of these were written in the Los Angeles press, but a full 153 articles were written in the non-Los Angeles newspapers, and there certainly would have been more had there not been a strike that prevented publication of the *New York Times* between September 17 and October 10.

Early news reports about the crisis in Watts tended to concentrate on (1) descriptions of the rioters and (2) primary explanations for the cause of the destruction. Within the mainstream press, the similarities mainly concerned the descriptions of the rioters and their actions, which were described as being "irrational," "hysterical," and "indiscriminate." In terms of their causal narratives, however, there were significant differences between the papers. The primary explanation in the *New York Times* was that Watts resulted from the incomplete extension of social rights and the breakdown of the African-American family. The *Chicago Tribune* explained the events of Watts as a breakdown in law and order, and also as a failure of Californian politicians to act with sufficiently swift or decisive force. The *Los Angeles Times* narrated the Watts crisis as being caused by a breakdown in law and order, and also by the "extremist discourse" of leaders of the civil rights and anti-war movements. By contrast, all three African-American papers explained the events of Watts as being caused by the racism and brutality of police officers, and by general white indifference toward African-American social problems. Where they differed was in their description of the rioters. The *Los Angeles Sentinel* and the *Chicago Defender* described them as lawless, shameless, and engaged in senseless violence; in other words, their actions were the wrong means toward achieving a desired end. On the other hand, the *New York Amsterdam News* described the destructive actions of the rioters as rational, measured, and focused, the most rational action possible by those who were persistently ignored by a racist society.

The differences in news reports about Watts did not split neatly along racial lines, but were also influenced by the insertion of the Watts crisis into other, ongoing public narratives about, race, nation, and civil society. There were important differences here; depending on the paper, Watts was linked to the Cold War fight against Communism (*Chicago Tribune*, *Los Angeles Times*), the civil rights campaign of the federal government (*New York Times*, *Los Angeles Sentinel*, *Chicago Defender*), the entire history of race relations in America (*New York Amsterdam News*), and the exceptional mistakes of a few individuals in Los Angeles (*Chicago Tribune*). Related to these different narrative linkages were variations regarding the central character oppositions of the different news narratives. For example, linkage to the Cold War narrative reinforced the opposition of pro-order vs. anti-order. By contrast, linkage to the federal civil rights campaign reinforced the opposition of pro-federal intervention vs. obstructing federal intervention. Because of these sorts of intertextual interactions, the causal narrative of the *New York Times* often looked more like that of the African-American press than the daily papers of Chicago or New York; the descriptions of the rioters in the *Chicago Defender* and *Los Angeles Sentinel* looked rather more like the mainstream press than those in the *New York Amsterdam News*.

While the variation in news coverage did not split neatly along racial lines, however, there were important points of difference that show why the black press was an important resource for African-Americans trying to counter the hegemonic nature of the dominant media and public spheres. In each city, the African-American news coverage of Watts responded to the most negative aspects of the mainstream coverage. In this way, the African-American press served a protective function – providing alternative interpretations against the most damaging representations made in the dominant public spheres, and a different set of issues for African-American residents of these cities to discuss. The Watts crisis sparked vigorous discussion within the African-American public sphere, and black residents actively sought out the black press to get a different perspective than the one they were used to seeing in the dominant media. The *Los Angeles Sentinel* distributed 61,000 issues of its August 19, 1965 issue (the first after the Watts uprisings) which, despite being double the paper's average circulation, still sold out on the first day.

The Los Angeles press

Initial reports in the *Los Angeles Times* were unambiguously critical of the rioters and unquestioningly supportive of the police. Its news reports described the rioters as "youthful," "boastful," "irrational," and "insane," and described the riot zone as "terrifying" and "hysterical."[8] A front-page editorial described how "the rioters were burning their city now, as the insane sometimes mutilate themselves."[9] Other "objective" news reports offered evidence for this evaluation; for instance, accounts from eyewitnesses reported that the rioters were impeding the rescue work of fire trucks and ambulances, and also through "false reports designed to lure vehicles into the riot area."[10] With such a negative coding of the rioters and their actions, there was a naturalization of support for the police, who were coded positively. This worked initially through the principle of semiotic opposition, where opposition to the rioters also meant opposition to their putative motivation characteristics. Editorial opinion in the *Los Angeles Times* reinforced this opposition early and often, contrasting the forces of order and the forces of disorder.

Race rioting has brought anarchy to a crowded area of south Los Angeles. Terrorism is spreading. Whatever its root causes, the terror which has gripped the city for three days and three nights must be halted forthwith. If the National Guardsmen belatedly sent to the relief of Chief Parker's outnumbered police, sheriff's deputies and California Highway patrolmen are not enough, additional hundreds must be provided at once . . . Only after sanity is restored can there be any meaningful talk about long-range cures of the basic problems involved.

(*Los Angeles Times*, August 14, 1965: A1)

There are no words to express the shock, the sick horror, that a civilized city feels at a moment like this. It could not happen in Los Angeles. But it did. And the shameful, senseless, bloody rioting continues unabated after the four ugliest days in our history. Decent citizens everywhere, regardless of color, can only pray that this anarchy will soon end. Meanwhile the community, watching, waiting, praying, becomes more aware each moment of the debt owed its heroic law enforcement and fire fighting personnel. These men deserve the highest praise for their splendid efforts under unbelievably difficult conditions.

(*Los Angeles Times*, August 15, 1965: A1)

The placement of editorials on the front page of the paper signaled that evaluation was the proper frame for talking about the crisis, and that the evaluation should be pro-order and directed against the rioters. In such an interpretive environment there was no possible defense for the rioters, all attempts to stop them were just, and any discussion of the riot's causes were premature and wrong-headed. *Los Angeles Times* editorials and news reports merged together into a single text, describing the rioters and their supporters as anti-civil, evil enemies of civil society. This cultural dynamic was reinforced by the public statements made by Los Angeles Police Chief William Parker. Parker claimed that the riots occurred because people lost respect for the law, and he refused to meet with civil rights spokesmen on the grounds that there were no effective leaders.[11] Additionally, Parker blamed "pseudo-leaders" of the African-American community for persuading the police not to crack down when rioting first broke out, but then not being able to control the rioters themselves.[12] Finally, Parker said that any attempt to blame police for the riots was a "vicious canard." The *Los Angeles Times* reported all of these statements uncritically, and reinforced them by linking criticism of the police to "Communist press agencies" worldwide.[13]

In this developing narrative of the *Los Angeles Times*, where Parker became the heroic figure challenging the "pseudo-leaders" of the African-American community, the civil rights movement itself came to be a part of the crisis, representing a tragic breakdown in civility and social order. Watts quickly became a point of narrative linkage for the *Los Angeles Times* and its public speakers to criticize all forms of civil disobedience, including the leaders of the civil rights, student, and anti-war movements.

Under the leadership of a self-proclaimed peace lover, they have preached non-violence but winked at violence. They have preached love but winked at hate. They have talked about rights but never responsibilities. They have taught their people that law and order are a pedestrian way to achieve results and that civil disobedience is a virtue if it gets things done faster.   (*Los Angeles Times*, August 18, 1965: B5)

It [the rioting] is very much likelier to happen so long as the nation coddles the teachings of the Mario Savios and the Martin Luther Kings, and their disciples who, seeking an honorable motivation for the exercise of their anarchic instincts, walk away from the bloodshed they have caused citing the liturgy of a black mass, which excuses on some ground or other their heinous deeds.

(*Los Angeles Times*, August 20, 1965: B6)

Within this interpretive environment, Watts as a topic of serious discussion was viewed as very dangerous and polluting, used by Communists and the fanatical proponents of disobedience. The way this narrative was developing, the crisis of Watts was not one of violence, unemployment, or police brutality; rather, the crisis was the introduction of "extremist discourse" into the public sphere. In other words, Watts represented a threat to controlled, rational, and civilized behavior, and the rioters were seen as the dependent dupes of extremist discourse propagated by civil rights leaders and Communists. For the *Los Angeles Times* and its readers Watts represented an epic struggle against the forces of evil. The heroes in this struggle were the police, the enemies were African-American leaders of the civil rights movement, and the sacrificial victim was the belief in the possibility of racial understanding or tolerance. This understanding of Watts was reflected in the opinions of white residents in Los Angeles, seventy-four percent of whom believed that Watts hurt the civil rights movement, seventy-one percent that it increased the gap between the races, and seventy-nine percent of whom supported Chief Parker.[14] It was in marked contrast to African-American opinion in Los Angeles, however, where fifty-eight percent of those surveyed anticipated a favorable effect to come from Watts, only twenty-three percent expected it to increase the gap between the races, and seventy-six percent were critical of Chief Parker.[15]

In attempting to re-narrate the Watts crisis, those writing in the *Los Angeles Sentinel* were faced with trying to counter several damaging plots and characterizations crafted in the *Los Angeles Times*: the plot of Communist influence, the plot of heroic police officers, the plot of ineffective African-American leaders, and the plot of insane rioters. The *Sentinel*'s news about Watts focused primarily on countering the plots of heroic policemen and of ineffective African-American leaders, and trying to re-frame the plot of insane rioters. The *Sentinel* did criticize the rioters, describing them as "lawless" and "shameful." But the *Sentinel*'s criticisms were made in the context of a search for possible motivations behind the violence, and ultimately were used as a starting point to get to a different narrative, one of police brutality and white racism. This strategy can be seen in the first editorials about Watts written in the *Los Angeles Sentinel*:

Basically, we believe that all self-respecting Negro citizens here deplore the burning of buildings, the lootings and shootings and its staggering toll in human lives and property damage which besieged our city last weekend, and also know the need of proper law enforcement to protect all of our citizens . . . The incident and the arrests which triggered the riot last Wednesday night were only incidental. Because the psychological fires of frustration had been smouldering in the minds of thousands of deprived citizens in Watts and other areas, and it was going to happen someday, anyhow . . . Certainly, it is easy to blame 'criminal elements' or a 'hoodlum fringe,' or even the Communists, when what is called for is some really deep soul-searching.
(*Los Angeles Sentinel*, August 19, 1965: A6)

They said it couldn't happen here but it did. In this case, the 'they' isn't the undefinable 'group pronoun' of fabricated stories or gossip. They are the leaders of our city government – the Mayor, the Chief of Police, members of the City Council, business and community leaders and just plain everyday citizens who have not been facing up to the facts. People who have been living in a dream world. A world in which they have ignored the fact that we here in Los Angeles have been sitting on a racial tinderbox for at least the last five years! . . . The reforms, the programs, the projects, and the grass-roots work which could have been inaugurated to prevent what has been the bloodiest and most disastrous U. S. race riot in history, never materialized, either because of official non-interest or the simple, isolated, unmovable fact of racial prejudice.
(*Los Angeles Sentinel*, August 19, 1965: A7)

These two editorials demonstrate a reflexive orientation to other public spheres, and a reversal of the narrative lines exhibited in the mainstream Los Angeles media. Where the mainstream media saw danger in "extremist discourse," the *Sentinel* saw danger in the lack of serious discourse. Where the rioters had been labeled as irrational and unmotivated, they were now symbolized by rational and deep-seated motivations (even if they were still negatively coded as uncontrolled and violent). And where Watts had turned the plot of the civil rights narrative to a discussion of its excesses, for the *Sentinel* it functioned to turn the civil rights narrative to a discussion of its incomplete realization. Rather than constructing an opposition between order and disorder, as was the case with the *Los Angeles Times*, the *Sentinel*'s reports mobilized a different opposition: between action and inaction, between reconstruction and blame.

In this narrative environment, where the plot development was in the direction of causes and solutions, the *Sentinel*'s news stories about Watts took one of two paths. The first was concerned primarily with the criticism of the Los Angeles Police Department and its chief, and explained the unrest in Watts as being caused by "resentment over the tactics of white police officers in minority communities."[16] From the beginning of its reports about Watts, those who were quoted in the *Sentinel* concentrated on the problem of Chief Parker and the Los Angeles Police Department.

Sparked by the Rev. H. H. Brookins, Assemblyman Mervin Dymally and other community leaders, an intensified move to oust Police Chief Parker is gaining momentum. The action, reflecting increasing resentment over the tactics of white police officers in minority communities, was planned as a protest against Parker's attitudes and expressed statements about Negroes. "Having worked closely with our law-abiding citizens, I am convinced that the removal of Police Chief Parker would be a major factor in curtailing the continued unrest and violence which has brought shame and disgrace to a city destined for greatness," Dr. Brookins said.

(*Los Angeles Sentinel*, August 19, 1965: A1)

In two conferences at the Governor's office in Los Angeles during the height of the rioting in South Los Angeles, leading members of the community asked "that Governor Brown remove the national guard from the leadership of Chief Parker and the Los Angeles force, and that the guard be placed under the leadership of a state or federal officer whose very name and presence are not part and parcel of the crisis facing our community."   (*Los Angeles Sentinel*, August 19, 1965: A9)

These criticisms of the police department placed the Watts crisis in the middle of an ongoing story about community-government and community-police relations. Here, Watts did not evince evidence of the excesses of civil disobedience, but rather the lack of real concern for civil rights on the part of local government officials. African-American leaders were represented as forces of order, while Los Angeles police and politicians were the forces of disorder. The problem was not with African-American leaders, but rather with Los Angeles politicians who refused to engage in a serious dialogue about race and urban crisis. In reversing the *Los Angeles Times*'s character oppositions, the *Los Angeles Sentinel* recalled a series of past events, molding them into a coherent sequence demonstrating the racism and inaction of Los Angeles politicians and its white constituents:

> For almost 10 years, warnings that disaster was inevitable have been voiced by sources both within and without the Los Angeles Negro community. Typical of numerous official reports was one that was issued in August of 1963 by the United States Commission on Human Rights which stressed the need for strong measures to relieve police oppression in the Los Angeles ghetto area. And since 1962, civil rights organizations have sought, through non-violent direct action, to dramatize the frustrations and sufferings of the minority community and to give the majority community opportunity to relieve these frustrations before they hardened into feelings of bitterness and rage. With the passage of Proposition 14, with continued unfair employment practices, with heartless delay in the administration of anti-poverty funds, the majority community has replied with a resounding NO, while city officials remained blind and deaf to all complaints of malpractices by the police, answering only with increased police force in the minority community.
>
> (*Los Angeles Sentinel*, August 26, 1965: A6)

> The simple and objective facts, and they are plain and ominous to anyone familiar with the area, are that poverty, law enforcement attitudes, and a general feeling of hopelessness, frustration, and being regarded as less than human were the major causes for the riots . . . It is apparent at this writing that these points are not clearly understood by the majority of the residents of this city. It is apparent that our Mayor, Samuel Yorty, and Chief of Police, William Parker, either do not want to recognize these facts or recognize them and do not want to give them credence. It is apparent that this is the same feeling of many of our other city, county, and state officials. By their deeds and through their words, it is apparent that they have really not profited from the terrible experience of the tragedy we've all just witnessed and lived through. They are further compounding the crime which they have been guilty of for years: a total apathy and disregard for what have been the area's problems.
>
> (*Los Angeles Sentinel*, September 2, 1965: A7)

The polarized interpretations of the crisis in the two newspapers did not only influence how local actors were represented; they also structured how state and federal politicians were inserted into the Watts narrative. The *Los Angeles Times* criticized both Governor Brown and President Johnson, for "glossing over the real reasons for the Los Angeles riots,"[17] and placed the expectations of political leadership in the hands of Mayor Yorty. For the *Los Angeles Sentinel*, on the other hand, hope for resolving the crisis lay in the hands of African-American community leaders, and the state and federal politicians who would help to overcome the racism of Los Angeles political leaders. Clearly, the early interpretations of Watts in the *Los Angeles Times* and *Los Angeles Sentinel* existed in a relationship of dispute and confrontation.

The Chicago press

The *Chicago Tribune* utilized many of the same narrative strategies as the *Los Angeles Times* to report about Watts, including the plot of Communist influence, the plot of heroic policemen, the plot of ineffective African-American leaders, and the plot of insane rioters. This should not be too surprising. The *Los Angeles Times* and *Chicago Tribune* were similar in orientation during the 1960s, in terms of their strong anti-Communism, their committed local chauvinism, their distrust of national government, and their coverage of African-Americans and African-American issues.[18] In addition, the city of Chicago experienced a period of civil unrest in the Garfield Park section of the city, which began the day after the Watts unrest and lasted for two days. This unrest encouraged an experiential investment in the Watts crisis, even though the two events were unrelated, and encouraged a similar deployment of deviance in the city's mainstream public spheres. In its initial description of the rioters, the *Tribune* was as critical as the *Los Angeles Times*, and echoed William Parker's labeling of African-American leaders as "demagogic pseudo-leaders."[19] The *Tribune* uncritically quoted Los Angeles Mayor Yorty's labeling of police brutality charges as "part of a big lie technique shouted all over the world by Communists, dupes, and demagogues,"[20] as well as his criticism of the "ghetto conditions" explanation as being "inaccurate and unfair."[21] News reports written as objective stories described the rioters as raging, frenzied, out-of-control "bands of Negroes [who] stormed and looted neighborhood business establishments, attacked policemen, motorists, and cars with bricks and bottles, and set fire to cars, stores, and residences."[22] The *Chicago Tribune*'s account told how the rioters destroyed white-owned and African-American businesses indiscriminately, chose liquor stores as their favorite targets, and "strolled drunkenly along the streets, firing shots and setting the torch."[23] In these types of descriptions, similar to those of the *Los Angeles Times*, all attempts to explain the actions of the rioters were either ignored or criticized. The *Tribune* described how, even after the National Guard was beginning to control the streets, the "disorders" were being prolonged by "terrorists" engaged in "guerilla warfare."[24]

The main point of initial reporting differences between the *Los Angeles Times* and the *Chicago Tribune* had to do with the evaluation of the Los Angeles police. Rather than criticizing the use of excessive force, as the African-American papers did, the *Tribune* criticized the police for using insufficiently swift or violent force to control the situation, and drew a comparison between the Chicago and Los Angeles police responses to provide "evidence" regarding the "merits" of force.

Clearest of the immediate lessons to be drawn from the shocking rioting in Los
Angeles is the need for swift, firm executive action at the earliest possible moment
after local authorities upholding law and order have lost control of a city's streets.
California national guardsmen were understandably embittered by Lt. Gov. Glenn
M. Anderson's hours of indecision . . . Fortunately, Chicago has not been nor is it
likely to be victimized by any such vacuum of authority . . . Hatred expressed in violence against persons and property will best be contained, as we began by saying,
when and where government authority is invoked with resolution and without hesi-
tation to clear the streets of berserk rioters.

(*Chicago Tribune*, August 15, 1965: A14)

The force of the "law and order" theme shaped the *Chicago Tribune*'s coverage of Watts throughout the period of the crisis, including its coverage of
President Johnson's reactions and his statements about Watts. Initially, the
Tribune focused upon Johnson's denunciation of the rioters, specifically his
argument that "killing, rioting, and looting are contrary to the best traditions of this country." In describing this statement, *Tribune* news reports
wrote that "White House aides said his [Johnson's] words were directed to
every community where racial trouble, actual or potential, exists."[25] But
President Johnson's statements were not limited to criticisms of the rioters.
In addition, Johnson directed a significant portion of his comments to discussions about the problems of poverty, the unfinished agenda of the civil
rights movement, and the need for federal intervention to solve the problems of race and urban crisis. It was these statements which had caused the
Los Angeles Times to criticize Johnson for "glossing over the real reasons
for the riots." Similarly, it was these statements which drew criticism from
the *Chicago Tribune*:

The President talked sense when he said of the Los Angeles riots, 'A rioter with a
Molotov cocktail in his hands is not fighting for civil rights any more than a klans-
man with a sheet on his back and a mask on his face' . . . Mr. Johnson would be
talking directly to the point if he continued to couch his discussions of racial violence in terms of law and order and personal responsibility . . . Yet this sociological
pap that everybody is guilty but the rioters is peddled pervasively . . . Despite the
contention of Mr. [Robert] Kennedy that the law may be ignored, and of the Rev.
Martin Luther King that the law may be disobeyed any time somebody thinks it
'unjust,' the law is for all of us and binding on all of us. If it isn't, the country is
finished.   (*Chicago Tribune*, August 28, 1965: A12)

Clearly, the *Chicago Tribune* reported about Watts through the same plot
devices as the *Los Angeles Times*: the plot of Communist influence, the plot
of heroic (insofar as they were sufficiently violent) police, the plot of
ineffective African-American leaders, and the plot of insane rioters. Given
this, one would expect similar narrative strategies deployed in the *Chicago*

Defender as were used in the *Los Angeles Sentinel*: the plot of police brutality and white racism, the plot of racist Los Angeles politicians, the plot
of effective federal intervention, and the plot of misguided rioters. This
was, in fact, how the *Chicago Defender* covered the Watts crisis, criticizing
the rioters much in the same way as the *Los Angeles Sentinel*. In an article
beginning with the heading "Civic Leaders Condemn Violence," the
Defender reproduced a public statement made by "four leading figures in
Chicago's Negro Community":

It is imperative that leaders and lieutenants of the civil rights groups of the Nation
make special efforts to restrain the violence which is surging in many communities.
We understand and sympathize with the pent-up frustrations which issue in dem-
onstrations and protests, but we vigorously denounce and categorically disapprove
violent and senseless attacks upon persons and property. Lawless and irresponsible
behavior beclouds the objectives of the civil rights movement, besmirches the image
created by those who have made sacrifices of liberty and even life, and surrenders
to the very evils of mob rule and injustice we all deplore.

(*Chicago Defender*, August 14, 1965: A1)

In a similar criticism, the *Defender* quoted Roy Wilkins calling the rioters
"hoodlums," and arguing that they were not members of his, Martin
Luther King's or Whitney Young's groups.[26] For African-American leaders
such as Wilkins, this realization was a source of concern and realization,
that there were no leaders who spoke for the disenfranchised inner-city
black residents living in Los Angeles. For King himself, Watts was a crucial
event suggesting the need to add an economic and class analysis to his civil
rights discourse.[27]

The *Chicago Defender*'s treatment of the violence was not only directed
inward toward the African-American community and its leaders, however;
it was also part of a reflexive dialogue against the *Chicago Tribune*. Just as
the *Los Angeles Sentinel* offered alternative interpretations of the crisis
which countered those in the *Los Angeles Times*, the *Chicago Defender*'s
reports were shaped through a dialogue of confrontation and dispute
against the *Chicago Tribune*. While the *Tribune*'s eyewitness reports
recounted indiscriminate and irrational destruction in Los Angeles, the
Defender's eyewitness accounts reported how the violence was being
focused against particular stores which exploited the African-American
community: "the stores hit were white-owned with few exceptions and
often had shoddy goods and comparatively high prices."[28] While the
Chicago Tribune emphasized that Watts could not have happened in
Chicago, the *Chicago Defender* quoted Congressman Adam Clayton
Powell, Jr.'s warning that every city was a potential Los Angeles.[29] Just like
the *Los Angeles Sentinel*, news reports in the *Chicago Defender* attempted

to re-frame the plot of insane rioters, and to emphasize that the urban revolt had been caused by the failure of mainstream society to listen to African-American leaders.

> Because the law of the land took so long to heed Roy Wilkins and Thurgood Marshall in their search for justice; because the rulers of the land took so long to endorse the non-violent tactics of Martin Luther King; because industry took so long to understand the common-sense advice of Lester Granger and Whitney Young; because of all this – a new Negro is striding the land. He is unafraid to die. He is intolerant of the virtues of patience . . . Someone – many someones – better learn to speak the language of this new Negro. The power structures of the cities and the states and the Federal Government better get the message which burns in the hearts of this new Negro. The civil rights leadership will have to learn to communicate with him better – and they can start by learning how to communicate with each other better.   (*Chicago Defender*, August 28, 1965: A10)

Those writing in the *Chicago Defender* recognized that the white indifference African-Americans typically confronted was likely to turn into white hostility after Watts, and might easily result in the "greatest wave of anti-Negro feeling which has ever swept across this nation . . . threatening the beach-heads of civil rights."[30] This suggested two discursive strategies for the African-American press and public spheres. On the one hand, African-American leaders would have to figure a way to bring African-American youth more fully into the African-American public spheres. On the other hand, the black press had to remain vigilant against mainstream public apathy toward racist politicians. Consistent with the latter goal, the *Defender* repeatedly criticized the inaction of Los Angeles politicians during the Watts crisis.

In re-describing Los Angeles politicians, the *Chicago Defender* utilized the same kind of historical event sequencing that the *Los Angeles Sentinel* had used to demonstrate the racism and insincerity of local politicians. In addition to criticizing Los Angeles Mayor Yorty, however, the *Chicago Defender* also included Chicago Mayor Daley in its historical story of political apathy and neglect. The *Defender* described how Los Angeles Mayor Yorty and Chicago Mayor Daley had "erred when they ignored the inter-agency efforts to form a summer task force," and also when they had ignored a 1962 report about police-minority group relations. After linking the two mayors as equally irresponsible, the news story went on to describe further the character attributes of Yorty.

> In essence, the report indicates that in 1962 when the state civil rights commission convened to hold hearings on "the relationships between the police and minority groups" there was opposition from both Mayor Yorty and the chief of police, William H. Parker. The mayor, considered irresponsible in many Washington quar-

ters, called the members of the state commission "communist dupes" and said the hearings would cater "to the dissidents" in the community. The NAACP led the groups that gave testimony. What were the complaints? Excessive violence at the time of arrests, greater arrests and surveillance in densely Negro and Mexican-American areas, police inability to distinguish between criminals and law-abiding minorities.   (*Chicago Defender*, August 21, 1965: A1)

As we can see from this news excerpt, the *Chicago Defender* attempted simultaneously to discredit the plots of Los Angeles political leadership and of Communist influence, and to position federal politicians and African-American leaders in the heroic character positions. The *Defender* also linked the events of Watts to fears about racism in white society and the need for continued vigilance by civil rights activists. One of the early descriptions about the social context in which the unrest occurred described how "most Negroes in the area believe an alarmingly high number of white policemen hold membership in the Birch Society and other right wing organizations."[31] This served to link the narrative of Watts to a *Defender* editorial the week before, which had pointed to the rise of the Goldwater Republicans and the John Birch Society in California, and to the corresponding need to mobilize the African-American vote against the conservative movement. By linking the Watts crisis to a history of conservative racist politics, news reports in the *Chicago Defender* undermined any assumptions that local politicians in Chicago or Los Angeles could be trusted.

After the tragic rioting late August in the Watts area of Los Angeles, the residents of that community were led to believe that many of the social and economic ills that had brought despair and frustration in their wake would be promptly attacked . . . Even the churches, business organizations and bi-racial groups interested in finding a solution to the problems find their efforts impeded by lack of coordination and planning. The result is a snail's pace approach, piece-meal solution to a volatile situation ready for another explosion. The people are impatient, and in many instances sullen. They think immediate measures to alleviate their conditions should have been instituted weeks ago. (*Chicago Defender*, October 23, 1965: A10)

Like in Los Angeles, one of the things that Chicago's African-American press accomplished during the Watts crisis was to challenge the interpretations made in the mainstream press, and to offer different understandings about the issues and the actors involved. African-Americans in the 1960s did not trust the mainstream press, as the Kerner Commission would discover, and they turned to the black press to find a different side to the story. This dynamic was even true in New York, despite the fact that the coverage of Watts in the *New York Times* was much more sympathetic to race and urban poverty than were the reports of the *Los Angeles Times* or *Chicago Tribune*.

The New York press

News coverage about Watts in the New York press differed in important ways from Los Angeles or Chicago. The *New York Times* did not rely on a plot of Communist influence or of heroic police in its news narrative. Instead, its news coverage was organized primarily around the plot of federal intervention and ineffective Los Angeles politicians, thereby overlapping in important respects with the *Chicago Defender* and *Los Angeles Sentinel*. Like those papers, the *New York Times* criticized Los Angeles politicians by constructing a historical sequence of events demonstrating the political errors of Los Angeles Mayor Yorty:

Federal officials said today they had warned Mayor Samuel W. Yorty of Los Angeles as long ago as the spring that there was potential danger of violence in his city. The Mayor, these sources said, refused the offer of a conciliator from the Community Relations Service to help Los Angeles through the summer. The warning and the offer of help came from officials dealing with urban problems under the President's Council on Equal Opportunity . . . Under the committee's program, conciliators from the Community Relations Service were assigned to nine cities deemed to be potential trouble spots for the summer months. The cities were New York, Newark, Rochester, Boston, Detroit, Cleveland, Philadelphia, Gary, Ind., and Oakland, Calif. In those cities, officials said, the conciliators have expedited Federal antipoverty grants to low-income areas and served as a channel for information among mayors and local human relations councils, civil rights groups and the Federal Government. In several instances, they said, these conciliators have been able to alert mayors to potentially serious situations. The nine cities served by the program so far have avoided major racial disturbances this summer.

(*New York Times*, August 17, 1965: A17)

While the *New York Times* narrative was similar to the African-American press in its criticism of Los Angeles politicians, it did not save any active or heroic character positions for African-Americans. Instead, the *New York Times* coverage emphasized the need for national leadership by President Johnson. In this representation, politicians and African-American residents in Los Angeles were both at fault, for impeding federal initiatives designed to solve the problems of race, poverty, and urban crisis. In the *New York Times* reports, the entire city of Los Angeles signified self-interest and divisiveness,[32] and the resolution of the crisis would have to come from figures outside of Los Angeles. Indeed, two such figures were quickly inserted into such character positions. The first was LeRoy Collins, who was described by the *Times* as a "race relations trouble shooter for the White House," and who was given credit for solving the local Los Angeles politicians' inability to secure federal anti-poverty funds.[33] The second was

John McCone, who, as we will see, was represented by the *New York Times* as a federal political actor. But the most important heroic character in the Watts narrative of the *New York Times* was President Lyndon Johnson who, in the *Times* story, contrasted the tragedy of the violence in Watts with the romance of federal civil rights programs.

The *New York Times*'s treatment of President Johnson's statements about Watts was unique among the six newspapers. Rather than emphasizing Johnson's criticisms of the rioters themselves – as did the *Los Angeles Times* and the *Chicago Tribune* – news reports in the *New York Times* instead constructed a narrative around Johnson's ongoing attempts to extend social rights.

President Johnson described the Los Angeles riots today as "tragic and shocking." He warned the rioters that their rights could not be won and their grievances remedied "through violence" . . . Mr. Johnson has been growing increasingly concerned with the problem of violence in America, as well as its causes. The Los Angeles situation is said to have reinforced his conviction that the Administration must open a broad attack on lawlessness and disorder as quickly as possible . . . Mr. Johnson is also said to be particularly chagrined and disturbed by the riots, as his statement suggests, because they have followed so closely the enactment of historic and far-reaching Administration legislation to guarantee Negro rights.

(*New York Times*, August 15, 1965: A1)

In this narrative, Watts was linked not only to other riots in Chicago and Springfield (Massachusetts), but also to a speech President Johnson had given about the African-American family in 1964 at Howard University. In constructing this type of narrative, the events of Watts were not to be explained as the tragic breakdown in civility, but rather as a consequence of the incomplete extension of social rights. While the *Times* linked Watts to Johnson's Howard University speech on four separate occasions, this historical metaphor was completely absent from all of the other newspapers. The first editorial about Watts in the *New York Times* illustrates well how Johnson's speech was linked to the uprisings in a coherent narrative of federal paternalism. While African-American violence was criticized, its significance was discounted, explained away as the result of an incomplete government project of racial and urban salvation. If African-Americans could exercise restraint and discipline, government programs would soon rescue them from their despair and frustration.

The orgy of death and destruction that has erupted in Los Angeles, Chicago and Springfield recall President Johnson's fears, expressed in his Howard University speech last spring, of 'destructive rebellion against the fabric of society.' The President pointed out that though the Negro has won his revolution for equal rights, the heritage of degradation and discrimination has brought a breakdown in family life and a sense of injustice that can give rise to anarchy and lawlessness. These are the common causes of the riots this week. They cannot be disarmed by the victory for legal equality and freedom. They are embedded so deeply and so explosively that even the most trivial incident can set them off . . . The Federal Government and the nation are committed to root out the factors that have produced Negro indifference, despair, and frustration. It is a long and expensive process, calling for better education, better housing, better opportunities, and all of the other strands of a free society that have been denied them so long. But this new phase in the Negro revolution also demands the kind of discipline and solidarity that the nation's Negroes exhibited in their successful battle for civil rights.

(*New York Times*, August 15, 1965: E8)

President Johnson was portrayed as the leader in a war against slum living conditions, summoning the nation to make a complete commitment. The "disarmament of the slums" would bring about "the triumph of hope and opportunity for all Americans."[34] There was a romantic sort of urgency to this need for extending social rights to those living in the African-American ghettos, as the following editorial conveys well:

The legal revolution in their status is inadequate by itself. The rights to vote, work and learn do not suffice for an impoverished, easily distinguished minority still forced by social pressures into a kind of segregation, which is economically unable to exercise full opportunities. The entire procedure of adjustment must be speeded up . . . We have demonstrated in past moments of national emergency an astonishing ability to move massively and fast. It is evident we are now again in a moment of national emergency. For the sake of our internal conscience we shall have to heal the causes of the turmoil.   (*New York Times*, August 18, 1865: A34)

The paternalism of the narrative, and its discounting of African-American agency, was typical of the *New York Times*. It evinced a toleration of African-Americans, but not a real engagement with their concerns. Indeed, the need to heal "our [white] internal conscience" was a more significant motivating factor than the desire to improve African-American lives or actually to engage African-Americans in discussions about matters of common concern. The Watts narrative of the *New York Times* failed to address the issue of police brutality that was such a central part of the African-American papers; it also failed to connect the Watts crisis to the deeper historical narrative of racial oppression in America. While it was more historical in its treatment than the *Chicago Tribune* or *Los Angeles Times*, the historical memory of the *New York Times* only began with the most recent interventions of national politicians into the civil rights and anti-poverty programs. It was against this type of paternalism and limited historical memory that the *New York Amsterdam News* responded.

Like the *Los Angeles Sentinel* and *Chicago Defender*, the Watts narrative of the *New York Amsterdam News* drew on a historically deep and continuous narrative of racial oppression. Absent a geographical experience of unrest, and absent a deployment of deviance in the city's main daily newspaper, the *Amsterdam News* developed its story line without ever criticizing the rioters themselves. Instead, news reports in the *Amsterdam News* described the rioters as rational, measured, and focused, and explained the cause of the uprising to be white indifference, police racism and brutality, and irresponsible politicians. These descriptions and explanations incorporated both editorial argument and "objective" accounts from eyewitnesses. The following excerpts, from the first two articles written about Watts in the *Amsterdam News*, are indicative of the objective type.

Los Angeles residents spoke to this reporter Tuesday after six days of rioting in the Negro section of town covering 20 square miles. Albert Hampton, vice president of the Family Savings and Loan Association in the city, told the Amsterdam News by telephone that he had just completed a tour of the riot-torn area and his observations indicated that only commercial properties were damaged while residences and churches were left unharmed. He appraised the looting heaviest in liquor stores, grocery stores next, jewelry and watch concerns next with furniture stores last on the list. No one was left homeless as far as he could ascertain, and Negro business structures were virtually left alone.

(*New York Amsterdam News*, August 21, 1965: A1)

One young Negro who sought to assess the cause of the riots said: "The riots will continue because I, as a Negro, am immediately considered a criminal and if I have a pretty woman with me, she's a tramp. That's the Watts' Negro status with the Los Angeles Police Department." Rev. E. L. Hicks, a Baptist minister, predicted: "There will be riots here until police brutality stops. The Governor may say it's over, but we work among the people and we know what is going on."

(*New York Amsterdam News*, August 21, 1965: A1)

If the actions of the rioters were both rational and reasonable, then there had to be an underlying cause for them: namely, a combination of white indifference and hostility toward African-American concerns. This explanation was elaborated in the *Amsterdam News* by a number of national African-American leaders – Roy Wilkins, Adam Clayton Powell, Jr., Martin Luther King, Jr., A. Philip Randolph, and James Farmer – all of whom wrote editorials about Watts in the *Amsterdam News* during the two weeks following the uprisings. In these editorials, Watts indicated a *national* crisis, caused by the refusal of white society to recognize the legitimate needs of the African-American community, and by the parallel refusal to allow African-Americans to participate fully in American society.

Negroes all over America are angry and they are furious. They are angry about the historical deprivations they have suffered at the hands of a largely callous and indifferent white society. They are furious about the debilitation and degradation of their leaders whenever these leaders were picked by black people themselves and not the white power structure . . . To deny human beings the most elemental rights . . . and then compound these denials with barbaric police brutality and officially condoned physical abuse is to lay the foundation for a sociological detonation of unbelievable proportions . . . Every black ghetto in this country is a potential Los Angeles only because the white power structure . . . has persistently rejected the efforts of black people to participate fully in the running of the total community.

(*New York Amsterdam News*, August 28, 1965: A1)

The non-violent movement in the South has meant little to them since we have been fighting for rights which theoretically are already theirs, therefore I believe what has happened in Los Angeles is of grave national significance. What we have witnessed in the Watts area is the beginning of a stirring of a deprived people in a society who have been bypassed by the progress of the past decade . . . To treat this situation as though it were merely the result of an irresponsible criminal element is to lead the Watts community into a potential holocaust. And so long as this stubborn attitude is maintained by responsible authorities, I can only see the situation worsening.

(*New York Amsterdam News*, August 28, 1965: A14)

In all of these accounts, the unifying thread was the idea that rioting was the *most rational* strategy of ghetto residents. It was not enough to wait for federal intervention, because mainstream society had historically only been motivated to act on the basis of "sudden and terrified fear" brought on by events such as Watts.[35] Similar events, such as the 1964 Harlem riots, were seen to have resulted in more favorable political and police appointments in New York.[36] The tragedy was that African-Americans had to destroy their own communities to get the attention of mainstream society, and even then the type of attention was of the wrong kind. As two editorials by James Farmer, the leader of Congress of Racial Equality (CORE) explained, the typical white understanding of civil uprisings such as Watts was based on a historical narrative which could only be viewed with bitter irony by those whose practical experience and historical memory allowed them to know better.

When violence explodes in an American Negro community, a number of automatic things happen, most of them born of ignorance and molded of the same bigotry that made this mess in the first place. First, white public officials go on record with "shock" and "surprise" that those nice Negroes who've been "getting everything, including the Nobel Peace Prize," are mad about anything at all . . . And second, a lot of folks, of all colors, grab the Kleig light to make pronouncements about "responsible leadership" and "savage behavior." What frightens and worries me about all of this is that the very ignorance reflected in these reactions sets the stage for further violence, indeed demonstrates that even after 300 years of trouble and seven years of rebellion, the vast majority of Americans simply refuse to believe that you are in trouble if you are born black – trouble that strides through your entire life. 		(*New York Amsterdam News*, August 28, 1965: A15)

The senseless but predictable horror of Los Angeles is not a lesson that Negroes must learn, we know it all too well, in all its bloody detail. It's a lesson burned into our history . . . our pride has been cauterized by hate and violence. We are the brothers and sisters of Nat Turner and Denmark Vesey. We are apprised of death, and whatever brotherhood and whatever love that can be found amongst us must be measured against a long memory; from the black chattel markets of New Orleans through the massacre of Negro troops at Fort Pillow to the ashes of children in a Birmingham house of God.
 		(*New York Amsterdam News*, September 18, 1965: A13)

Clearly, the *Amsterdam News* narrative of Watts had nothing to do with complaints about a breakdown in respect for the law, or with the dangers of civil disobedience and putatively irresponsible African-American leaders – as the *Los Angeles Times* and the *Chicago Tribune* suggested – but rather with the refusal of white society to recognize the historical origins and the historical continuity of racial crisis. In this sense, the coverage of the *Amsterdam News* was similar to that of the other African-American papers. But African-American news coverage of Watts evinced a dialogical relationship of confrontation and dispute against mainstream press coverage. And in this respect, the *Amsterdam News* had a different set of news texts against which to argue. Because the *New York Times* had itself re-framed the plot of "insane rioters" to a plot of the incomplete extension of social rights, the *Amsterdam News* did not have to do this. Instead, its news narratives focused on the historical depth of white racism and paternalism.

The McCone commission

I have so far examined the main plots around which news coverage of the Watts crisis was organized. While there were important differences among the newspapers, all of them structured their stories around the description of the rioters and the causes for the uprisings. News narratives are flexible, however, and can change with the weaving in of a new event into the ongoing story. The McCone Commission, which held hearings daily in Los Angeles for almost two months, releasing an eighty-six page report about the uprisings in December 2, 1965, offered just such an event sequence. The commission's hearings took place at a pre-announced time, in a central location in downtown Los Angeles, and usually involved "official sources." All of these qualities made the commission's activities more likely to be considered newsworthy.[37] But events organized by the McCone Commission did not become part of the Watts narrative in every newspaper, and its narration differed greatly among those papers in which it was included. The *Chicago Tribune* and *New York Amsterdam News* wrote nothing about the McCone Commission; the other papers wrote about it with varying concentrations and through varying cultural forms.

How are we to understand the lack of coverage in the *Chicago Tribune* and *New York Amsterdam News*? One possible explanation is that resource constraints prevented coverage. This may explain the lack of coverage in the *New York Amsterdam News*, but it does not explain why the *Chicago Defender* (with equal resource constraints) did cover the hearings, or why the *Chicago Tribune* (with no significant resource constraints) failed to. A better explanation is that the Watts narratives of these two papers did not need to include this new event, and, furthermore, that the editorial structure of their narratives did not allow for the hearings to be inserted coherently. As there were already more than enough anti-heroes in all of the news narratives, the events of the McCone Commission were most likely to be seen as newsworthy when they could help to develop a heroic plot. Because the *Chicago Defender* and *New York Amsterdam News* both had criticized Los Angeles as well as national politicians, the hearings were not seen as part of a potential narrative of political redemption. Indeed, they were not seen as newsworthy at all.

This explanation – that the commission hearings were only newsworthy if they could help to develop a heroic plot – fits the other newspapers' coverage as well. The *Chicago Defender*, for example, inserted the hearings into the plot of effective federal intervention, noting that "the Commission has put its finger on the sociological causes that brought on the disorders in Watts . . . [but it] was wrong in not articulating the obligations of governmental and organized social agencies to come quickly to grips with inflammable conditions before they burst into almost irrepressible conflagration."[38] This interpretation was consistent with the *Defender*'s arguments that mainstream society had failed to listen to the warnings by African-American leaders concerning race and the urban crisis. In other words, the inclusion of the McCone Commission report reinforced the heroic character positions already developed in earlier news reports. The *New York Times* incorporated its news about the McCone Commission in a similar way, inserting it into the earlier narrative which praised federal legislation and federal intervention while criticizing Los Angeles politicians:

it [the report] is fair notice that inefficiency in administration in the antipoverty program is intolerable and it gives a sense of urgency to the need for radical improvement in such areas as education, job training and racial tolerance.

(*New York Times*, December 8, 1965: A46)

Linking the McCone Commission to the federal efforts against local inefficiency in Los Angeles, the *New York Times* reported that half of the funding for the commission had been provided by a national agency, the Ford Foundation.[39] Its description of the commission's head, John McCone, emphasized that he had been a former director of the Central Intelligence Agency. Clearly, it was the national politicians who were the heroes in the Watts narrative of the *New York Times*; and opposite them stood the anti-heroes – Los Angeles politicians, who were too suspicious, too unrealistic, and too factionalized.

The most interesting news coverage of the McCone Commission hearings can be found in the *Los Angeles Times*. Initially, the main Watts narrative of the *Los Angeles Times* had emphasized the heroic character of Police Chief Parker and the Los Angeles Police Department, and had criticized as evil and wrong-headed all attempts to discuss underlying social causes or solutions for the civil unrest. Initial reports about the McCone Commission were folded neatly into this interpretive frame, as the *Los Angeles Times* recounted the reservations which many political leaders had about the hearings. Governor Brown, who had formed the McCone Commission, testified on the first day of the hearings; what the *Los Angeles Times* emphasized was his concern about whether the residents of Watts would be willing to cooperate or come forward with information.[40] This was in tune with the *Los Angeles Times* depiction of African-Americans in Watts as deceitful and untrustworthy. In addition, the *Los Angeles Times* continued to publish editorials explaining the importance of law and order, the need to support the police, and the political backlash that was sure to befall Governor Brown as a result of the continued focus on Watts.

Once a consistent form of including the hearings had been found, the fit between the institutional location of the hearings and the news routines of *Los Angeles Times*' journalists led to many more stories. The hearings, however, were oriented precisely toward the question the *Los Angeles Times* had warned was so dangerous: specifically, the question of underlying causes. The newsworthiness of the commission hearings, combined with the expressed focus of those hearings, allowed for a transformation in the narration of the Watts crisis in the *Los Angeles Times*. A daily parade of officials offered testimony about the various causes of the riots and the solutions to prevent future ones. When they emerged from the hearings, they were willing to summarize their arguments for an inquiring press, which then incorporated each new event into the ongoing news narrative about Watts. These extensions of the plot included considerations of law enforcement methods, failures to implement anti-poverty programs, worsening of segregation in housing and schools, and the passage of Proposition 14. The suggestions of solutions also extended beyond the *Los Angeles Times*'s previously narrow concern for law and order, encompassing arguments about the need for a rapid influx of new jobs, the construction of a university campus in Watts, and even the development of a task force of sociologists to be set up to help rural immigrants adjust to life in the city. In this extended news narrative about Watts, public expectations began to echo the claim made by Congressman Augustus Hawkins as he finished his testimony on the second day of the hearings: "We cannot have politics as usual, business as usual or commission reports as usual."[41] John A. Buggs, director of the County Human Relations Commission, stated publicly after his testimony that "there is an air of great expectation and great hope that the McCone Commission will come up with some solutions to the problems of jobs, discrimination, housing and education."[42] And toward the end of the hearings, John McCone suggested that perhaps the commission should become a semi-permanent institution, remaining active for at least two years in order to make sure its recommendations were put into practice.[43] The important thing to note is that the hearings were interpreted through a narrative of local political leadership; all of the recommendations were understood as things that could be implemented by Los Angeles Mayor Yorty.

While the incorporation of the McCone Commission events broadened the Watts narrative in the *Los Angeles Times*, by suggesting heroic actions that could be taken by local political actors, Mayor Yorty did not change his symbolic strategies accordingly. As a result, his status as the pre-eminent heroic character in the narrative began to weaken. Yorty continued to criticize all those officials who criticized Los Angeles government or police officers in any way, and failed to provide any explanations or solutions that did not involve blame. When Yorty compounded this failure by not paying attention to the changing public narrative about Watts, leaving for a trip to Vietnam the week before the McCone Commission was to release its report, the *Times* criticized him in an editorial for a failure of leadership.[44]

Thus, when the McCone Commission released its report on December 2, it did so in a cultural climate where the symbolic status of Mayor Yorty was undergoing deflation in the *Los Angeles Times*. This had an effect on the way the paper incorporated the report into its ongoing narrative about Watts. Basically, the commission and its report took the symbolic position previously occupied by Yorty, so that anyone who criticized the report became a threat to the resolution of the crisis. The report was still interpreted within the frame of heroic political leadership by Los Angeles leaders, and a putative lack of leadership by local African-American leaders. The first editorial after the release of the McCone report explained that the "sense of urgency conveyed by the report . . . is real, it is vital, and it grows stronger every day."[45] On the other hand, those who opposed the report's recommendations were selfish, ineffective pseudo-leaders.

Money, co-operation, commitment, and responsible leadership at all levels are demanded, with this last perhaps the most important of all . . . where it [leadership] must begin is where it has so far been most conspicuously lacking, with the chief executive officer of this city, Mayor Yorty. Leadership, the mayor should be reminded, by definition requires being in the forefront. It cannot be exercised through a political speech in San Francisco, or on a tour of exotic capitals 6,000 miles from home.   (*Los Angeles Times*, December 7, 1965: B4)

Clogged bureaucratic arteries are going to have to be forced open, to speed implementation . . . Most of all, perhaps, there is a need for coordination and leadership, to get things moving and to keep them on the right track. Such immediate leadership and inspiration must emerge at the local level, for this after all is where the problem dwells.   (*Los Angeles Times*, December 8, 1965: B4)

Several points from these editorial arguments are worthy of further comment. Most importantly, the *Los Angeles Times* limited the important character positions to local actors – political leaders who did not criticize the McCone Commission report. This is significant for three reasons. The first is that it allowed for a potential recasting of Mayor Yorty back to a positive character sketch; if the mayor exercised decisive leadership, he would get the central symbolic reward as the "chief executive officer" of the city. The second is that it narrated all critics of the commission report as selfish and egotistical threats to the urgent need for reform as outlined by the report. This was significant because many African-American leaders, both locally and nationally, were critical of the report and its recommendations. The third is that the editorials denied any significant positive character positions to African-American residents of the Watts community. Instead, the *Los Angeles Times* called for a change in African-American attitudes, which were described as so "suspicious" and "hostile" that they "help inevitably to shape reciprocating attitudes on the part of the police."[46] In this explanation, African-Americans came to Los Angeles with preformed hostilities against the police, and through these supposedly unreasonable attitudes they provoked police hostility.

In the end, the release of the McCone Commission report did not, for the *Los Angeles Times*, improve the symbolic position of African-American residents of Watts. If rural immigrants needed help adjusting to Watts, this was the job of academics, rather than leaders of the African-American community. Changes in law enforcement methods, anti-poverty programs, and new jobs were all the province of white political and intellectual elites. This does not deny the fact that the incorporation of the McCone hearings produced a somewhat less punitive Watts narrative. But it did so in a way that failed to alter the negative characterization of African-Americans.

For the *Los Angeles Sentinel*, the events of the McCone Commission were equally newsworthy; rather than opening up the Watts narrative, however, they instead provided extra support for the plot of police brutality, white indifference, and the politics of blame. Here, the benefit of the commission and its report was not so much its "sense of urgency" or the need of leadership on the part of Mayor Yorty. Rather, the report served to publicize things to the mainstream society that the African-American community already knew. The McCone Commission did not "solve" the problems of racial Los Angeles, as the *Los Angeles Times* narrative had suggested. For the *Los Angeles Sentinel*, what the commission report accomplished was to open up the mainstream public spheres to a more subtle discussion of race and urban crisis. In a city where African-Americans were almost invisible to white society, the simple fact of this increased visibility provided cause for hope:

While the McCone Commission report was lacking in specifics on a panacea for the many problems in impoverished areas, it did accomplish two things: 1. It exposed to the nation, the state, and our total population the tragic evils of unemployment, educational retardation and alleged police malpractices in minority neighborhoods, conditions which most of us who work in our own communities already knew about. 2. It has focused more attention than ever before on the serious challenge facing our entire city if quick action is not taken on a training and job placement program for the thousands of unemployed youths and adults in minority communities.   (*Los Angeles Sentinel*, December 16, 1965: A6)

No one can honestly and truthfully say that he is happy that Watts occurred. No one can say that he was happy with the violence, the death, or the destruction which were a product of the bloody days. But, neither can anyone sincerely believe that since it did occur, the holocaust did not result in an improvement of conditions for the Negro in Los Angeles. Many doors which have been closed to Negroes have since opened and many who were not aware, really aware, of the plight of thousands in their midst have done some soul-searching and re-evaluation.

(*Los Angeles Sentinel*, December 30, 1965: A7)

The African-American community's hopeful and romantic expectations about the effects of the Watts crisis allowed for the building of common solidarities that could transcend previous political divisions, creating a united front behind the mayoral candidacy of Thomas Bradley, and against Yorty (who had received considerable African-American support in the 1965 mayoral election). Research by Tomlinson and Sears indicated that fifty-eight percent of African-Americans in Los Angeles felt that there would be positive results from Watts.[47] In sum, the cultural construction of Watts in the African-American public sphere of Los Angeles invigorated a new racial project, oriented more toward political power than ethnic assimilation.

Racial formation, Watts, and multiple publics

As Omi and Winant point out, racial movements are built on the terrain of civil society.[48] First, movement leaders re-narrate the story of civil society, turning the utopian romantic narrative against itself and arguing that their own self-emancipation constitutes the central dramatic challenge to civil society's ideals. Next, they seek to extend this new public narrative into the discourse of other public spheres, including those of the dominant society. This allows the movement leaders to make reformist demands on state policies and institutions, on the grounds that they are inconsistent with the narrative of civil society, newly-redefined. This is precisely why the civil rights movement was so important to American civil society. Omi and Winant describe how civil rights leaders such as Robert Moses and Martin Luther King, Jr. redefined "the moral, spiritual, and political leadership of American society. They represented not only their own centuries-long struggle for freedom, but the highest and noblest aspirations of white America as well."[49]

Importantly, these alternative interpretations of American civil society did not occur first in the mainstream public spheres organized by such newspapers as the *New York Times*, *Chicago Tribune*, and *Los Angeles Times*; rather, they tended to get articulated in African-American public spheres organized by black papers such as the *New York Amsterdam News*, *Chicago Defender*, and *Los Angeles Sentinel*. During the 1960s, African-American leaders spoke frequently in the African-American press and the specifically African-American public spheres. The result of their participation in the smaller, more "limited" publics was often more beneficial for the purposes of political formation than speaking in the larger, more hegemonic publics of mainstream civil society. The reason for this is that the African-American newspapers were more open to narratives which empowered the African-American community. This was clearly the case during the Watts crisis in Los Angeles, where the intensive publicity surrounding the crisis was constructed in the *Los Angeles Sentinel* through a genre of romantic hope about the future, and where the binding force of solidarity which emerged out of Watts produced a much more vibrant and powerful political project within Los Angeles' African-American community. Before Watts, Los Angeles' African-American community was divided into two opposing camps; after Watts, it was united.

But while Watts brought the urban racial crisis squarely into the public arena, it did not cause any significant overlap between African-American and mainstream news narratives about race and civil society. All three mainstream newspapers presented similar descriptions of the rioters as irrational, hysterical, and insane (although the *New York Times* did not exhibit nearly as much interest in describing the rioters as the other papers). On the other hand, all African-American papers explained the causes of the uprisings as being white indifference, police brutality, and racism. These structured similarities, which exist despite other significant differences, suggest that the mobilization of race in the 1960s produced a stratified focus that increased racial tensions. In the white public sphere, the alignment of black rioters with the profane discourse of civil society undermined their ability to participate rationally and actively in the search for resolution. Black leaders who spoke in the mainstream press had to spend much of their time discussing the actions of the rioters before they ever got the chance to talk about underlying social causes, and they were more likely to get media publicity if they first criticized the rioters. In the black public sphere, the identification of white society with racism and indifference, combined with the mainstream public focus on the putative irrationality of black rioters, produced an increasing distrust of the mainstream media. Thus, while the black public sphere during the 1960s was successful in providing a space for forming new collective projects and new unions, it was less successful in increasing tolerance and engagement with those in the more dominant publics.

4

The Rodney King beating

On March 3, 1991, an African-American motorist, Rodney King, was pulled over for speeding. After a brief chase, King was met by twenty-one police officers, including members of the California Highway Patrol and the Los Angeles Police Department. In full view of all who were present, King was severely beaten by three white LAPD officers, in the presence of a sergeant and the remaining seventeen officers. Unknown to the police officers, the event was videotaped by an amateur cameraman, George Holliday, sold to a local television station, and subsequently broadcast on television thousands of times. Since then, the Rodney King case has become the defining instance of police brutality in Los Angeles, despite the fact that the city paid more than $20 million between 1986–1990 in judgments, settlements, and jury verdicts against Los Angeles police officers in over 300 lawsuits dealing with the excessive use of force.

Despite the frequency with which the Rodney King videotape was broadcast, the build-up to crisis was more gradual than during the uprisings of 1965 or 1992. This can be seen by examining news coverage during the first week after the precipitating events for the three crises. For the six newspapers of the study, the first week's news coverage totaled 203 articles for the 1965 Watts uprisings and 375 articles for the 1992 uprisings, but only forty-one articles during the first week of the 1991 Rodney King crisis. Indeed, it is quite possible that any of the other excessive force cases could have yielded social dramas of the magnitude of Rodney King, just as the impact of the Rodney King beating might not have exceeded that of the cases preceding it.

This is not to deny the fact that the event contained all the necessary symbolic elements to construct a narrative of crisis. First, the videotape of the beating – which was recorded by an amateur cameraman, an ordinary citizen of civil society – showed visual and technical proof of the event: in a sense, a video-text, which itself placed the actors in relations of similarity and opposition to one another. The videotape served a naturalizing function for the subsequent interpretations that would be made. Second, the primary image of the videotape, the brutality of the white officers toward the African-American victim, Rodney King, was easily related to earlier historic images of white police violence against African-Americans. Finally, there existed a history of conflict between Police Chief Daryl Gates and minority groups in Los Angeles.[1] The Los Angeles police had been a polarizing force since before Watts; demonstrating the racial divide in public perceptions, they were consistently praised by white residents of the city, and criticized by African-American residents.[2] With the release of the Rodney King videotape, however, Daryl Gates and his police department came under nearly-universal media criticism. Rather than calling for closer police control of ghetto communities, public figures began calling for more control over the police. Noting this shift in interpretation, those in the African-American public sphere watched expectantly, waiting to see if mainstream civil society would be willing to grant African-Americans more power and control over their communities.

In addition to the cultural history which enabled the Rodney King beating to develop into a crisis, there were a number of additional events which shaped the contours of the 1991 crisis and the way it was discussed in the public spheres of civil society. These events are summarized in Table 4.1. The first of these events took place rather quickly, when Police Chief Daryl Gates called the beating an "aberration," a statement that outraged many activists and critics of the police department, and placed a spotlight on the quality of its leadership. Indeed, the questions surrounding the leadership of Daryl Gates erupted into a crisis of its own when the Police Commission – on the urging of Mayor Bradley – temporarily removed Police Chief Gates from his position. The Police Commission's action was met with extreme criticism from the members of the City Council, who instigated court action to have Gates reinstated. With the growing conflict between the Police Commission and City Council, the crisis of leadership in the Los Angeles Police Department seemed to many to be exacerbated by a crisis of leadership in Los Angeles politics more generally.

In addition to the political furor surrounding Police Chief Gates, the contours of the Rodney King crisis were also impacted by the formation of four separate "official investigations" into the beating: one by the grand jury, one by the FBI, one by Daryl Gates's Arguelles Commission, and one by Mayor Thomas Bradley's Christopher Commission. These investigations culminated with the July 9 release of the report about the police department by the Christopher Commission (which had merged with the

Table 4.1. *Events surrounding the Rodney King crisis, March–September 1991*

3/3/91	Rodney King is beaten by members of the Los Angeles Police Department, and recorded on videotape by amateur cameraman George Holliday.
3/6/91	Police Chief Daryl Gates calls the beating an "aberration."
3/11/91	A grand jury investigation is formed to look into the beating of Rodney King.
3/12/91	An FBI probe is formed to investigate the beating of Rodney King.
3/14/91	Four Los Angeles police officers are indicted for the beating of Rodney King.
3/30/91	Daryl Gates forms the Arguelles Commission to investigate the beating of Rodney King.
3/30/91	Tom Bradley forms the Christopher Commission to investigate the beating of Rodney King.
4/4/91	The Police Commission, on the urging of Mayor Tom Bradley, removes Daryl Gates from his position as police chief.
4/5/91	Arguelles Commission and Christopher Commission are merged into an expanded Christopher Commission.
4/6/91	The City Council, after criticizing the Police Commission's action, reinstates Daryl Gates to his position as police chief.
7/9/91	The Christopher Commission releases the results of its investigation, the "Report of the Independent Commission on the Los Angeles Police Department.
7/12/91	Daryl Gates announces that he will retire as police chief.
7/14/91	Daryl Gates announces that he might not retire until 1993.
7/17/91	City Councilmen John Ferraro and Joel Wachs make a public call for the resignation of Daryl Gates.
7/22/91	Daryl Gates announces that he will resign as police chief in April 1992.

Arguelles Commission). The report was highly critical of Chief Gates; found a systematic failure to control officers with repeated complaints of excessive force; discovered significant racism and bias within the department itself; and found tactics of intimidation designed to discourage public citizens trying to make complaints.[3] The commission's report led to a concerted effort on the part of the local political elite to get Gates to commit to a retirement date, which he finally did on July 22.

These additional events extended the duration of the Rodney King crisis and increased its dramatic impact. Indeed, the number of twists to the plot helped to maintain a palpable tension between romantic and tragic narratives, as we will see, and kept public attention fixed on the crisis for longer than might otherwise have been the case. Between March 7 and September 4, a total of 633 articles were written about the crisis in the six newspapers of the study – more, in fact, than were written during the equivalent period of the 1965 Watts crisis. Seventy-eight percent of these were written in the Los Angeles press, but a full 139 articles were written in the non-Los Angeles newspapers.

Early constructions of the crisis in the daily press

The earliest reports about the beating came from the daily press and the television media. The *Los Angeles Times* provided the most intensive initial coverage, totaling fifty-five articles about the beating during the first two weeks. Other daily newspapers also covered the story in great detail, with twenty-one stories in the *New York Times* and fifteen in the *Chicago Tribune* during the initial two-week period. *ABC News* produced eight separate stories about the Rodney King crisis during this period, including a special sixty-minute episode of "Primetime Live." All of these news outlets represented the beating as a "shocking" event, criticized the police officers for using their powers illegitimately, and described them as being irrational and excitable in their work. Accounts from witnesses reported that the officers were "laughing and chuckling [after the beating], like they had just had a party."[4] These interpretations were not presented as evaluations, but were placed within the descriptive frame of the news account, each account attributed to a source. At the same time, the polluting, counter-democratic discourse of civil society was operating within the text: through quotations, editorials, and descriptions. The following descriptions of the event appeared in the *Los Angeles Times* during the first days of the crisis:

... accounts ... suggested that what should have been a relatively simple arrest ... escalated wildly out of control   (*Los Angeles Times*, March 7, 1991: A21)

The violent images of white police officers pounding an apparently defenseless black man have raised the ire of civil rights groups
                                        (*Los Angeles Times*, March 7, 1991: A22)

The beating of King, videotaped by an amateur photographer, has sparked an outcry over police misconduct in Los Angeles, as well as calls for the resignation of Chief Daryl F. Gates. The images of white police officers pummeling the black motorist with their batons were aired by television stations across the country.
                                        (*Los Angeles Times*, March 9, 1991: B1)

Similar reports of outrage and public indignation were echoed in the initial reports of the *New York Times, Chicago Tribune*, and *ABC News*:

A two-minute amateur videotape of the beating of a black motorist by a group of police officers has jarred Los Angeles and revived charges that the police department has failed to confront an alleged pattern of police brutality and official abuse of minorities among its officers.   (*New York Times*, March 7, 1991: A1)

It's a case of brutality that's making headlines around the world in a spark of growing rage in the black community. Today that rage took the form of a major protest against the LA Police Department sponsored by the NAACP.
(*ABC News*, March 9, 1991)

Outrage mounted Wednesday over the videotaped police beating of an unarmed black motorist with thousands of angry calls to police headquarters, the mayor's office and civil rights activists. The startling video, shot from a balcony by a resident and shown nationwide on network television news programs, showed officers using an electric stun gun to subdue Rodney King, then clubbing the prone man as he begged for mercy.   (*Chicago Tribune*, March 7, 1991: A10)

While all of these descriptions were attributed to "accounts," "civil rights groups," and "images aired by television stations" – thus remaining within the constraint of news objectivity and the routine practices of using official sources – the descriptive words *violent, wildly, pounding, pummeling*, and *brutality* operated to place the actors in symbolic relations to each other and to the discourse of civil society. In other cases, editorial accounts mobilized the "reality effect" of the videotape to symbolically tarnish the police officers, as is evident from the following excerpts from the *Chicago Tribune* and the *New York Times*, respectively.

By now, most of the nation must have seen or heard of the videotape shot by a nearby resident as King, a 25-year-old parolee, was arrested on a Los Angeles street last week after what the police said was a high speed chase. Viewing it is roughly akin to watching a wolfpack take down a deer.

(*Chicago Tribune*, March 11, 1991: A12)

It has been three days now since television gave America a portrait of horror: a renegade band of Los Angeles policemen savagely kicking and beating a suspect lying on the pavement . . . What the 15 officers in Los Angeles dispensed was sickening summary injustice; the national jury awaits a proper response.
(*New York Times*, March 8, 1991: A28)

Along with the construction of the event as a crisis came a specification of those violations depicted by the video images: violations of fairness, openness, and justice. News reports described the anti-hero attributes of the police officers, adding to earlier descriptions of their "uncontrolled and irrational" motivations. The event of the beating, when linked to the videotape, was understood as a way to expose the evil that existed in the police department. An editorial in the *Los Angeles Times* proclaimed that "this time, the police witnesses, knowing about the videotape, will probably not compound their offense by lying about what really happened."[5] Similar questions were asked in the *Chicago Tribune, New York Times*, and *ABC News*. This type of news coverage, exposing the secrecy and brutality of the officers, was used by local leaders as well as "objective" news reporters:

It exploded onto Los Angeles television screens last week. The scene: three Los Angeles police officers involved in a merciless, relentless, brutal beating of a Black man as he lay face down on the ground, while 12 officers observed in tacit approval.
(*Los Angeles Times*, March 14, 1991: A1)

"This is not an isolated incident!" thundered Jose de Sosa, the rally's organizer and president of the San Fernando chapter of the NAACP. "This is the type of thing that occurs under the cover of darkness throughout our city."
(*Los Angeles Times*, March 10, 1991: B1)

The police officers were condemned through visual images as well as linguistic discourse. On the one hand, the images of the videotape served to highlight the dark fact of police brutality. On the other, the news reports presented the videotape as proof of the deceitfulness of the police department. In this double-sense, the police officers lost credibility by the videotape, and the sense of crisis was strengthened.

Still, if it was merely a problem of a few individuals in need of administrative control, a crisis need not have ensued. True, the fact that such an event could have occurred was represented as evidence of a fundamental problem in officer selection and training, and by itself brought some criticism of the police organization. But the real threat to reputation of the police was constructed through portrayals of Police Chief Daryl Gates as being unaccountable, racist, and ego-driven. From March 7–11, there were four editorials in the *Los Angeles Times* about the beating, but none focused on Gates or the institution of the police department. From March 12–14, however, there were six editorials about the crisis and all focused on Gates and the question of the integrity of the LAPD. The following two excerpts are typical of editorial opinion during the second week of the crisis:

. . . [t]he people of Los Angeles have been unable to hold their chief of police accountable for anything – not his racial slurs or racial stereotyping; not his openly-expressed contempt for the public, juries and the Constitution he is sworn to uphold; not his spying on political enemies or cover-up of that espionage.
(*Los Angeles Times*, March 12, 1991: B7)

Chief Gates is responsible for inflammatory comments, for the actions of his officers and for the $8 million in taxpayer money paid out last year to satisfy complaints against the department. But because of rigid civil service protections, the police chief is not accountable to the mayor, the City Council or to the city's voters.

(*Los Angeles Times*, March 13, 1991: B6)

Attached to Daryl Gates in these two excerpts were many different attributes, and all were damaging to his symbolic status. Gates was cast in opposition to the public, the Constitution, the mayor and the City Council and on the same side as the LAPD officers, who had already been tarnished. Gates and the LAPD were also opposed to the mayor and the City Council, who in turn benefited by their semiotic contiguity to the public and the Constitution.

In the daily presses of New York and Chicago there was the same level of criticism against Police Chief Daryl Gates, but the positioning and description of characters differed in several important respects. For the *Chicago Tribune*, the censuring of Gates and the police department extended to include all politicians in Los Angeles, whose inability to regulate the police was taken as a sign of official weakness. Understood as an impersonal, fragmented mass society with no strong community ties, the city of Los Angeles itself came to be portrayed negatively; the more community-centered city of Chicago was represented as the opposite of Los Angeles, and was thereby shown in a positive light.[6]

Given the long history of racial allegations against members of the department, and the chief's apparent inability to curb his men, the head that should roll now sits squarely on the stiff neck of Chief Gates . . . Indeed, it is likely that the official toleration of these outrages – both by Gates and Mayor Tom Bradley, himself an ex-policeman – is the main reason it continues. Any number of bad police departments . . . have cleaned up their acts after the appointment of chiefs who made it clear they would not tolerate police brutality.   (*Chicago Tribune*, March 14, 1991: A27)

These perceptions [of injustice] have not been eased by a police department that traditionally takes a heavy-handed, high-tech approach to law enforcement instead of a people-oriented approach that encourages beat patrols, community cooperation and intensive human-relations training. Yet this more enlightened approach has helped reduce crime and brutality complaints in Chicago and many other communities, including some near Los Angeles, that have experienced severe police brutality complaints in the past. How does one break the cycle of distrust that leads to more crime? There may be no greater prescription than grass-roots organization.

(*Chicago Tribune*, March 13, 1991: A23)

In this type of comparison, the Rodney King crisis provided a device for praising Chicago and its leaders. Even the images of police brutality became a vehicle for praising Chicago police, as the *Tribune* compared the increased self-reflection the videotape was causing among community leaders and local police in Chicago to the inaction of the Los Angeles police department.[7] Similar forms of news coverage were found in the *New York Times* (though less centrally), where the home city was viewed favorably against the mass society of Los Angeles and its unaccountable institutions. When Police Chief Gates was compared to New York police commissioners, the comparison consistently worked to the benefit of the New York police;[8] the same was true regarding the comparison of Los Angeles and New York City municipal governments.[9]

Rather than turning to the local community leaders as the figures best able to solve the type of crisis the Rodney King beating represented, stories in the *New York Times* highlighted the actions taken by national figures such as the Attorney General, the Congressional Black Caucus and the FBI chief:

In a meeting with news executives today, Attorney General Dick Thornburgh emphasized that the indictments in Los Angeles on local charges of assault and other counts would be supplemented by an inquiry involving the Federal Bureau of Investigation . . . The Reconstruction-era statutes likely to be used by the Government, one of which was enacted to cripple the Ku Klux Klan, give the F. B. I. a reason to enter brutality cases, especially those in which local prosecutors may be close to the police.   (*New York Times*, March 16, 1991: A8)

Outraged over the videotaped beating of a suspect by the Los Angeles police last week, members of the Congressional Black Caucus asked the Justice Department today to conduct a wide-ranging inquiry into police brutality in the city . . . several lawmakers said today . . . a broad Federal investigation was necessary because the local authorities had been unable to halt what they referred to as a 'pattern of abuse' by the police.   (*New York Times*, March 13, 1991: A22)

Interestingly, the *Chicago Tribune* also reported about the Congressional Black Caucus's urging of a federal investigation into police brutality, but connected it to the narrative of local community power. While commending Attorney General Richard Thornburgh for recognizing what "community spokesmen have long contended . . . not just in Los Angeles but in cities across the country," *Tribune* editorials criticized federal officials for a tendency to minimize the problem, questioned what the investigation would do with the findings, and argued that "in this nation, law enforcement is primarily – and properly – a local responsibility . . . [where] in the last analysis, it is the locals who must make it happen."[10]

Thus, in the early reports about the Rodney King crisis within the daily press, the anti-heroes had fairly similar characteristics, but those of the heroes were quite different. For the *Los Angeles Times*, the heroic actors were the local government leaders, who benefited by a process of semiotic and political opposition to Gates and the Los Angeles police department. For the *Chicago Tribune* the hero was the collective local community, opposed to the putative mass society of Los Angeles. For the *New York Times*, most of the heroic character positions were reserved for national politicians. Like the *Tribune*, the New York paper used Los Angeles as a point of negative comparison, comparing the glossy Hollywood fantasy image of Los Angeles law enforcement against the realist and grainy amateur videotape.[11]

These character oppositions, which developed in the initial Rodney King narratives of the three newspapers, reinforced specific self-representations about each news organization's public voice. The *Chicago Tribune* and *Los Angeles Times*, viewing themselves as the voice of their respective cities, placed political actors from their respective cities in the heroic character positions. The *New York Times*, viewing itself as the leading news voice of the nation, reserved the heroic character positions for national political leaders, and used the Rodney King narrative to expose the dangers of local autonomy, particularly in racial matters. These differences in character opposition mirrored those from the Watts narratives of 1965, despite the significant nationalization of the Chicago and Los Angeles daily newspapers between 1968 and 1990. Regardless of the fact that the three papers looked much more similar in terms of news-gathering resources, journalist staffing, and bureau placement, they continued to evince important differences in their news narratives, differences which related to the specific cultural histories between press and public sphere.

Narrative tension and the elaboration of the crisis

With the event having been constructed as a crisis, it began to unfold through a tension between two competing narrative forms, which are summarized in Table 4.2. On one side was a romantic "drama of redemption" pitting the heroic actors, however defined, against the anti-heroes of the Los Angeles Police Department and its leader, Daryl Gates. In the *Chicago Tribune* and the *New York Times*, the identification of the anti-heroes extended to include the entire city of Los Angeles. In all of these narratives, the heroic actors were not constructed through any sort of positive discourse, but rather through a semiotic opposition to Gates, the LAPD, and (for the non-Los Angeles press) the putative mass society of Los Angeles. This occurred on several different levels. Semiotically, it operated through opposition, where every term implies and entails its opposite. In this case, symbolic opposition to Gates benefited the heroic figures. Politically, it worked because of the need for an identifiable legitimate authority. This political dynamic was expressed quite well in a *Los Angeles Sentinel* editorial, which argued, "This community has had enough police brutality and if the chief of police won't stop it, then the commission must, and if not, the mayor and the City Council must take definitive action."[12]

In the *Los Angeles Sentinel*, however, the actual composition of the romantic narrative differed in important respects from that of the *Los Angeles Times* or the other mainstream news media. An important reason for this was the construction of a second romantic narrative in which the African-American community itself was cast as the hero. In this "romance of the community," the hero was portrayed not through mere semiotic opposition, but through actual and positive discourse. Employing a style common to the African-American press, the newspaper invoked the ideals of American society while criticizing the existing one. In opposition to mainstream society, it represented the African-American community as the true voice of unity and morality, and hence as the only agent able to truly resolve the crisis. We can see the construction of this second romantic narrative in the following excerpts from the *Los Angeles Sentinel*:

> Rarely, if ever, has an issue so united the Black community in the way the March 3 Rodney King incident has done. The savage beating of King has inspired Los Angeles' Black community to speak with one voice.
>
> (*Los Angels Sentinel*, March 14, 1991: A1)

> We must not allow ourselves to be set apart in this battle. Justice must be served and we must, at least in part, be the instruments of that justice.
>
> (*Los Angeles Sentinel*, March 28, 1991: A7)

> The African-American community itself has a distinct role in the accountability equation. In fact, the community represents the proverbial bottom line: it is the ultimate determinant of values and enforcers of acceptable standards.
>
> (*Los Angeles Sentinel*, April 11, 1991: A6)

In this romantic narrative, the beating of Rodney King became a watershed, unleashing the potential power of the African-American community. While Daryl Gates and the LAPD were still the villains of this narrative, there were new heroes. Furthermore, this second romantic narrative was much more accommodating of the public sphere goals of cultural autonomy, as described in Chapter 1.

In progressive union with the romantic narratives, both Los Angeles newspapers also used a tragic frame to interpret some of the events surrounding the crisis. In a tragic narrative, as Frye notes, the drama must make a *tragic point*; that is, while the protagonist must be of a properly heroic stature, the development of the plot is one of ultimate failure.[13] Thus, in the *Los Angeles Times* the public – what Sherwood has called the

Table 4.2. *Narrative forms of crisis construction during the 1991 Rodney King crisis*

Narrative form	Heroes	Descriptions of heroes	Anti-heroes	Descriptions of anti-heroes
L.A. Times:				
Romance....	mayor, City Council	semiotic opposition to anti-heroes	Gates, LAPD	out of control, irrational, deceitful, not accountable
Tragedy....	"the world," "the people"	isolated, factions	white, middle-class citizens	passive, horrified
L.A. Sentinel:				
Romance....	local government	semiotic opposition to anti-heroes	Gates, LAPD	brutal, merciless, secretive
Romance....	African-American community	unified, moral, active	Gates, LAPD	brutal, merciless, secretive
Tragedy....	African-American community	ironic memory	white, mainstream society	racist, insincere
New York Times:				
Romance....	national government leaders	national laws, historical precedent; semiotic opposition to anti-heroes	Gates, LAPD; Los Angeles mass society	savage, out of control, deceitful; powerless, corrupt
Chicago Tribune:				
Romance....	local community, grassroots organization	human scale; semiotic opposition to anti-heroes	Gates, LAPD; Los Angeles mass society	savage, out of control, deceitful; powerless, corrupt
Amsterdam News:				
Tragedy....	African-American community	ironic memory	white, mainstream society	racist, insincere
Chicago Defender:				
Tragedy....	African-American community	ironic memory	white, mainstream society	racist, insincere

heroic actor of the "drama of democracy" – became represented as a series of factions, and it became more difficult to imagine a plot development where a new actor could successfully step in and do battle with Gates and the police department.[14] Within the tragic genre, reaction to the beating was interpreted through a narrative of class, racial, and ethnic segregation rather than public unity. As an editorial in the *Los Angeles Times* lamented, "It is profoundly revealing that while middle-class viewers recoiled in horror at the brutal footage, the victim, like many others familiar with police behavior in poor and minority neighborhoods, considered himself lucky that the police did not kill him."[15]

These types of accounts in the *Los Angeles Times* represented a "tragedy of fate," in the sense of resigned acceptance, a tragedy "already there and already evil."[16] In a narrative context where the local politicians were the heroes, and where the newspaper viewed itself as the voice (and supporter) of the city, a story of racial segregation offered too much disjuncture to be incorporated into the romantic narrative. A factionalized city could not heal itself. By contrast, a narrative which allowed for heroic characters to emerge from outside the city could still be told through the romantic genre. Such was the case with the *ABC News* narrative. In its reports about the crisis, the problems of racism and factionalization in the city of Los Angeles could be resolved through the actions of national politicians:

They were wrestling with a tough question at the White House today, one which has been on the public mind for more than two weeks: How do you enforce law and order when those accused are policemen? A question of course triggered by the videotape of Los Angeles police beating a black motorist. Today the President met with his Attorney General Dick Thornburgh to talk about cracking down on police brutality . . . The Justice Department does not intend to reopen all 15,000 police brutality cases filed in the last six years, but it will look for patterns of abuse to determine whether there should be changes in the way police are trained . . . In Los Angeles today one group of citizens announced it would try to launch a voter recall of Chief Gates, while another group announced it would try to hold a rally in support of the Chief, a sign of polarization in a troubled city. From the person on the street to the President of the United States, outrage has been the common reaction to the videotaped beating of Rodney King. But in minority communities there is another reaction, that King's beating is nothing new . . . The feeling that white police are out to get minorities is widespread in Los Angeles.

(*ABC News*, March 21, 1991)

The point is that the reports of factionalism did not necessarily lead to any single narrative form; the "tragedy of fate" in the *Los Angeles Times* was caused by an inability to incorporate the new plot into the ongoing Rodney King narrative. For *ABC News*, where the reports of factionalization in Los

Angeles supported the romantic notions of a national government, there was no need for any change in narrative form.

Along similar lines, the development of a tragic frame did not necessarily lead to a fatalistic understanding, as it had for the *Los Angeles Times* (and as it did in the news reports of the *Chicago Defender*, and *New York Amsterdam News*). News reports in the *Los Angeles Sentinel* combined elements of tragedy and irony, calling up other recent instances of brutality against African-Americans. News reports in the *Sentinel* juxtaposed the outrage over and collective attention to the Rodney King beating with the relative lack of attention concerning another beating case whose trial had begun on the same day. The trial stemmed from the "Don Jackson case," a 1989 event where two Long Beach police officers were captured on videotape pushing an off-duty, African-American police officer through a plateglass window, "followed by the sight of Jackson being slammed onto the hood of their patrol car, after a 'routine' traffic stop."[17] While the *Los Angeles Times* had given the Don Jackson story significant coverage in 1989, writing twelve articles about it, it failed to make the same immediate textual attachment to the Rodney King beating in 1991. While the *Los Angeles Times* and *Chicago Tribune* failed to make the connection to the Don Jackson case, both the *New York Times* (March 7, 1991, p. A18) and *ABC News* (March 20, 1991) did. For the *New York Times* and *ABC News*, the reference to Don Jackson was used to highlight the national investigations of Congress and the FBI. For the *Los Angeles Sentinel*, however, the Don Jackson story served as a plot device to deepen the historical context of the Rodney King crisis. In a feature interview, Brotherhood Crusade leader Danny Bakewell noted: "When I saw what happened to that brother on television, I thought I was watching a scene out of the distant past: a Ku Klux Klan lynch mob at work."[18] By recalling other instances of brutality against African-Americans, writers for the *Los Angeles Sentinel* placed the event of the beating in the middle of a long and continuous narrative, rather than at the beginning of a new one.

The *Chicago Defender* and *New York Amsterdam News* also made use of a deeper historical frame to construct their Rodney King narratives, and did so through the use of the tragic genre. Unlike the *Los Angeles Sentinel*, however, these historical narratives did not contain any hope of local-community edification, but were written singularly as tragic tales of white indifference. In the *Chicago Defender*, there was the same type of irony-tinged tragic story told by the *Los Angeles Sentinel*, where the African-American leadership, press, and community had been fighting the issue for some hundred years, but had been largely ignored by the mainstream media and white society.

The charge of police brutality is an old charge made by Blacks in most areas of the nation. The Black press has been fighting this issue for 100 years. In most cases the charges are ignored by the mainstream media. The big media bosses have generally taken the position the police are falsely accused . . . In the case of Los Angeles, there is no way to whitewash the cops. They are shown kicking and beating a helpless Black man lying on the ground . . . There is a streak of savagery in our society which most often manifests itself in racial conflicts. One of the great crusades of the NAACP for the first 50 years of its existence was for the enactment of a federal anti-lynching bill. We no longer fear lynching by white mobs of hooded men. Nevertheless, the lynch mentality is still alive and well in many quarters . . . Until we face up to the hypocrisy in our society, we will continue to make over-moralistic statements that are totally divorced from reality.

(*Los Angeles Sentinel*, March 23, 1991: A22)

While joining the other newspapers in criticizing Daryl Gates and the Los Angeles Police Department, the *Chicago Defender* emphasized the historical continuity of police brutality rather than the particular aspects of the Rodney King beating. None of the significant events of the case found their way into the *Defender*'s reports. This includes the temporary removal of Gates by the Police Commission and his reinstatement by the City Council; the release of the Christopher Commission report; and the final announcement by Gates that he would resign from his position. Instead, the narrative line of white indifference was maintained, and given historical explanation as being regulated by a cycle of outrage and loss of attention.[19]

The same strategy of narrating the Rodney King crisis in terms of a more general story of white indifference and hostility dominated the news coverage of the *New York Amsterdam News*, where the specific events of the case were devalued in favor of the more general narrative. In the *Amsterdam News*, however, the general narrative was a more biting and tragic one. Here, the videotape was constructed as part of a long and continuous tragic story of brutality, a story which transcended space, time, and even nation in the continuity of its evil.

It was a stark, brutal scene right out of Selma of the '60s or contemporary Soweto. Like a klaven of kluxers, a squadron of uniformed white cops surrounded a black man, while three of the throng took turns beating and kicking him. The only unique thing about this felonious assault by a dozen or so members of the Los Angeles Police Department early Sunday morning (March 3) was that it was all graphically captured on videotape by an amateur photographer.

(*New York Amsterdam News*, March 16, 1991: A4)

The totality of racist oppression and indifference extended in this narrative, across American history, from local politics to national politics, and even international conflict. In direct opposition to the dominant construction of the crisis of the non-Los Angeles mainstream press, where Los Angeles was an aberrant case to be used to edify the local community or the federal government, the *Amsterdam News* argued that Gates and Los Angeles were interchangeable with any other American politician or community.

Nor is Chief Gates' 'aberration' confined to Los Angeles. Many Black New Yorkers say they expect an increased number of assaults on minorities as the general mood of militarism grows and police ape the swagger and menace of the military after its trouncing of Iraq.   (*New York Amsterdam News*, March 16, 1991: A4)

If things become too hot, if he becomes too much of an embarrassment, they will retire him on a hefty pension and replace him with someone else . . . the real problem is the systematic contempt and disdain for all Blacks and Chicanos that allows not only countless instances of brutality to go unpunished but accepts as normal the ongoing national concept that Blacks and Hispanics are not entitled to full protection under the law, legal recourse, or even basic services . . . The Watts riots in Los Angeles started over a similar incident . . . Police the world over tell lies. They are taught how to lie by senior officers . . . In New York the situation warranted the Kerner Commission report, which was ignored by former Mayor Ed Koch. In Los Angeles, several watchdog groups have filed repeated lawsuits against police with limited success.   (*New York Amsterdam News*, March 30, 1991: A28)

Even the videotape of the beating, which had such an unquestioned ontological realism in the other news reports, became devalued in the *Amsterdam News* in terms of its potential effectiveness. The *Amsterdam News* predicted that the videotape would create more police violence, as the police would "include video takers as criminals and go after them and destroy their cameras and evidence, then say they were interfering with police procedure."[20]

There is an interesting paradox in the more sweeping and historical context of the *Chicago Defender* and *New York Amsterdam News* narratives. On the one hand, these narratives placed the Rodney King crisis in the middle of the most central dramatic challenge of American history, that of racial oppression. One would think that this was a positive move because it allowed for the re-narration of that history, and also for the orientation of present actors toward possible ways of providing a resolution and denouement to the epic narrative. Surprisingly, however, the insertion of the crisis into this deeper historical context was followed by a loss of attention to the immediate events surrounding the present crisis. Neither the *Chicago Defender* nor the *New York Amsterdam News* offered any news coverage or editorial on the Christopher Commission or the release of its report, despite its criticism of police practices, its instrumental role in removing Gates from his office, and its role in producing a public discussion about police racism in metropolitan cities. The narration of a long, historical tragedy, as it turned out, was not at all effective in encouraging an extended discussion about matters of common concern. Indeed, in the next chapter on the 1992 crisis, we will see this same use of historical tragedy within the daily mainstream press, and the same public sphere disengagement following the consolidation of that narrative frame.

Genre strategies and the formation of official investigations

As Victor Turner has described, once a breach develops into a crisis, the political elite will often attempt certain "redressive actions" in order to try to maintain the romantic narrative (where they were the heroic figures) and to deflate the tragic one.[21] These actions often take the form of official investigations, which have the cultural attributes of being independent, rule-regulated, and impersonal: that is, aligned with the semiotic code of democratic institutions. Yet, just like the construction of the crisis, the success of these attempts is neither automatic nor guaranteed. In fact, the initial attempts to resolve the Rodney King crisis through "official investigation" failed miserably. The first attempt was a grand jury investigation, begun the week after the beating. This investigation ultimately led to the trial of LAPD officers Briseno, Powell, Koon, and Wind. Despite the fact that it produced these indictments, however, the grand jury investigation was not selected by any of the news media as a significant event in their developing plots about the Rodney King crisis. There are several possible reasons for this. The first is that the indictments lacked temporal immediacy, in the sense that they could only provide a symbolic end in the far distant future, after the conclusion of a lengthy criminal trial. The second reason, and perhaps the more significant one, is that the grand jury actions did not follow any of the plot lines of the various news narratives. They did not involve the local government, the national government, or the African-American community as heroes; they did not address the problem of the police chief; and they left unresolved the questions of fragmentation and segregation. While the sequence of events following from the grand jury investigation eventually led to the extremely meaningful "not guilty" verdict of 1992, the initial event was insignificant to the narration of the crisis.

Perhaps the more interesting case was that of the FBI probe, begun March 12. This action did get incorporated in a more significant fashion in the different news narratives of the various presses, although in substantially different ways. In both Los Angeles newspapers, the FBI probe was evaluated negatively. In the *Los Angeles Sentinel*'s romantic narratives, the FBI probe failed to include the African-American community. In relation

to the other romantic frames, the national-level FBI probe could only res-
urrect the image of the police department by tarnishing that of the political actors cast as the romantic heroes: the Mayor and the City Council.
Resolution of the crisis by the FBI would have placed the political leaders
of Los Angeles in a symbolic position of dependence, and the crisis would
have ended with a new genre and a new plot: a comedy about the city's political leadership. The city's leaders would have been symbolically transformed
from active leaders to *imposters* who, unable to fulfill the requirements of
their office, would have been viewed instead as "blocking characters."[22]
While this comedy could still have been constructed as a narrative of inclusion, through the reconciliation or conversion of the imposter characters,
it would have necessarily decreased political legitimacy for local government. The FBI probe was quickly criticized for being divisive and coercive,
particularly in the *Los Angeles Times* where the "romance of local government" resonated most strongly. While the police officers were usually represented together with Daryl Gates as the anti-heroes, when reporting
about the FBI probe the *Los Angeles Times* linked Gates to the FBI and the
police officers to the symbols of citizenship and rights.[23] Even the *New York
Times*, which initially had narrated the FBI probe in a positive light –
linking its right to conduct investigations back to the attempt to cripple the
Ku Klux Klan during the Reconstruction period[24] – ultimately was swayed
by the symbols of citizenship and rights which had been successfully
attached to the Los Angeles police officers. After a March 30, 1991 story
titled "Officers' Rights Hinder F.B.I. Inquiry into Beating," the *New York
Times* ceased coverage of the FBI inquiry.

Of all the political attempts at redressive action, however, the one which
failed most completely, and with the greatest effect for the discursive environment surrounding the Rodney King crisis, was the effort by Mayor
Thomas Bradley to remove Gates from his position as police chief. Initially,
Bradley had refused to call for Gates's removal. But the failure of the FBI
and the grand jury investigations, as well as growing public opinion against
Gates, led Bradley to change his mind. Bradley made a public call for Gates
to resign, and projected his resignation as a means of healing for the city
and as a way for Gates to purify himself for the good of the public. He
urged Gates to resign "for the good of the LAPD and the welfare of all of
Los Angeles,"[25] and by doing so to show "uncommon courage."[26]

When Gates refused to step down from his position, the Police
Commission, on Bradley's urging, temporarily removed Daryl Gates from
his duties as police chief. This action, far from resolving the crisis, only
inflamed it, reinforcing and re-affirming the tragic narratives. The City

Council criticized the Police Commission for being dependent on Bradley, attacked Bradley for being motivated by power instead of the public good, and described the action as "illegal" and "irresponsible."[27] One prominent City Council member, Joel Wachs, linked the action to the Watergate crisis, calling it "a shocking abuse of our time-honored system of government."[28] The Police Commission (which had been virtually powerless until Bradley's mayoral victory in 1973) responded that "the action we have taken is on sound legal grounds and the court will back us."[29] Bradley tried to connect this emerging crisis with the larger Rodney King crisis, where, particularly in the Los Angeles press, he was the hero, Gates was the villain, and any action against Gates was therefore a heroic act:

> It is my hope that today's Police Commission action will give us all time to bridge the differences that have grown between us since the Rodney King incident," he [Bradley] said . . . The Police Commission is using a well-established procedure.
>
> (*Los Angeles Times*, April 5, 1991: A23)

> "I acted in good faith on what I felt were legitimate concerns," Bradley said Saturday. "There was divisiveness in the city. The chief was at the center of the storm of protests and so long as he remained in the position it was not likely to change."
>
> (*Los Angeles Times*, April 7, 1991: A30)

While it was certainly understandable for Bradley to link the Police Commission's action to the larger Rodney King crisis, the pollution of power and ego proved to be more powerful than his metaphor of healing or his discourse of procedure. The *Los Angeles Times* increasingly described the mayor as "working behind the scenes" and "cranking up the political pressure," descriptive terms which resonated with the counter-democratic code of motives and relationships. On April 6, just one month after the beating, the *Los Angeles Times* reported the results of a poll showing that sixty percent of those surveyed believed that "the mayor was trying to further his political aspirations rather than . . . to mend a divided city."[30] While Bradley had been successful in making the removal of Gates a turning point for the Rodney King crisis, the direction that the narrative was taking was surely not what he had wanted.

Narrative updating amidst failed attempts at resolution

As I have shown above, none of the initial attempts to resolve the crisis were successful. The grand jury investigation was largely ignored by the press, the FBI probe was eventually de-emphasized after being criticized by the Los Angeles press, and the conflict between the City Council and the Police Commission did little except hurt the mayor's approval ratings. News reports in the *Los Angeles Times* responded to these failed actions of the political elite by updating the two narrative constructions and shifting the relative importance accorded to each genre. On the one hand, reports from "civic leaders" strengthened the tragic narrative of factionalism, claiming: "The intense fight over Gates' tenure has further polarized the city, politicized the issue and obscured the fundamental questions of brutality, racism, and police training raised by the King beating."[31] On the other hand, other reports weakened the romance of local government, noting with irony the lack of heroism among city leaders. As an editorial in the *Los Angeles Times* noted, "The Rodney King beating has brought to the surface ugly problems in Los Angeles: not only the allegations of police brutality, but the now exposed factionalism among races and ethnic groups and the tensions between longtime city powers who fear too much change and new line city powers who fear too little."[32] In this new plot, the event of the beating was not only linked to the problems of police brutality, but also to the weakness of local leaders.

Table 4.3 summarizes the discursive environment that surrounded these failed attempts at resolution. For the *Los Angeles Times*, the romantic "drama of redemption" – positing local government as hero – had devolved into a *satire* of romance, where "a slight shift of perspective . . . and the solid earth becomes an intolerable horror . . . [showing] man as a venomous rodent."[33] In this satirical form the romance threatened to turn into bitter tragedy, but without the usual sympathy for the tragic figure. Charged with the task of cleansing society of the evil of Police Chief Gates and the LAPD, local government leaders instead were painted as selfish, egotistical, and deceitful. As a result, the tragic genre resonated more strongly in the *Los Angeles Times*.

In the other newspapers, where the local government was not the central heroic figure, the conflict between the Police Commission and the City Council was not as critical an event for their Rodney King narratives. For example, in the *Los Angeles Sentinel*, the tragic form resonated strongly during this period, but the romance of the African-American community continued to exert a powerful influence on the interpretation of the crisis. In this plot, the *Los Angeles Sentinel* continued to represent the African-American community as a unified group who needed to demand their right to economic and political empowerment.[34] This need for heroic action on the part of the African-American community was opposed to the police department, as reports in the *Sentinel* editorialized about the commonality of unpunished police brutality, and reported that African-American police officers had to deal with racist behavior from other police officers in their daily police routines.[35]

Table 4.3. *Narrative forms surrounding failed attempts at resolution during the 1991 Rodney King crisis*

Narrative form	Heroes	Descriptions of heroes	Anti-heroes	Descriptions of anti-heroes
L.A. Times:				
Romantic satire . . .	mayor, City Council, Police Commission	selfish, egotistical, deceitful	Gates, LAPD	out of control, irrational, deceitful, not accountable
Tragedy. . . .	"the world," "the people"	isolated, factions	white, middle-class citizens	passive, distracted, insincere
L.A. Sentinel:				
Romance. . . .	mayor, Police Commission	semiotic opposition to anti-heroes	Gates, LAPD, City Council	brutal, merciless, secretive
Romance. . . .	African-American community	unified, moral, active	Gates, LAPD	brutal, merciless, secretive
Tragedy. . . .	African-American community	ironic memory	white, mainstream society	racist, insincere
New York Times:				
Romantic	mayor, City Council, Police Commission	selfish, egotistical, deceitful	Los Angeles mass society	powerless, corrupt
Chicago Tribune:				
Romance. . . .	local community	human scale; semiotic opposition	Los Angeles mass society	powerless, corrupt
Amsterdam News:				
Tragedy. . . .	African-American community	ironic memory	white, mainstream society	racist, insincere
Chicago Defender:				
no news coverage				

Within such a narrative context, where the negative characteristics of the police department continued to be described through the romantic genre, the conflict between the Police Commission and City Council had a different meaning. News reports in the *Los Angeles Sentinel* placed Bradley and the Police Commission in a heroic context in which Gates and the City Council were the anti-heroes. There was no causal link here between the event and "factionalism." Rather, the *Sentinel* accepted the discourse of procedure and the metaphor of healing in its representation of the Police Commission's decision to remove Gates.[36] By contrast, when the City Council reinstated Gates, the *Los Angeles Sentinel* described the Council members through the same attributes used for the police officers: deceit and unreasonableness.

With regard to the council's decision to pay the police chief's legal fees . . . That probably will be millions of dollars out of the tax payer's pocket . . . I guess the City Council will have to answer to their voters about their decision to pay what could be millions in legal fees on the chief's behalf.

(*Los Angeles Sentinel*, May 2, 1991: A14)

This last proviso, regarding monetary damages, seems a hollow gesture to lend authenticity to the city council action, since Gates out of his own mouth states that he seeks no money damages.   (*Los Angeles Sentinel*, April 11, 1991: A6)

Thus, during this period the romantic narratives of the *Los Angeles Sentinel* remained relatively stable, clearly identifying the heroes and the anti-heroes of the growing crisis. In fact, while white support for Mayor Bradley decreased from forty-nine to forty-one percent after the temporary removal of Police Chief Gates, African-American support for Bradley actually increased during this period, from fifty-four to sixty-four percent.[37] In a discursive environment where the conflict between the City Council and Mayor Bradley was presented in such unambiguous terms, the tragic-irony of the narrative also remained stable. Within this frame, the *Sentinel*'s monitoring of the mainstream media meant that it began to interpret the reactions of the mainstream community, where support for Bradley had dropped, in an increasingly negative light. The *Los Angeles Sentinel* began to evaluate the mainstream public, and its reactions to the crisis, through the critical discourse of factionalism and falsity. The following news excerpt is indicative of this shift:

While America pretended to be in shock, Black America was not shocked at all . . . the attack on Rodney King is a part of the historical pattern of violent oppression of Africans in America which has been visited upon our people ever since we arrived here in a condition of involuntary servitude.

(*Los Angeles Sentinel*, April 11, 1991: A7)

In this type of interpretation, anyone who would be surprised by the beating in effect denied the history of racism and slavery. This monitoring of the mainstream media led to the continuing resonance of the tragic-irony in the *Los Angeles Sentinel* narrative.

Thus, at the end of these failed attempts to resolve the crisis, there was a shift in narration toward the more negative genres of tragedy, irony, and satire. In the *Los Angeles Times*, the political conflict reduced the romance of the political elite into a satire, where the politicians were motivated more by personal ego than the requirements of office. In the *Chicago Tribune*, the lack of police accountability and civilian control in Los Angeles had "sent the unfortunate message to many law-abiding people throughout the country . . . that the police cannot be trusted," and clouded the "reality" that "most police officers are honest, hardworking, and incensed by what happened."[38] In the *New York Times*, the political infighting among Los Angeles politicians was causing the beating itself to recede into the background, creating a situation where "politics has taken precedence over policy, and investigations of the police department have taken second place to a struggle for dominance in city government."[39] In the *Los Angeles Sentinel*, the preoccupation of the mainstream public sphere with the politicization of the crisis reinforced nagging fears about white insincerity. And in the *New York Amsterdam News*, even the Police Commission's effort to remove Gates was viewed ironically, because "what the Rodney King incident really means is that police officials may be accountable for widely publicized and well documented patrol misconduct – otherwise it's business as usual. This is so because the federal courts have made it unlikely that police commanders will be held responsible for even the most blatantly systematic police brutality off-camera."[40]

The Christopher Commission and the move toward resolution

Resolution of the crisis would, for the discursive community of the *Los Angeles Times*, require the creation of a new hero; for the *Los Angeles Sentinel*, it would require that this new hero be attached to the African-American community, if not that it be the African-American community itself. The "hero" who was eventually to satisfy the conditions of both communities was the Christopher Commission and its Report of the Independent Commission on the Los Angeles Police Department, released to the public on July 9, 1991. The Christopher Commission comprised representatives from all institutional branches of "elite" civil society. It was co-chaired by John Arguelles, a retired State Supreme Court judge, and by Warren Christopher, a former deputy attorney general and deputy secretary of State. Also included in the commission were two university professors, a college president, three accomplished lawyers, the president of the Los Angeles County Bar, and a corporate executive.

Despite these inclusions, a symbolic sign of fairness, the Christopher Commission was not automatically cast in an heroic role. It had originally been formed as two separate investigations: the Arguelles Commission, formed by Daryl Gates, and the Christopher Commission, instituted by Mayor Bradley. Like the investigations preceding them, both commissions were initially presented in a negative light by the *Los Angeles Times*, for being politically motivated and dependent. The Arguelles Commission was portrayed as being tied too closely to Gates, the Christopher commission too closely to Bradley. The decisive move toward symbolic resolution of the crisis came with the merging of the two commissions into an expanded Christopher Commission. As an event, the merging of the two commissions presented an opportunity for new narrations of the crisis to be made. Both Arguelles and Christopher made numerous public statements about the merged commission as an independent, cooperative, and objective body, whose orientation was directed toward the good of the public. They represented their merged commission as a movement away from the tragedy of factionalism and back toward the romance of local government. As the following excerpts demonstrate, their efforts were reflected in the *Los Angeles Times*:

The heads of the panels . . . said they were seeking to distance themselves from the clash as the Police Commission forced Gates to take a leave.

(*Los Angeles Times*, April 5, 1991: A23)

"I think it would be good for everybody if we could come up with some kind of coordinated effort," said retired State Supreme Court Justice John Arguelles, the head of Gates' five-member civilian panel. "There are [now] two committees that might be perceived as having independent agendas that they might want to advance."

(*Los Angeles Times*, April 2, 1991: A1)

"In order to maximize the commission's contribution to the community," Christopher and Arguelles said in a joint statement, "we must concentrate on making an objective and thorough study of the long-term issues without being drawn into the controversy over the tenure of Chief Gates."

(*Los Angeles Times*, April 5, 1991: A23)

In an environment dominated by satirical and tragic interpretations, even this merged commission was understood skeptically, and its report was forecast by some to be an "impressive study . . . that ends up just sitting on somebody's shelf."[41] Nevertheless, when the Christopher Commission's report was released on July 9 – completed "within a restricted time frame because delay would not be in the public interest"[42] – media coverage of the crisis surged. In the *Los Angeles Times*, while there were three articles about the Rodney King crisis during the week before the release of the report, there were forty-eight articles in the subsequent week; in the *Los Angeles Sentinel*, the density of articles increased from three articles to nine, over the same period of time. But the report did not only provoke a quantitative change in media discourse; it also engendered a qualitative shift. The event became a turning point for all of the narrative understandings in the Los Angeles press about the Rodney King crisis. In the *Los Angeles Times*, it was interpreted through a religious metaphor of revelation strengthening the romantic narrative:

Just as the Rodney G. King videotape gave the American public an unfiltered glimpse of police brutality, so did the Christopher Commission open a window Tuesday on the working lives of Los Angeles police, exposing strains of racism, violence, and callousness toward the public they are sworn to protect.

(*Los Angeles Times*, July 10, 1991: A10)

Throughout the inquiry, both men said, they were acutely aware of the high expectations for their efforts. Arguelles talked of producing a report that would be seen as 'visionary.' (*Los Angeles Times*, July 10, 1991: A17)

The *Los Angeles Times* began to interpret the release of the Christopher Commission report as a symbolic completion of the crisis that was triggered by the videotape. If the videotape provided the beginning of the narrative, the report enabled its conclusion. With this interpretive shift the satirical and tragic frames disappeared from the reports of the *Los Angeles Times*. At this point, the discursive environment of the paper began to resemble a cultural situation that Turner has called "reaggregation."[43] While figures of authority had previously been shown as divided and politically-motivated, they were now represented as being open and cooperative, unified in their support of the Christopher Commission report, and motivated by the duty of office and concern for the public. Attention also shifted back to Police Chief Gates, who was portrayed as increasingly ego-driven and out of touch with the public. As the following news reports demonstrate, the sharp opposition drawn between Gates and the remaining political leaders helped to increase the legitimacy of those leaders:

"It appears as though a pattern is beginning to develop at Parker Center to punish or harass those who cooperated with the Christopher Commission and to intimidate others from cooperating in the future," [City Councilman] Yaroslovsky said. "This is an untenable situation, which the Police Commission should immediately move to restore." (*Los Angeles Times*, July 16, 1991: A7)

The councilmen's good faith should not be trifled with by Gates. He can either cooperate with the council members and business leaders who would try to work with
him on a transition or he can try to fight the many lined up against him.

(*Los Angeles Times*, July 17, 1991: B10)

Over a turbulent 10-day period, some of the most prominent political, business, and
labor leaders wrestled with a difficult mission: how to persuade Police Chief Daryl
Gates to commit to a retirement date.   (*Los Angeles Times*, July 24, 1991: A1)

Former political adversaries, such as the Police Commission and the City
Council, were now calling on one another to help in a common cause.
Business and labor leaders, who had previously not been significant players
in the social drama, were reported to be joining the unified effort. Articles
in the *Los Angeles Times* reported that police departments in other areas,
such as those in Pasadena, Long Beach, Santa Monica, Maywood, and the
Los Angeles Sheriff's Office, were also conforming with the Christopher
Commission reforms. Finally, when two of Gates's strongest supporters –
City Councilmen John Ferraro and Joel Wachs – called for his resignation,
the symbolization of political unity was virtually complete, at least for the
Los Angeles Times.

Table 4.4 summarizes the discursive environment surrounding the release
of the Christopher Commission report. For the *Los Angeles Times*, as I
have suggested, this period witnessed a strong narrative consolidation of an
exclusively romantic frame. Acting as a bridge to unify the previously
divided members of the local government and the political elite, the
Christopher Commission was presented as an objective and visionary
body enabling the unification and cooperation of local government leaders.
At the same time, the unification of local government coincided with a
strengthening opposition to Police Chief Gates. When Gates finally
announced his resignation, the police department became purged of the
figure around whom much of the symbolic pollution had concentrated.
Public focus began to turn to the upcoming trial of the four officers
indicted, the conviction of whom would signal complete redemption for the
political leaders of Los Angeles, legitimacy for its institutions, and moral
upliftment for its citizens. Rather than treating the trial as a separate event,
the *Los Angeles Times* and its public understood it as the final chapter of
the narrative, clearly expecting the result to be the conviction of the officers.
As for the other narrative forms that had previously been used by the *Los
Angeles Times* – the tragedy of isolation, and the satire of politicization –
they appeared to disappear in a case of collective memory-loss.

In the *Los Angeles Sentinel*, however, collective memory continued to
play a significant role in the coverage of the crisis. We can see this from the

Table 4.4. Narrative forms after the release of the Christopher Commission report

Narrative form	Heroes	Descriptions of heroes	Anti-heroes	Descriptions of anti-heroes
L.A. Times:				
Romance. . . .	Christopher Commission, mayor, City Council, Police Commission	independent, objective, unified, cooperative, "visionary"	Daryl Gates	ego-driven, coercive, obstructing, deceitful
L.A. Sentinel:				
Romance. . . .	Christopher Commission	objective, forthright, recognition of African-American grievances	Gates, LAPD	oppressive, exclusionary, racist
Romance. . . .	African-American community	unified, moral, active, vindicated	Gates, LAPD, City Council	greedy, politically-motivated, obstructing reforms
Tragedy. . . .	African-American community	ironic memory	white citizens	false pride, misled, insincere
New York Times:				
Romance. . . .	national leaders, Christopher Commission report	rational, oriented toward the public good and the duty of office	Los Angeles mass society	corrupt, oriented toward self-interest and image
Chicago Tribune:				
Romance. . . .	local community	human scale; semiotic opposition to anti-heroes	Los Angeles mass society	powerless, corrupt, inept
Amsterdam News: no news coverage				
Chicago Defender:				
Tragedy. . . .	African-American community	ironic memory	white, mainstream society	racist, insincere

earliest events leading up to the release of the Christopher Commission report. In its evaluations of the separate Christopher and Arguelles Commissions, the *Sentinel* identified the latter with Gates and the former with Bradley, and used the appropriate sides of the bifurcating discourse of civil society to interpret them. The *Sentinel* reported about the merging of the two commissions in a manner far different than the *Los Angeles Times*, as the following news report demonstrates:

Earlier Gates said that his Arguelles Commission would cooperate with Bradley's Christopher Commission. Subsequent reports indicate that the Arguelles Commission has had difficulty in attracting panel members and that the two commissions would merge – a prospect not too much to the liking of the Brotherhood Crusades' Danny Bakewell or acting Police Commission President Melanie Lomax.
(*Los Angeles Sentinel*, April 4, 1991: A3)

The *Los Angeles Sentinel* interpreted the possibility of a merger between the two commissions as being necessitated by the weakness of the Arguelles Commission. The Arguelles Commission was interpreted as something to be avoided, and as a potential danger to the purity of the Christopher Commission.

Nevertheless, when the merged commission's report was released, the *Los Angeles Sentinel* described it as a "window of opportunity,"[44] and as an investigation of "extensiveness . . . forthrightness . . . and validity."[45] In this respect it mirrored the *Los Angeles Times*. At the same time, however, the *Sentinel* did not construct the commission's report as a bridge toward the legitimation of local government leaders, but rather as a justification for the longstanding criticisms made by the African-American community. In this respect, the event of the Christopher Commission report was linked to the romance of the African-American community. John Mack, executive director of the L. A. Urban League, argued that the report "confirmed what we already know: that racism is rampant in the LAPD."[46] By attaching the event to the romantic narrative of the African-American community, the *Los Angeles Sentinel* reinforced the heroic role of the black community at the same time that it extended such a role to the Commission and its report. If local leaders wanted to be cast as heroes in the *Sentinel* narrative, they would have to include the African-American community in the resolution of the crisis, and would have to recognize that community's collective memory.

Notably, the focus in the *Sentinel* was on the reform recommendations, the findings of bias, and the issue of racism, rather than on the unity of the political leadership in its quest to remove Gates. Rather than supporting the political and business leadership, the *Sentinel*'s support for the

Commission included City Councilman Michael Woo, Brotherhood Crusade leader Danny Bakewell, the African-American Peace Officer Association, as well as "community leaders and various community coalitions long critical of Chief Gates and the practices and politics of the LAPD."[47] Those writing in and for the *Los Angeles Sentinel* did not readily forgive the political leaders, the police department, or "white society." They continued to depict the police department as being remote and racist, and continued to identify police departments in other areas (such as the Lynwood Sheriff's Office) as being racist. The memory of police oppression, always available for the *Sentinel*, was again brought forth as new incidents of brutality were revealed. As the following excerpts demonstrate, the *Los Angeles Sentinel* continued to present the political system and mainstream society as dangers to the successful resolution of the crisis:

After the Rodney King beating, the barrage of nationwide media publicity and public disgust lulled citizens into a false sense of pride and complacency, encouraging them to believe that impending recommendations on LAPD practices and politics would serve to turn the department's mentality around. Then along came the Vernell Ramsey case – another Black Foothill victim alleging excessive force by the LAPD.   (*Los Angeles Sentinel*, September 19, 1991: A1)

Recent City Council debates – 13 so far – over Christopher Commission recommendations have led to a barrage of complaints from community leaders and various coalitions. One of the main arguments has been the issue of power. Critics charge that the City Council has too much and has become lackadaisical about responsibly exercising its duties.   (*Los Angeles Sentinel*, August 22, 1991: A1)

Thus, as we see in Table 4.4, there was no real narrative consolidation in the *Los Angeles Sentinel* after the release of the Christopher Commission report. The romance of the African-American community continued to be the dominant genre for reporting about the crisis. It was supplemented by a "romance of the Christopher Commission," where the commission was constructed in relations of similarity to the African-American community instead of being attached to local government. Local government leaders, and the City Council in particular, were viewed largely as a threat to the resolution of the crisis. Similarly, the tragic-irony in the narrative persisted. White citizens were interpreted as being not sufficiently concerned or vigilant to ensure that the reforms would be enacted. In other words, while the *Los Angeles Times* had interpreted the commission report as a link to political leadership and public unity, the *Los Angeles Sentinel* had narrated it as a link to African-American leadership and public complacency. In doing so, both newspapers were following the logical development of their narratives during the course of events.

The non-Los Angeles press also incorporated the Christopher Commission's report into their news coverage of the Rodney King crisis in a manner consistent with the narrative logic that had developed in each. In the *Chicago Tribune*, the Christopher Commission was neither the agent of political unity nor the agent of justification for longstanding African-American criticisms; rather; it was an independent commission whose effectiveness would be prevented by the political ineptitude of Los Angeles mass society. Describing the commission's recommendations, commentators in the *Tribune* claimed that "Los Angeles may be at a unique disadvantage in trying to respond to them."[48] Reports of Gates's eventual decision to step down as police chief were not linked to themes of political unity but rather to a mayor who was "powerless to force him out."[49] Even the Christopher Commission report, which was described by the Los Angeles press as "objective" and "visionary," was described by the *Tribune* as weak and dependent.

> The panel's call for a new chief was the report's biggest surprise. It didn't mention the matter until page 227, the next-to-last page . . . The report broadly criticized the department's leadership, but never singled out Gates for blame . . . At a news conference, Christopher was vague about how and when Gates should step aside.
>
> (*Chicago Tribune*, July 10, 1991: A3)

In this type of description, where Los Angeles symbolized an anti-democratic mass society where there was neither effective community support nor political leadership, the Christopher Commission was not seen to be so important or visionary. Thus, the attention in the *Chicago Tribune* turned to the trial of the officers, as a referendum on whether the local judicial system was any better than the other civil institutions of Los Angeles.

In the *New York Times* and *ABC News*, the Christopher Commission was presented in a positive way, through the "theme of ascent" typical of the romantic genre. Both, however, narrated the release of the report as an important and powerful indictment with *national* consequences and *national* voices of acclamation.

> In Washington, Hubert Williams, president of the Police Foundation, a private research group, called the report a milestone. 'The Rodney King incident has changed the way to look at police,' he said, 'and this report will cause other cities to look more closely at their police problems. We'll see positive changes in the attitudes of police officers and less tolerance by citizens.' The report was also welcomed by minority and civil liberties leaders [none named in the article] who said it lent credence to longstanding complaints that the police routinely violated the rights of the poor and minorities, dispensing summary justice at the curb.
>
> (*New York Times*, July 10, 1991: A1)

Former New York Police Commissioner Patrick Murphy says police all across the
nation will have to pay attention to the Christopher Commission. "It will not be a
case of well we've seen 100 other reports, ho hum. I think this is going to have an
effect on most cities in the country."   (*ABC News*, July 9, 1991)

In this understanding of the Christopher Commission report, the national
impact was emphasized, thus allowing for a return to the original romantic form of the *New York Times*' Rodney King narrative. For example, news
stories described how the commission's recommendations were already
having important effects "far beyond Los Angeles," such as in New York,
where the chief of the Transit Authority Police had already distributed
summaries of the report to seventy-five senior officers and had planned a
meeting to discuss it.[50] Stories in both the *New York Times* and *ABC News*
described how the Kansas City Police Department – influenced by the
Christopher Commission report – had instituted a system to try to identify
problem officers.[51] Even the crisis over the tenure of Police Chief Gates,
whom the report had encouraged to resign, was related to an earlier
national figure, J. Edgar Hoover. In this historical metaphor, a story in the
New York Times described how "Hoover's example caused Congress to
limit his successors to one 10-year term. No doubt Chief Gates's obduracy
will have the same result in Los Angeles."[52]

Narrative variations: race, nation, region

Even though American journalism experienced significant forces of nationalization between the 1960s and 1990s, the news coverage of the Rodney
King beating demonstrates that there are still multiple news publics. There
were substantial regional variations among the news narratives of the *New
York Times*, *Los Angeles Times*, and *Chicago Tribune*. While the *Los
Angeles Times* reserved the heroic character positions of its news narratives
for Los Angeles politicians, the *New York Times* and *Chicago Tribune*
described those same politicians as ineffective and anti-civil anti-heroes,
and criticized the city of Los Angeles through mass society imagery. The
New York Times, like *ABC News*, narrated the crisis with a national perspective, in which national politicians occupied the heroic character positions, and where the conclusion to the story emphasized the national
significance of the Christopher Commission report. The *Chicago Tribune*'s
narrative of local community power, in which Los Angeles was portrayed
negatively, and through a process of semiotic opposition, was to the benefit
of Chicago.

Despite these regional variations, there were still some important structural similarities in the news coverage of the mainstream press. While all of

the mainstream media began their respective Rodney King narratives through a focus on police brutality, they ended their stories through plots which emphasized politics. For the *Los Angeles Times*, the Rodney King beating showed that the political system in Los Angeles worked, that it could respond effectively to an out-of-control police department. For the *Chicago Tribune*, the Rodney King beating proved that the political system in Los Angeles did not work, but the problem was specific to Los Angeles and did not concern other cities. For the *New York Times* and *ABC News*, the crisis also revealed that the political system in Los Angeles did not work, but that its ineffectiveness was countered by an effective national political system. While all of these news media came to different conclusions about the Rodney King crisis, they shared certain formal properties in the way they understood the crisis: through a romantic ending, emphasizing a particular normative vision of politics, and where the concerns of African-Americans and African-American leaders could be met through normal political channels.

The Rodney King beating also showed that African-Americans could not rely on the mainstream press to change their public stance on stories about race and civil society. While there was certainly more than one story-line in the mainstream media, none of them emphasized African-American concerns about white insincerity or African-American empowerment, nor did they deal with the history of police brutality in a significant or engaged manner. In order to discuss these concerns, African-Americans had to turn to the black press and public spheres, where there were a different set of public narratives, and where the romantic forms of narration were tempered with significant elements of irony and tragedy. While the crisis ended with the release of the Christopher Commission report in most of the mainstream publics, in the African-American publics discussion about the crisis of civil society continued.

The Rodney King beating uncovered one additional crisis of civil society: namely, the weakened ability of the black press to operate as a public sphere. Among the African-American papers, only the *Los Angeles Sentinel* provided extended coverage of the events surrounding the Rodney King crisis. African-Americans living in New York and Chicago were unable to rely on the black press in their respective cities if they wanted to get detailed information about the crisis. This lack of coverage is understood better in relative terms than absolute terms. It was natural that there would be more articles about the crisis in the Los Angeles press. Yet, while the *Los Angeles Sentinel* wrote thirty-eight percent as many articles about the Rodney King crisis as the *Los Angeles Times*, the African-American papers in New York and Chicago only wrote about ten percent as many articles as the major metropolitan papers in their respective cities. And while the *New York Times* and *Chicago Tribune* wrote nearly twenty percent as many articles about the crisis as the *Los Angeles Times*, the *New York Amsterdam News* and *Chicago Defender* only wrote about five percent as many articles as the *Los Angeles Sentinel*. In the place of detailed coverage, what the readers of the *Chicago Defender* and *New York Amsterdam News* got were sporadic, extremely general, and highly tragic forms of news coverage, forcing them to turn to the mainstream media for most of their information about the Rodney King beating.

5

Rodney King 1992

As academic opinion has begun to register about the 1992 uprisings in Los Angeles, several different interpretations have emerged. Omi and Winant have argued that the uprisings drew attention to the continuing importance of race, and also to the limits of racialized domestic politics played by Presidents Reagan and Bush during the 1980s.[1] Watts has argued that the 1991 beating of Rodney King, by providing "moral capital in a racial struggle," led African-Americans to suspend disbelief and to expect a just verdict from the trial; the not-guilty verdicts, and the uprisings that followed, acted to rob them of their illusory feelings of hope.[2] Cornel West has argued that "the astonishing disappearance of the event from public dialogue is testimony to just how painful and distressing a serious engagement with race is."[3] According to West, serious discussions about "race matters" – and also *why* race matters – tend to get short-circuited by overly-simplistic notions of race proffered by both liberals and conservatives in their attempts to win the allegiance of the suburban white voter. The events of urban upheaval in Los Angeles were not mentioned a single time in the presidential debates of 1992, testifying how difficult it was to fit the issues raised during the crisis into the standard political tropes.[4] Although different in their emphasis, all three opinions shared a belief that the 1992 uprisings provided a "reality check" regarding the state of American race relations.

This chapter considers the different media narratives which developed about race and civil society after the return of not-guilty verdicts in the trial of Los Angeles police officers Powell, Wind, Briseno, and Koon.[5] For mainstream journalists, the not-guilty verdicts deflated the liberal-progressive belief in the power of news publicity; if exposing wrongdoing in the press could not by itself bring about reform, then it was more difficult for journalists to understand their role in the liberal public sphere as romantically or heroically as they might have liked.[6] For African-American journalists, and particularly for those writing in the black press, such a deflation of the journalistic role reinforced an ongoing suspicion about the racialized limits of the public sphere.

While the 1992 crisis may have provided a "reality check" regarding the state of race relations, it was ultimately narrated in the media through the use of the tragic genre. The directions that the tragic plots took were multiform, but included the recognition that none of the problems of the 1960s urban underclass had been solved; that middle-class blacks who had benefited from the effects of the civil rights movement still suffered rampant racism in their everyday routines; that riots destroyed the very communities in greatest need of help; and that the political rhetoric of fear and blame was insufficient to lead to any improvements. In the African-American press, while these tragic narratives were also utilized to cover the story, they were supplemented by an additional tragedy: the tragedy of the white response to urban crisis, and the tragic persistence of white racism in American history. Romance was undercoded throughout the crisis in all the news publics, encouraging a sense of tragic resignation, fatalism, and, ultimately, inaction. It was this prevalence of tragic discourse which made the Rodney King crisis so dangerous for the political public sphere, and which created the sense of hopelessness about the possibility of racial understanding. Indeed, the use of the tragic form to talk about racial crisis persisted long after the Rodney King crisis was over, extending to include both the "Reginald Denny" and O. J. Simpson trials.

If news coverage of the 1992 crisis was crafted overwhelmingly through the use of tragic discourse, it was unusually lengthy, detailed, and expansive. The Rodney King crisis of 1992 created a period of public focus and attention on race equaled by few events in recent American history. A Times-Mirror opinion poll taken one week after the verdict found that ninety-two percent of those surveyed were following the Los Angeles events either closely or very closely, a figure even greater than public attention to the Persian Gulf War.[7] Measured by news density, the 1992 crisis received much more public attention than those of 1965 or 1991. In the initial five weeks after the verdict, 799 articles were written in the six newspapers included in this study about the events surrounding the 1992 urban uprisings in Los Angeles. By contrast, there were only 264 articles during the same initial period of the 1991 social drama of Rodney King, and only 432 articles for the Watts crisis of 1965. In all, there were 1030 articles written about the 1992 crisis during the first twelve weeks after the verdict. News coverage concentrated first on the verdicts, then on the causes underlying the uprising, and finally on the threat that racial division posed for civil society.

Early news narratives: the verdicts

Public reactions to the verdict were generally disapproving, and became even more critical when expressed openly. Opinion polls found a racialized, though mostly negative, response to the verdict. In Los Angeles, 96.3 percent of African-Americans and 65.1 percent of whites disagreed with the verdict.[8] A national *Newsweek*/Gallup poll reported that ninety-two percent of blacks and seventy-three percent of whites disagreed with the verdict.[9] In the news media, however, response to the verdict was almost universally critical, for whites as well as blacks. Scores of political and community leaders made public statements criticizing the outcome of the trial. Mayor Bradley said he was left "speechless" by the "senseless" verdicts, and complained that "the system let us down."[10] Benjamin Hooks, the executive director of the NAACP, called the verdicts an "outrageous mockery of justice."[11] New York Governor Mario Cuomo called the verdicts "an apparent, egregious miscarriage."[12] Opinion polls,[13] phone calls and letters,[14] community leaders[15] and "man-on-the-street" interviews[16] quickly registered the strong public disagreement with the jury's verdict.

Reports about the verdict and the negative public reaction to it dominated mainstream media attention. Between April 30 and May 13, the *Los Angeles Times* wrote 290 articles about the Rodney King crisis, the *New York Times* wrote 105 articles, and the *Chicago Tribune* wrote 103 articles. *ABC World News Tonight* covered the Rodney King crisis as its lead story for eight consecutive evenings, between April 29 and May 6. All of these news organizations reported on the verdict by linking it to the videotaped beating of Rodney King. Initial descriptions contrasted the images of the videotape with the verdict returned by the jurors, depicting the latter much as they had once represented the former: as a "shocking" event, requiring public condemnation:

This is one of those cases in which the first reaction is one of slack-jawed amazement. How could that jury, if they looked at the same videotaped beating that we've all seen a dozen times or more on television, how could they look at that and then vote for acquittal?   (Ted Koppel, *ABC News*, April 29, 1992)

Outrage and indignation swept the city Wednesday as citizens rich and poor, black and white, struggled to reconcile the acquittals of four Los Angeles Police Department officers with the alarming, violent images captured on a late-night videotape.   (*Los Angeles Times*, April 30, 1992: A1)

The videotaped beating that shocked the nation failed to convince a jury that the white police officers who repeatedly kicked and clubbed black motorist Rodney King were guilty of assault.   (*Chicago Tribune*, April 30, 1992: A1)

Four Los Angeles police officers were acquitted of assault today in the videotaped beating of a black motorist that stunned the nation.

(*New York Times*, April 30, 1992: A1)

In these descriptions, where public opinion was strongly opposed to the verdict, the jurors came to be identified with the counter-democratic discourse of civil society, representing the anti-civil anti-heroes who had short-circuited the anticipated resolution of the Rodney King crisis crafted in most news narratives in 1991. Now, the decision to move the trial out of Los Angeles county – a July 23, 1991 event that received scant attention in the media at the time it took place – was recounted as a decisive event determining the outcome of the verdict, because it left the determination of justice in the hands of irrational, hysterical, racist, and fearful Simi Valley residents. Some news stories focused on the general difficulty of convicting police for brutality, because prosecutors typically had to rely on those same officers in their typical criminal prosecutions; this led to the suggestion that a special prosecutor be reserved for police brutality cases.[17] More common, however, were the following types of condemnations of Simi Valley and the people who lived there:

The case may have been decided the day Superior Court Judge Stanley M. Weisberg ordered the trial moved from Los Angeles to Simi Valley, an overwhelmingly white, conservative community long known as a popular home for law enforcement officers . . . "Given this jury, they might have still acquitted the defendants and ordered King to jail," said New York University law professor Burt Neuborne. "This was a jury of people who ran away from Los Angeles to get away from Rodney King."   (*Los Angeles Times*, April 30, 1992: A18)

The very layout of the streets in this well-to-do suburb speaks volumes about how unwelcome strangers are here, about how much safety means to the 100,000 people, most of them white, who have crossed the mountain range and then the Ventura County line to escape the chaos and discomfort of the people.

(*New York Times*, May 4, 1992: B7)

Simi Valley residents are 88 percent white; just one and a half percent of the people who live here are black. [Professor Melvin Oliver, UCLA Sociologist]: "It's where people who don't want the problems of Los Angeles move, and, of course, they tend to be white."   (*ABC News*, April 29, 1992)

In the African-American press the verdicts were also met with outrage, but the news reports focused their criticism on the judicial system itself, rather than isolating the Simi Valley jurors.[18] Fears about the racial prejudice of the jury were expressed before the verdict came out, indicating that African-Americans had not completely suspended disbelief about the possibility of getting justice in the courts. Shock and outrage about the verdict were disassociated from any sense of surprise in the African-American press. Even before the verdict, news reports in the African-American press described how the public was ignoring the Rodney King trial, how the lawyers in the case had played the videotaped beating so many times it had lost its effectiveness, how justice was in the hands of an all-white jury, and how nobody in mainstream civil society seemed to be paying attention to any of these dangerous signs of potential racial injustice.[19] The verdicts were simply an affirmation of white insincerity, racism, and the cynical politics of blame.

Even when the evidence is as compelling as a videotape of the brutality, White America finds a way to ignore this reality, just as the nation has closed its eyes to the rampant racism that daily ravages the lives of African-Americans . . . Black America's quest for justice has been fruitless, and justice . . . seems unable to decide in our behalf, particularly when White law officers stand accused of assaulting a Black man.
(*New York Amsterdam News*, May 9, 1992: A6)

This not-guilty verdict was sown and harvested in White racism, a racism imbibed as holy water by its White creators and defenders, an aspergillum used to sprinkle and anoint the faithful in holy communion, a racism apotheosized in pulpits, glorified in editorial pages, magnified in movies and television, sanctified in school textbooks. African-Americans do not now, have not in the past, will not in the future enjoy full citizenship in America – under its present structure.
(*New York Amsterdam News*, May 16, 1992: A13)

Don't you realize that the inhumanity that the world witnessed over and over again this past year on videotape is an image that we have seen over and over again, year after year; that the only change is the name of the victims? Don't you realize that when we finally lash out in exasperation, we emulate models that you have established over the course of your history? . . . Do you understand our disdain for your hypocrisy when you celebrated the disobedience in Tien-Anmin Square, Moscow, Warsaw and Manilla because it furthered your goals, but cried out for 'cooler heads' in Watts, Detroit, Johannesburg and South Central L. A. because it furthered ours?
(*Los Angeles Sentinel*, May 7, 1992: A6)

The verdict in the Rodney King trial reaffirmed for the world what Africans in America already know. Racism is alive and well in the U. S. Like the Dred Scott Decision in 1857, the decision in the King case proclaimed loudly and clearly that Black people have no rights which a racist and exploitative system is compelled to respect.
(*Los Angeles Sentinel*, May 21, 1992: A7)

It is clear, then, that those in the black press and public sphere did not suspend disbelief as they awaited the jury verdict. Grounded in a history of exclusion, antipathy, and distrust toward mainstream civil society, the black press provided a different forum for discussing matters of common concern, a different agenda, a different story about justice and civil society.

In African-American newspapers, there was no liberal-progressive belief that the mere act of publicity could bring about social progress. There was no belief that the verdict was an aberration, any more than there had been a belief that the beating of Rodney King was an aberration. The verdicts confirmed what had been feared all along: that racial justice was illusory, and that white society was not concerned about racial oppression. From such an understanding, white outrage and criticism of the verdicts was evidence precisely of the lack of attention and vigilance which had been warned about in the 1991 Rodney King narrative. As an *ABC News/ Washington Post* poll reported the day after the verdicts, seventy-nine percent of African-Americans believed that Washington only paid attention to black issues after blacks resort to violence; only thirty-nine percent of whites agreed.[20] From the beginning, African-American understandings of the 1992 Rodney King crisis were tied to concerns about white racism.

These interpretive differences can be seen by examining the different uses of historical memory in the African-American and mainstream press. In the mainstream press, the 1992 uprisings provoked memories about the Kerner Commission and other *political* attempts to address race and urban crisis. But it was precisely these political attempts by the white elite which were criticized in black newspapers for contributing to the problems of racial injustice. For these African-American papers, the uprisings provoked memories of racial injustice caused by insincere white politicians and racist white jurors: the Missouri Compromise of 1820, the Kansas-Nebraska Act of 1854, the Dred Scott decision of 1857, the California Constitutional Convention of 1847, and previous legal injustices in trials such as the Emmett Till and Medgar Evers murders. The *New York Amsterdam News* went so far as to report that "nowhere in the annals of American history has a highly publicized case of White police brutality against a Black man ended in conviction."[21] These were much more damaging historical metaphors, because they equated contemporary times with ante-bellum America, and implied that little, if anything, had changed since then in the area of race relations. This historical narrative was linked not so much to despair over political ineffectiveness as to a more general despair about white racism and insincerity. At issue in the black press were the cynical and racist politics of blame which had deprived African-American communities of much-needed economic resources.

Early news narratives: descriptions of the rioters

The 1992 crisis was not precipitated by a single act of racial injustice; what will be remembered as vividly as the public outrage over the verdicts were the public acts of protest and destruction in cities throughout north America. In Los Angeles the destruction was most devastating, lasting for three days and resulting in fifty-two deaths, 2,383 injuries, 16,291 arrests, over 500 fires, and property damage estimated in the range of $785 million–$1 billion.[22] Public opinion polls indicated a strongly critical evaluation of the rioters. As a May 2 Gallup poll indicated, seventy-four percent of blacks and seventy-nine percent of whites were critical of the violence. In fact, this poll indicated that more whites disapproved of the rioting than disapproved of the verdicts. Given this polling context, how would the mainstream media report about the violence and destruction?

One of the most surprising things about the news coverage of the Los Angeles uprisings was that the *Chicago Defender* and *Los Angeles Sentinel* were more critical of the rioters than those writing in the mainstream press. The *Chicago Defender* described the rioting as "totally wrong and [it] should not be justified by any responsible person."[23] The *Los Angeles Sentinel* warned, a week before the verdict was reached, that "the Rodney King affair contains the seeds for African-American copping out; i.e., not dealing with the real causes of the problems, but succumbing to a sort of Watts rebellion mentality, where wanton destruction and momentary catharsis substitute for soundness and reason as the major reaction to crisis."[24] As the following two excerpts illustrate, the *Sentinel* and the *Defender* incorporated their descriptions of the rioters into a larger tragic narrative of self-destruction.

The recent two days of rioting and devastation that took place in South Central Los Angeles are a sad, sad commentary on the state of affairs of Black America. It had nothing to do with the verdict in the Rodney King case or the verdict handed down by Judge Joyce Karlin in the case of Soon Ja Du. The real underlying factor was and still is economics. The people of South Central Los Angeles and the African-American community nationwide have failed to become supportive of themselves. The African-American community in this country has become a race of 'beggars and leeches.' We can blame no one but ourselves.

(*Chicago Defender*, May 9, 1992: A47)

The failure of the jury in Simi Valley to find the four officers guilty was the first problem. This, however, is a problem that will only be solved by time and patience . . . The anger we all felt at the rendering of the Rodney King verdict was strong . . . But to take out that anger and frustration on innocent people was pure folly . . . It makes no sense, no matter how angry and hurt we may have been, to destroy ourselves in our rage.

(*Los Angeles Sentinel*, May 7, 1992: A7)

These critical evaluations in the *Chicago Defender* and *Los Angeles Sentinel* were similar to those made in 1965 during the Watts uprisings; the destruction was the wrong means toward expressing protest, because it destroyed much-needed African-American infrastructure. But there was a crucial difference between 1965 and 1992. In 1965, African-American public statements made in Chicago and Los Angeles were made in a discursive environment dominated by criticism of the rioters in the mainstream press of Chicago and Los Angeles. In 1992, however, the "deployment of deviance" against the rioters was almost completely missing from the mainstream media.[25]

Surprisingly, the initial news narratives about the violence in the mainstream press mostly avoided criticizing the rioters and their actions. Instead, the narrative of public outrage and criticism of the verdicts served to unite the rioters and the public together against the jurors and residents of Simi Valley. Rather than emphasizing a law-and-order theme, as the *Los Angeles Times* and *Chicago Tribune* had done during the 1965 Watts uprisings, all of the mainstream news narratives about the 1992 uprisings were crafted in a way that focused, for the most part sympathetically, on the motivations of the rioters. In fact, during the 1992 crisis the rioters were given a voice they do not usually receive in the mainstream media. The following exchange between Ted Koppel and three Los Angeles gang members is illustrative:

Koppel: This last weekend was different. I sat in a church basement after Nightline ended last Friday, while a lot of very eloquent but angry people bounced their frustrations off me. It wasn't anything personal; I just happened to be the most visible white person around. You'll understand when you see it. And then on Saturday I spent most of the afternoon with a bunch of murderers, drug dealers, robbers and probably the architects of quite a few crimes I've never even thought of, and I'm only slightly embarrassed to say that I liked them very much and was extremely impressed with a great deal of what they had to say, and the passion with which they said it . . .

3rd gang member: We still don't understand how it get shipped from Van Nuys to Simi Valley, population majority Caucasian. Where do all the police live at? Simi Valley. How did that happen? The jury, was they from Simi Valley? Possibly they was from Simi Valley. Some of they kids or grandsons could have been police. See what I'm saying? Some of them could have been them got they X's on they face, and from the triple K. We don't never know. That's unfair, man. That's not Rodney King's peers. That's nobody's peers.

Koppel: And I think a lot of people around the country are saying the same thing that you were just saying. How did that trial get moved out to Simi Valley? A lot of people asking that question, a lot people don't think that's fair.

2nd gang member: Then ask it right now, then. Are we on TV right now?

3rd gang member: We can't answer it.

Koppel: Well, go ahead and answer it. Why not?

1st gang member: Why did it get moved? Is that the question, really? You're really asking me something that simple, that small? And we all know why it got moved. They could have had it downtown anywhere. Anywhere. Could have had it close to Rodney King's house, maybe he would have went to the trial then. White folk moved that for a reason. They want – they didn't have to move it. They didn't have to move it. We could have had it right here, listen to everything, 28 days, all that old [expletive deleted] they was going through. Could have had it right here. They could have found them guilty on every charge, everything would have been fine.

(*ABC News*, Nightline, April 30, 1992)

This exchange is remarkable in the way it crafted such a strong agreement between Los Angeles gang members, Ted Koppel, and the American public. Insofar as the focus remained on the Simi Valley jurors, the narrative about the destructive actions of the rioters remained surprisingly open to the possibility of understanding. This granting of voice to those who typically remain voiceless was a short-lived phenomenon – a result, as will become clearer later in the chapter, of the difficulty of sustaining tragic discourse in the public sphere, and particularly in the political public sphere. But the important point to make is that the early news stories were far more sympathetic toward the rioters than one would expect from the Gallup poll results. If there was disapproval of the violence, it was overshadowed and overwhelmed for a time by the disapproval of the verdicts and the focus of blame on the Simi Valley jurors. In the *Los Angeles Times*, early news stories made repeated mentions about an "awakening of conscience" among residents of South Central Los Angeles in the initial days after the restoration of calm to the city's streets.

When the emergency eased Sunday, Hollywood Division officers began checking out their leads, and were startled by the results: more neighbors began turning in neighbors; most people confronted readily gave up their loot; and others – upon seeing police officers – quietly put out their share of the loot in hallways, in planters, on stoops.   (*Los Angeles Times*, May 5, 1992: A3)

At the Roman Catholic archdiocese, Cardinal Roger M. Mahony's amnesty program – which promised no repercussions for looters who return what they stole to their local parish – had similar success. While adults turned in furniture and clothing, a child with a guilty conscience handed over a stolen candy bar.   (*Los Angeles Times*, May 6, 1992: A6)

While these types of representations are significant and unexpected, it is important to recognize that this humanization of Los Angeles rioters and gang members took place within a very specific narrative context, in which the rioters' actions became a part of the plot against the backdrop of different anti-heroes, such as the Simi Valley jurors. When describing the uprisings themselves, outside of this narrative context, news reports in the mainstream media tended to rely on the polluting discourse of civil society to describe the actors involved. For example, "simple" (i.e., non-contextualized) descriptions of the uprisings in the *Los Angeles Times* and *Chicago Tribune* described the rioters as largely composed of criminals and opportunists,[26] while the *New York Times* described the scene as reminiscent of a "street party" or a "carnival,"[27] and *ABC News* described the "rage" as "mindless, infectious and random."[28] But these types of descriptions were exceptional; more common among the initial news stories were those which reported about the violence within the larger context of the verdicts, the police, and the public outrage. In fact, most of the initial news reports about the violence blamed the Los Angeles police more than they blamed the rioters, by contrasting the police aggressiveness in beating Rodney King with the passive way they handled the uprisings:

The L. A. police, who had been present in large numbers to subdue Rodney King, were unaccountably absent during these assaults, which reportedly took place over a period of several hours.   (*Chicago Tribune*, May 1, 1992: A16)

"The department was impotent, paralyzed by its own guilt over the King incident and misconduct documented by the Christopher Commission," said Joseph McNamara, the former police chief of San Jose, who is now a fellow at the Hoover Institute in Palo Alto, Calif.   (*New York Times*, May 5, 1992: A25)

Police spokesmen have said they didn't respond at first because they were too busy escorting fire trucks, yet these last sequences on the video obtained by *ABC News* show fire trucks unescorted by any police driving right through the intersection, leaving the fires there to burn themselves out. Los Angeles Fire Department sources say they had no police protection anywhere initially, and had to delay responding as a result. The fact is, the rioting went virtually unchecked in its first 24 hours.
(*ABC News*, May 6, 1992)

[California state Supreme Court Justice] Arabian said much of the public now suffers not only from a fear of excessive force by officers but also from concern that police, because of low morale and a hostile environment, will not react aggressively to crime. "This fear became a reality during the recent riots," Arabian said . . . "Any slower response and we would have seen photos of policemen posted on milk containers and listed as missing."   (*Los Angeles Times*, May 8, 1992: A1)

The same types of criticisms were leveled against Police Chief Daryl Gates, whose aggressive and combative style was contrasted with his indecisive and timid reaction to the urban uprisings. Gates was roundly criticized for being motivated by ego and self-interest, particularly because he chose to remain at a fund-raiser (organized in opposition to local referendums concerning the proposed changes in the police department, recommended by the Christopher Commission) while the uprisings were beginning.

The initial news reports about the uprisings, then, showed a surprising amount of narrative diversity and openness toward understanding the lives of inner-city blacks. The shock of the verdicts opened up media access to a wider spectrum of voices, and opened up the public sphere to a wider diversity of narratives than was typical during ordinary news days. This openness was to last only for a short time, however. As the mainstream news media continued to report about the 1992 crisis, they came increasingly to rely on the genre of tragedy: the tragedy of urban neglect, the tragedy of history, the tragedy of politics, and the tragedy of racial division and legal paralysis. The recourse to the tragic form had a deflationary effect on the narrative environment of the public sphere, which ultimately served to weaken the force of the narrative diversity and the liberalized access of the mainstream public spheres.

The tragedy of urban neglect and the tragedy of history

In a fashion similar to what happened in the *New York Times* and the African-American press during the 1965 Watts crisis, the refusal to describe the rioters as irrational pushed the narrative about the unrest toward a discussion of underlying causes. For the case of Rodney King 1992, this narrative movement was articulated through a number of historical metaphors linking the uprisings to the tragic failure by politicians, and society as a whole, to respond adequately to the problems of the urban underclass. In all of the mainstream news narratives, the 1992 crisis flashed-back to the urban crises of the 1960s, to the 1968 Kerner Commission report, and to other, more historically distant crises and commissions. Viewed as a systemic and historical problem, the 1992 crisis had systemic and historical causes. This type of explanation for racial crisis was new to the *Los Angeles Times* and *Chicago Tribune*; as we recall from Chapter 3, both newspapers had explained Watts as being caused by civil disobedience, extremist discourse, and a breakdown in law and order. In 1992, however, their causal narrative about racial crisis included a discussion about the incomplete extension of social rights. This new explanation extended back to include other racial crises in the past, and involved a re-description of the 1965 Watts crisis.

The redefinition of the 1960s in the *Los Angeles Times* and *Chicago Tribune* was the result of two different factors: (1) the nationalization of news culture, described in Chapter 2; and (2) the narrative logic of the Rodney King beating, where the naturalized images of the videotape produced an expectation about the outcome for the verdict. On this latter point, the "surprise ending" of the Rodney King story produced a period of liminality and heightened reflexivity. The result was that, by the end of the second week of the crisis, the dominant types of news narratives were those concerned with laying out the tragic history of race and urban crisis.

Twenty-four years after the commission to investigate the riots of 1967 issued its strong warning, America watched as Los Angeles erupted in riots that, in a few short days, wrecked the domestic peace and revived once again the race question that has plagued American history since the nation's birth . . . Even after all these years of apparent progress, of affirmative action and equal opportunity, of an expanding black middle class and of a decline in the kind of boiling race hatred that filled the screens of the first video generation in the 1960s, racism remains the nation's incurable malignancy.   (*Chicago Tribune*, May 10, 1992: A1)

The battles in the streets of Los Angeles have ended, and the political battles have begun. At their core is the nation's most famous report on urban violence, which looked at burning cities a quarter century ago and called for a major Government effort to heal them . . . Since then everything has changed, and nothing has changed. Today, the Kerner Commission serves as a monument to a more optimistic era when the nation felt it had the will and the ability to heal its urban ills . . . If that era of optimism, prosperity and commitment has left the nation with cities mired in poverty, violence, and despair, what is the current environment likely to produce?   (*New York Times*, May 8, 1992: A19)

Like the wail of a police siren in the night, the searing image of the nation's second-largest city in flames has jolted America awake, forcing people all across the country to look at the realities of race and urban tension that have been all but ignored for almost twenty years. The country now faces a historic decision, whether Americans want to stop ignoring the anger and despair and social disintegration that many see as the root causes of urban and racial strife and instead resume the effort begun in the late 1960s to find solutions.   (*Los Angeles Times*, May 3, 1992: A1)

Several things are notable about these news reports. First, all three were written in the period following shortly after the end of the violence, a period described by the *New York Times* as a "surrealistic calm." Second, there was a common connection made between the crises and commissions of the 1960s and the urban uprisings of 1992. Third, all of the descriptions contrasted the optimism and prosperity of the 1960s with the apathy and pessimism of the 1990s. The general explanation, given by all three newspapers, was that the energy and optimism of the 1960s had faded during the 1970s and 1980s, and had been replaced by cynical politicians who used race as a divisive issue, to be used to win elections by playing on the racial fears of suburban whites.

"I don't think politics has dealt honestly with race in 25 years," said Senator Bill Bradley, Democrat of New Jersey. "Republicans have used race in a divisive way to get votes, speaking in code words to targeted audiences. Democrats have essentially ignored self-destructive behavior of parts of the minority population and covered that self-destructive behavior in a cloak of silence and self-denial."

(*New York Times*, May 8, 1992: A19)

The lawlessness that the entire world saw last week did not begin in South Los Angeles. The lawlessness did not even begin with the brutal clubbing of Rodney King and the verdict of jurors in Simi Valley . . . The lawlessness began with the clubbing of black America, the conscious and criminal neglect and fashionable racism characteristic of the Age of Greed over which Ronald Reagan and George Bush have presided.   (*Los Angeles Times*, May 5, 1992: B7)

The historical connection between the 1960s and 1990s was narrated through multiple forms of tragedy. On the one hand, there was the sense that, if the problem of the urban underclass could not be resolved in the idealistic and prosperous past, then there was no hope for the apathetic and cynical present. This sense of resignation was reinforced by recalling the Kerner Commission's 1968 warning that the nation was being split into two separate societies;[29] by citing census statistics to show that the residents of south central Los Angeles actually lived in worse poverty than they had in 1965;[30] and through editorials, written by prominent sociologists such as Melvin Oliver and William Julius Wilson, describing the despair confronting those living in the urban underclass in the 1990s.[31] All beliefs that there had been any progress or accomplishment in race relations were deflated. Even the rise of the middle-class black population was interpreted tragically, as eleven separate articles in the three daily newspapers focused on the daily racism which middle-class African-Americans had to endure. The stories ranged from descriptions of black policemen who were treated as dangerous criminals when not in their uniform; college students expected to speak for their race; television personalities mistaken for doormen; doctors and lawyers who were regularly stopped by the police, and who feared that they could easily become the next victim of police brutality.

The genre of tragedy encourages an expectation of failure and resignation by creating a sense of historical continuity so deep as to be unchangeable. This was precisely the context into which historical stories about race, class, and urban space were narrated. The *New York Times* and *ABC News* had numerous stories and editorials about the decline of neighborhood and community centers, the rise in incarceration for young black men, and the increasingly intractable poverty of urban poor blacks. Opinion pieces in the *Los Angeles Times* stressed the problem of the urban underclass and the migration of the black middle class out of the inner cities. Both papers wrote editorials lamenting the fact that the 1968 Kerner Commission's recommendations had been largely ignored. Encoded within a tragic genre, this deepening of historical context actually served to undermine the belief in effective collective action. Ironically, the inclusion of racist American history into the narrative ended up replacing the linear time of progressive history with a cyclical time of inevitable return, which deflated the hopes and pretensions of progressive politics.[32]

Urban America has learned the hard way that racial rage does not take place in a vacuum, nor does it lie dormant after its first eruption. If there is a sense of unease after the explosion in south central Los Angeles, blame it on history. [voice-over] "The scenes by now are all too familiar, the violence, the anger, the bloodshed, and the senseless destruction of property. What has also become only too familiar is the analysis, linking, as this report does, the mob spirit and its murderous manifestations to the bitter race feelings that had grown up between the whites and the blacks." If that sounds just a little off-key, a tiny bit dated, you're right. The quote comes from an analysis written in 1918, by a group of experts commissioned by Congress to study the riots of 1917 in East St. Louis, and to draft a report.

(*ABC News*, May 7, 1992)

If the mainstream media's tragic narrative of urban neglect was encoded within a cyclical time of inevitable return, the African-American press narratives of urban neglect were written within a more definite historical time related to more definite structural changes. Since the 1960s, as a result of black middle class mobility and increased black middle class participation in mainstream civic life, the formerly class-integrated black communities had became increasingly class segregated. The *Los Angeles Sentinel, Chicago Defender*, and *New York Amsterdam News* all wrote about the urban crisis in a way that linked race and class, and which included significant criticism of African-American leaders who were thought to be "out of touch" with non-bourgeois blacks.[33] The *Amsterdam News* was the most strident in these criticisms, implicating "Black America's political elite" for acting according to their class interest as opposed to their racial interests. In the last article it wrote about the Rodney King crisis in 1992, the *Amsterdam News* explained how "Blacks have been told for generations that if another African-American from the upper-middle class is appointed to a high position . . . that the entire race is empowered"; the problem was that this belief "ignores that class identity and ideological commitments frequently outweigh racial membership."[34] In explaining the urban crisis as a failure of African-American leadership, those in the African-American press maintained an emphasis on African-American empowerment; despite the similarity in cultural form, then (through the use of tragic discourse), the African-American press continued to offer alternative interpretations and alternative ways of thinking about racial crisis in civil society.

The tragedy of politics

In a tragic narrative, the protagonist or hero ultimately fails in his or her mission, either because of the inevitability of fate or the violation of a moral law. Where narratives about politics and politicians are concerned, either cause of failure threatens a loss of legitimacy. Either they are ineffective, or they are immoral. This was the cultural environment in which George Bush and Bill Clinton had to make public interventions to try to resolve the 1992 Rodney King crisis. As will become apparent, it was not a hospitable environment.

As was the case with the Watts uprisings of 1965 and the Rodney King beating of 1991, the narrative environment in the mainstream media served to constrain the political actions available to the elite in responding to the 1992 Los Angeles uprisings, and also affected the public evaluation of those actions. Much as Samuel Yorty's failure to respond to a changing narrative context in 1965 had caused his symbolic deflation in the news reports of the *Los Angeles Times*, a parallel failure led to the symbolic deflation of the Bush administration in the daily newspapers of New York, Chicago, and Los Angeles. All three newspapers had reported, during the first days after the uprisings, that the events in Los Angeles would dominate the political landscape and serve as one of the most important issues in the presidential election.[35] President Bush and his main Democratic challenger, Bill Clinton, both visited Los Angeles within a week after the verdict: Clinton on May 3, Bush on May 7. Bush, being the incumbent politician and a key actor in the narrative that tied the urban problems of the present to the divisive and cynical politics of the 1980s, was from the beginning at a symbolic disadvantage. Even before Bush had made any definitive statements about the crisis, and before his statements had been evaluated in the media, he was already being symbolically positioned by the tragic narrative of cynical politics, and his actions were described as tentative, passive, and uncertain.

When Bush did begin to comment about the Rodney King crisis, he made three types of public statements. The first was to criticize the rioters and to appeal for law and order. The second was to dispatch federal Justice Department officials to California to pursue the possible federal prosecutions of the four acquitted officers. The third was to blame the problems of the urban underclass on the welfare policies of the 1960s. This combination of discursive strategies proved disastrous for Bush's public approval ratings. A *Times/Mirror* poll, according to the *Los Angeles Times*, found that "the Los Angeles riots have sharply reduced support for President Bush."[36] A *New York Times/CBS News* poll found that forty-three percent of whites and sixty-six percent of blacks were dissatisfied with the way Bush had

handled the Los Angeles situation; even worse, fifty-four percent of whites
and seventy-eight percent of blacks disapproved of the way Bush was hand-
ling race relations more generally.[37] While there were slight differences in
each newspaper, the conclusions were similar; the politicization of the crisis
reinforced the sense of tragic resignation. The *New York Times*, which as
we recall from the Watts crisis of 1965 had been the most committed to the
extension of social rights, was the most singularly critical of Bush, describing his early response to the 1992 crisis in the following manner:

> The comments [by Bush] spread over eight hours, left the impression that the White
> House was scrambling to keep atop public reaction to the verdict in the brutality
> case. As the day progressed, the President moved further from his initial expression
> of 'frustration' about the King verdict and began condemning the rioters. In his last
> appearance of the day . . . the President did not mention the verdict at all . . . On
> Wednesday evening, as smoke first began to curl above Los Angeles, Mr. Bush had
> told reporters only that "what's needed now is calm and respect for the law."
>
> (*New York Times*, May 1, 1992: A22)

As for the second political strategy of the Bush administration, the dis-
patching of federal officials to Los Angeles to begin inquiries into federal
prosecutions against the acquitted Los Angeles police officers, the *New
York Times* only wrote two articles about this event during the first five
weeks of the crisis. The first, written May 1, only mentioned Bush once and
instead focused on Attorney General William Barr, as well as the historical
precedent for undertaking a federal prosecution. By the time the second
article about the federal investigation appeared in the paper, on May 6, it
was described as part of an orchestrated attempt on the part of Bush to
demonstrate concern about urban issues, at the same time as he maintained
a law-and-order position and did not plan any significant new government
programs. In other words, Bush was described as an insincere politician,
concerned more with his public appearance than finding real solutions.

The political strategy which received the most attention in the *New York
Times* was that by which Bush attempted to blame the urban crisis on the
welfare programs of the 1960s. In the news narrative of the *New York
Times*, Bush was described as having made a conscious and calculated decision, after deliberations with his advisors, to mobilize the politics of division and blame. The following three news excerpts illustrate how the *New
York Times* interpreted this decision.

> Deep into a difficult political campaign and facing what some aides now call a
> domestic Persian Gulf crisis, President Bush will meet with his top domestic advis-
> ors Monday morning to begin mapping his response to the civic and physical wreck-
> age of the Los Angeles riots. Mr. Bush is being pressed to quickly address the

broader social ailments underlying last week's upheaval . . . [and] is under considerable political pressure to prove his leadership on the issue.

(*New York Times*, May 4, 1992: B9)

The White House said today that the riots last week in Los Angeles were a result of social welfare programs that Congress enacted in the 1960s and '70s, but it refused to say publicly whether President Bush would offer any detailed alternative to those 'failed' policies in coming weeks.   (*New York Times*, May 5, 1992: A1)

Mr. Bush has apparently taken the counsel of his more conservative advisers and decided to emphasize the need for re-establishing civil peace, rather than immediately embracing vast new urban development programs of the kind advocated by civil rights leaders in recent days. According to a senior White House source, he discarded a more accommodating text for his national television speech Friday night in favor of a restatement of the law-and-order creed that helped elect Richard M. Nixon and Ronald Reagan and, four years ago, Mr. Bush himself.

(*New York Times*, May 5, 1992: A26)

The point of these reports was clear: Bush had chosen to take an extreme, self-interested, and politicized response to the Los Angeles crisis, even though some of his aides had provided him with more reasonable suggestions. Bush's proposed solutions, dealing mainly with urban enterprise zones, were described as an idea of a Bush aide (housing secretary Jack Kemp), who for three years had been "shut out of the President's inner circle, ridiculed by the budget director and sent to fight lonely battles on Capitol Hill without White House reinforcements."[38] When Bush arrived to tour the damage in south central Los Angeles, reports in the *New York Times* described it as an ineffective trip where the urban residents were able to see through Bush's insincerity.

Mr. Bush came with the quiet of dawn and left with a whoosh of his motorcade at 9:59 A.M., almost before anybody knew he was in the 'hood.

(*New York Times*, May 8, 1992: A1)

Those who talked with Mr. Bush in several meetings today were polite, but their tone was unmistakable. They were educating the President about problems and tragedies with which they believed he was unfamiliar. Mr. Bush, clearly chastened by the unfamiliar experience of such raw emotion, responded with talk of racial harmony and promises of new urban policies . . . At other times, Mr. Bush seemed to be reaching for elusive words as he tried to craft a message around the notion that people are responsible for each other.   (*New York Times*, May 8, 1992: A1)

In the African-American press, reports about President Bush's attempts to resolve the crisis were reported in a form similar to that of the *New York Times*: too late, too insincere, too politically motivated. Bush's trip to Los Angeles was described as "missing the point," because he had been ignoring the exact same problems in Washington D. C. for years. Bush's "misguided social policies" were contrasted with the "successful" Great Society programs, and presented as the real causes for economically deprived black communities in Los Angeles, Chicago, Harlem, the Bronx, and throughout the nation.[39] Ultimately, as the *Chicago Defender* wrote in a May 16 editorial, the cause of the 1992 crisis was the President's lack of concern for the poor and minority residents of the nation.[40]

If Bush was having a hard time maintaining political legitimacy in the wake of the uprisings, however, Clinton fared only slightly better. Clinton was only slightly less eager to criticize the rioters, and just as willing to engage in the politics of blame. As a result, he was easily included in the tragic narrative of politicization and blame. In fact, the same *New York Times/CBS News* poll which found public dissatisfaction with Bush, found that only twenty-six percent of whites and forty-one percent of blacks were satisfied with Bill Clinton's response to the Rodney King crisis, reflecting the general sense of resignation typical of tragedy. Within two weeks after the rioting, both political figures had been criticized for a failure of leadership.

With the war on the streets of Los Angeles in a cease-fire, Americans caught their breath last week, turning to their President and their leading would-be President for insight, leadership and a plan for the future. What they got were old, relatively modest proposals and plenty of it's-not-our-fault, it's-theirs finger-pointing.

(*New York Times*, May 10, 1992: D1)

In the face of this gathering calamity, who has heard an authentic and imaginative word from any political leader? As what's left of the American social contract unravels, we seem paralyzed both by the muteness of our politicians and our own sense of resignation and powerlessness.   (*Los Angeles Times*, May 10, 1992: M1)

Only a day after President Bush and Congressional leaders met to display a spirit of bipartisanship in dealing with the aftermath of the Los Angeles riots, Republicans and Democrats returned to their normal political maneuvering today and demonstrated that they remained far apart on urban policy.

(*New York Times*, May 14, 1992: A20)

The construction of the political contest was basically the same in the *Los Angeles Times*, *ABC News*, and the *New York Times*. Bush was criticized more vehemently, but Clinton's symbolic position suffered by his inclusion in the tragic narrative of political self-interest. Since this narrative undermined the possibility of a political solution to the crisis, it blocked the favored romantic plot for the political public sphere, leaving only the tragic temporality of cyclical return. An *ABC News* story on the political visits to south central Los Angeles captured this sense of cyclical time well, noting how, "Older residents who remember the Watts riots of the 60's also remember that a lot of politicians paid a visit then. And, they say, nothing changed."[41]

For the *Chicago Tribune*, the tragedy of politics was refracted through a plot developed during the 1991 crisis: the loss of community, the loss of citizen participation, and the difference between Los Angeles and Chicago. Even before the trial, a story comparing the Los Angeles and Chicago police noted that Los Angeles had "a very different department from Chicago and most other large cities" and that "police experts nationwide, as well as local politicians, community leaders and residents, say the Chicago Police Department's history, ethos, and makeup make it far less disposed to the type of violence perpetrated by police against King."[42] After the trial and the uprisings, Los Angeles became a negative object lesson about the dangers of mass society, and, by implication, a positive story about Chicago's strong community solidarity:

Los Angeles has broken apart. People shake their heads, wring their hands; they say L.A. has fractured. But what Los Angeles gave America for decades was precisely a notion of a city of separate lives . . . The irony is this. L. A. was constructed for most of this century as a place, a paradoxical city of separateness. This was its optimism and the source of its youthful indifference. Now the city has lost its childish innocence with the realization that lives are related.

(*Chicago Tribune*, May 20, 1992: A17)

Like its 1991 Rodney King narrative, the *Chicago Tribune* aligned the national government with the local government of Los Angeles, labeled both of them ineffective, and contrasted them to a more community-centered and activated Chicago. While early editorials in the *Chicago Tribune* had expressed the hope that the uprisings would have positive benefits if they engaged citizens in more community involvement,[43] this sense of hope had disappeared by the end of May. Editorials described the federal government's efforts during the 1960s as "failures [which] paralyzed the nation by convincing people the government can't do anything to solve the problems of the inner cities,"[44] described the American voters as too short-sighted and distracted to still remember Los Angeles by election time,[45] and described politicians as too cynical and too manipulative to work to create new solutions to old problems.[46] Even though it took a different route to get to the same conclusion, the *Chicago Tribune*'s narrative of politics had the same ending: cynical, manipulative, and ineffective politicians.

The tragedy of racial division and legal paralysis

One result of the jury verdict and the uprisings in Los Angeles was the public recognition that the supposed realism and transparency of video images were in fact mediated through competing and racialized worldviews. The seeds of this recognition were planted, of course, with the not-guilty verdicts handed down by the Simi Valley jury; it was reinforced further by the recognition that there were, indeed, "raced ways of seeing" the uprisings. In focus-group discussions about the Los Angeles uprisings, African-American informants interpreted the television images of the uprisings as legitimate protest against racial and economic injustice; white and Latino informants, by contrast, interpreted the events primarily as criminal activities by anti-civil opportunists.[47] The recognition of these racial and ethnic differences in interpretation presented obvious complicating factors for public sphere engagement, because they encouraged the reification of collective identities, and discouraged real discussion and deliberation among *individuals* regarding matters of common racial concern.

Despite these complications, the consequences of recognizing that there were racialized interpretations were contingent, and depended on how they impacted the form and substance of public discourse in civil society. One possibility was that the recognition would lead to a greater commitment in favor of engagement and deliberation between different racial groups and across racially-divided public spheres. This did not happen. Instead, the recognition that there were "raced ways of seeing" was linked to the tragic plots of the 1992 Rodney King crisis, thereby deflating hopes about racial understanding and racial justice even further. Journalists had periodically noted the existence of racially organized interpretations, of course, when writing about other incidents of racial crisis. As Chapter 4 demonstrated, news reports in the daily press contrasted the shock and outrage that the beating of Rodney King provoked in white society with the opinions of many African-Americans that Rodney King was lucky the police had not killed him. But the 1992 Rodney King narrative made the tragedy of racial division more threatening to the civic ideals of legal impartiality and discursive neutrality. The not-guilty verdicts in the first trial of the police officers charged with beating Rodney King brought the recognition that white racism threatened legal impartiality. Two additional trials – the trial of the four men accused of beating Reginald Denny, and the federal trial of the Los Angeles police officers charged with beating Rodney King – dramatized even further the danger of racial division for the legal institutions of civil society.

From the beginning, the Reginald Denny trial was linked to the second Rodney King trial as part of a tragic tale of racial difference and racial division. Damian Williams, Henry Watson, Antoine Miller, and Gary Williams – four African-Americans charged with the videotaped beating of a white man, Reginald Denny, during the 1992 Los Angeles uprisings – remained in custody during their trial, unable to raise bail which ranged from between \$500,000 and \$580,000 each. Stacey Koon, Lawrence Powell, Theodore Briseno, and Timothy Wind – four white police officers charged with the videotaped beating of a black man, Rodney King – were each released on \$5,000 bond. These disparities were too obvious to be ignored, and led to the fear that either trial could result in a repeat of the 1992 uprisings. The *Chicago Tribune* described the federal trial against the Los Angeles police officers as "LA's Tragedy in Many Acts," writing that "a number of things could happen as a result of this case, most of them bad."[48] Its news reports described African-American support of the "LA Four" in the Denny beating trial as signaling the seemingly unbridgeable gap between white and black citizens, writing that "To many whites, the police officers have become persecuted victims. Many blacks view the gang members the same way."[49] The *Los Angeles Times*, writing about the removal of a black judge from the Denny beating trial, wrote that the trial "reinforced the impression among many in the black community that the legal system will twist itself inside out to deny justice to African-Americans."[50] The seemingly unbridgeable gap between white and black citizens became a dominant trope in reporting about both trials, as did the threat that this racial divide presented to the legal system more generally.[51]

In courthouses across America, justice is portrayed as a blindfolded woman carrying a set of scales, impartial and fair, but these days, don't try to sell that image in south central Los Angeles where many see the criminal justice system as just one more way for whites to oppress blacks. One month after the riots, the mood in L. A.'s poorest neighborhoods is, by all accounts, still angry, and just as the verdict in the Rodney King case was the flash point that started the looting, some community leaders say the courtroom may be the cause of more rioting.

(*ABC News*, June 5, 1992)

Six months after the worst urban unrest of this century, Los Angeles remains a city divided, its residents separated by deep fissures that have split along racial, economic and geographic lines. At a time when fragmentation and Balkanization have become civic buzzwords, Angelenos increasingly see their neighbors as being resentful or indifferent toward people of other races, more suspicious even than in the immediate aftermath of the riots . . . Twice as many blacks as whites expect the trial against those accused of beating Reginald O. Denny to be biased against the defendants. Twice as many whites as blacks say the trial of the police officers accused of beating King will be biased against the officers.

(*Los Angeles Times*, November 16, 1992: JJ4)

In coming to this conclusion about racial division and the threat it presented to civil society, the mainstream news narrative came closer to the tragic narrative of white racism which had been a prominent feature of

African-American news narratives about all three racial crises. But whereas the African-American press had emphasized the tragic role legal injustice played in creating racial division, the mainstream press was emphasizing the tragic role racial division played in preventing impartial legal justice. For the mainstream narrative, the promise of civil society seemed to mean the guarantee of an impartial, rule-regulated legal system. For the African-American narrative, however, the promise of civil society was linked, as it had been during the 1991 crisis, to the question of African-American participation and empowerment. The failure by the mainstream media narratives to conceptualize the issue of participation and empowerment reinforced the tragic narrative of white insincerity and racism in the media narratives of the African-American press.

By monitoring the public statements made by politicians and others in the mainstream public spheres throughout the 1992 crisis, those writing in the African-American press were easily able to build upon the tragic narrative of white insincerity and racism which had been so prominent a feature during all three crises. News reports and editorials in the African-American press criticized the mainstream press for calling Mayor Bradley ineffective and powerless;[52] for dehumanizing the rioters by calling them "savages," "thugs," and "animals";[53] for spreading distrust and misinformation about the truce between the major African-American gangs in Los Angeles;[54] and for constructing black-Korean relations as a "problem," focusing on tensions and downplaying cooperation.[55] Mainstream society was criticized for opting to find a scapegoat rather than real solutions.[56] In addition, there were numerous other articles pointing to erroneous public statements made by police officials, politicians, and journalists. Similar to the 1965 and 1991 crises, monitoring of the mainstream press reinforced suspicions about white insincerity, as well as the complicity of "the media" in producing symbolic violence against African-Americans:

Everybody is so busy trying to 'rebuild LA' and figure out what were the real causes for the Los Angeles rebellion. But the real root of the problem has not and probably will not be addressed which is the media's portrayal of minorities, in particular African-Americans . . . I know that no matter how destructive the actions of my people were to the city of Los Angeles, the media's assault would do irreparable damage to the character of an entire race.(*Los Angeles Sentinel*, July 23, 1992: B6)

While it was clear that there were competing accounts of the crisis, what was different about the 1992 Los Angeles uprisings was that all of the competing interpretations were narrated through a single cultural form. No longer opposed by any competing cultural form, the tragic mood encouraged resignation, fragmentation, and the loss of hope.

The persistence of tragedy

The tragic mode of reporting the 1992 Rodney King crisis persisted even in the face of new events which might have led to a more positive and romantic interpretation of the crisis. One such event was the release of the Webster Commission report on the causes of the uprisings. In the past, commission reports had served to re-focus public attention on the crisis, encouraging one more round of public discussion, and often providing a mechanism of successful closure for ending the crisis (at least in the mainstream press). In terms of its make-up, the Webster Commission was similar to most other commissions investigating civil crises, in that it comprised elite representatives of government and civil society. William Webster was a former director of the FBI; Hubert Williams, co-chair of the commission, was the president of the Police Foundation in Washington, D. C. Rather than offering the possibility of a new plot with new heroes, however, the events surrounding the Webster Commission were inserted into the tragic narratives which had dominated the media environment throughout the 1992 Rodney King crisis. The *Los Angeles Sentinel* incorporated the Webster Commission into its narrative of white insincerity and racism, writing that the commission "will almost certainly produce an inherently conservative and whitewashed report protective of existing institutions, in particular the authority and behavior of the LAPD."[57] The *Los Angeles Times* reported that the commission's public meetings about the police response to the uprisings "degenerated into a shouting match . . . as activists seized the opportunity to promote their own disparate causes."[58] When the report was released in October 1992, anonymous sources warned that "a deepening city budget crisis and mayoral politicking threaten to undermine promises to implement the reforms."[59] What was remembered most about the Webster commission was that it was unable to counteract the forces of political failure and racial division.[60]

Another event which failed to produce any formal changes in public narratives about Los Angeles and race relations was the transition of leadership of the Los Angeles Police Department. When Willie Williams was sworn into office as the new police chief, the event offered an opportunity to close the old narratives of the Rodney King crisis, which had involved Daryl Gates so centrally, and to re-interpret the crisis around themes of hope and change. Because Williams was the first African-American ever to serve as the police chief in Los Angeles, there was a chance for the event to encourage hope in African-American as well as mainstream news publics. But while Williams was described through the more positive imagery of hope and change, the *event* of the transition only seemed to reinforce the sense of tragedy and crisis swirling around Los Angeles. The *New York Times*, *Los Angeles Times*, and *Los Angeles Sentinel* all reported that Williams's ability to improve the department would most likely be blocked by political infighting, police factions, a demoralized staff that was too small to institute more progressive police practices, and a budget crisis that would stifle any attempts at systemic change.[61] Regardless of the event, it seemed that nothing could shake the sense of resignation about race and civil society – racial division and distrust, it seemed, were to be permanent features of American life.

If the tragic form had come to dominate interpretations of racial crisis after the Rodney King uprisings, it was reinforced immeasurably by the O. J. Simpson affair. Everything about the O. J. Simpson case reinforced the tragic understanding of race in American civil society.[62] On June 17, 1994, some ninety-five million Americans watched the low-speed chase between Simpson and the Los Angeles police. [63] From the beginning, mainstream news media covered the story from an almost exclusively racial angle, emphasizing the racially polarized attitudes toward Simpson, the police investigation, and the likelihood of a fair trial. The polling organizations of the largest news organizations went into overdrive, polling the American public about these issues and finding the racially-divided attitudes the media had been reporting about since 1992. Less than a week after Simpson's arrest, African-American leaders were complaining that "Simpson had already been tried and convicted by the white press."[64]

By the time the trial began on September 26, 1994, it was clear that not only race, but Rodney King, would provide the setting behind which the O. J. Simpson drama would unfold. Every move Judge Lance Ito made during the trial was understood in the media through a comparison with the first Rodney King beating trial; every mention of the Los Angeles Police Department brought back memories of the 1991 videotape. As Gibbs has argued, one of the most significant components of the Simpson defense team strategy was to keep the memory of Rodney King vivid and recurrent: "More than any single factor, Cochran had evoked the memory of Rodney King, the innocent victim of a vicious LAPD beating, police conspiracy, and subsequent cover-up only four years previously . . . For the defense during the yearlong trial, Rodney King was indeed the thirteenth juror, unobserved in the jury box but clearly visible in the imaginations of the black jurors." [65]

When the verdict was announced on October 3, 1995 – more than a year after the start of the trial – it was an event anticipated and watched by more than 107 million Americans; more than ninety percent of all television sets in use were tuned to channels broadcasting the verdict.[66] For weeks before it was announced, the expectation was that the verdict would only serve to exacerbate racial distrust and animosity, so it was not surprising that the theme of racial division continued to dominate news coverage after Simpson was acquitted. Television cameras focused on the celebration of African-Americans and the anger of whites, largely ignoring those whose opinions did not fit the narrative of racial division, and largely ignoring the voices of Asians and Latinos.[67] An opinion poll taken immediately after the verdict found that eighty-five percent of African-Americans agreed with the not-guilty verdict, while only thirty-two percent of whites agreed with it.[68] But these survey results reflected vastly different interpretations. For whites, the verdict was wrong because of a belief that racial division had destroyed the institution of legal impartiality. This was the same tragedy of racial division which had been emphasized in mainstream media accounts of the 1992 Rodney King crisis. For African-Americans, on the other hand, the verdict was correct because it vindicated longstanding complaints about police practices, because it sent a message to racist police officers, and because it raised the possibility that it was indeed possible for African-Americans to get a fair trial.

As journalists wrote and public figures commented on the meaning of the verdict and the public reactions to it, they relied on the same narratives that had developed during the 1992 Rodney King crisis. Mainstream newspapers dutifully reported about the racialized interpretations of the verdict, incorporating their reports and editorials into the tragic form through which they had become so accustomed to writing about race and civil society. The O. J. Simpson case became another event in the Rodney King saga; while the Rodney King uprisings had uncovered deep-seated racial division and distrust, the O. J. Simpson verdict seemed to show that the divisions were even worse than had been imagined.

It was over a quarter of a century ago that there was anything like this verdict, an event of overwhelming public interest that happened to come at a precisely scheduled moment, an event that would cause millions to stop whatever they were doing, to find a television set, to sit down and to watch. And that distant event was astronaut Neil Armstrong's walk on the moon, and it was remarkable in the way it brought people together. Today's event, the verdict in the O. J. Simpson trial, is remarkable in the way it has not only separated people, in the way it has cleanly divided Americans, black and white.   (*ABC News*, October 3, 1995)

Does racism remain so endemic and corrosive that it becomes an occasion for delirious celebration within the African-American community when the justice system exonerates one of their own, even one whom many blacks acknowledge probably committed the crime? The answer was as close as the split-screen. Yes. Racial alienation, in which perception and reality are impossible to separate, really is that bad.
(*Chicago Tribune*, October 8, 1995: A1)

The stunning pictures of blacks cheering while whites muttered or choked back tears when the verdict was announced chillingly captured the widening separation of interests that increasingly defines American life in the 1990s . . . "What this episode does is deepen the polarization," said Will Marshall, president of the Progressive Policy Institute, a centrist think tank in Washington. "It is really a terrible blow to the idea of a civic culture to which we owe allegiance that transcends our racial and ethnic identity."   (*Los Angeles Times*, October 9, 1995: A5)

If Neil Armstrong's moon landing was the epitome of the American dream, the O. J. Simpson verdict was the epitome of the American nightmare. What held these two events together in a relationship of binary opposition was the idealized image of a universal solidarity, that could transcend particular identities and exclusions. Of course, this idealized image of civil society as "transcending our racial and ethnic identity" had always meant something very different in the African-American public spheres. After all, claims to universal solidarity had been used to criticize African-American claims for civil rights during both World Wars and during much of the Cold War. Such claims also tended to ignore the fact that, for most of American history, African-Americans had been excluded on the basis of the very same racial identities that were being decried after the Simpson verdict.

White claims to universal solidarity had always wrung hollow in the African-American public sphere, and the Simpson affair was no different. African-American news accounts noted how "the force and intensity of whites' reaction to the Simpson verdict is reminiscent of southern whites, not too long ago, who clamored for the heads of accused African-Americans even before they were brought to trial."[69] Those in the African-American press criticized white journalists for prejudging Simpson, for writing about the case as if it were a "modern-day Othello," and for pandering to the historical chords of racism that existed in white communities throughout the nation.[70] Finally, African-American newspapers criticized the analyses by white pundits, who claimed that the Simpson verdict had increased racial antagonism. Offering an alternative interpretation of the meaning of the verdicts, those in the African-American press emphasized how the verdict exposed the racial divisions and the white racism that had always existed, but which had been hidden and suppressed from mainstream society.

The most disturbing aspect of the Simpson media spin is the propaganda that the verdict has worsened race relations. That's ridiculous. All the verdict has done is given many white Americans an opportunity to express secretly held, racially motivated, attitudes toward black Americans. The Simpson verdict could never trigger the kind of intense white backlash that the country is now experiencing. This backlash is the result of long held feelings, rising to be expressed at a time when it's acceptable to be "mad" at black people.

(*Los Angeles Sentinel*, October 18, 1995: A12)

Racial divisions accentuated by the Simpson trial mirror those of society. Most whites are castigating the jury for doing its job, the speed of the verdicts notwithstanding. This is no accident and should come as no surprise. What is truly scary is that virtually nothing is being done to reconcile differences among and between hugely diverse populations. Neither government nor the private sector is mobilizing to deal with factors underlying the disparate reactions to the Simpson trial which simply reflects current reality.

(*Los Angeles Sentinel*, November 1, 1995: A7)

The different meanings attributed to the verdict reveal an interesting paradox that lay at the heart of race, media, and the crisis of civil society. In African-American as well as mainstream publics, the O. J. Simpson verdict demonstrated the need in civil society for trust and engagement across lines of difference. As a *New York Times* editorial said "Our aim should be to build trust: for everyone's sake."[71] Indeed, whites as well as blacks recognized the need to open up a dialogue in order to increase trust between racial groups. But what was to be the communicative geography of this dialogue? Was dialogue to occur solely on the terrain of the mainstream press and public spheres, or was it to extend into the black public spheres as well? Was it to begin from the event of the moon landing, and representations of a past time of universal solidarity; or was it to include a longer history, grounded in a collective memory of exclusion and white racism? Like Watts in 1965 and the Rodney King crises of 1991 and 1992, public communication about the Simpson affair continued the long pattern of separation and bifurcation. What was needed was an opening up of the public spheres, so that conversations about matters of racial concern might be able to incorporate new narratives and new points of difference. This opening up was unlikely as long as tragedy dominated the narration of racial crisis, and it was unlikely as long as the larger mainstream publics remained unaware of the contours of the debates taking place within the smaller African-American publics.

Conclusion

The outcomes of public communication depend in large part on the communicative geography of civil society – that is, the extent and the quality of interactions between different publics, and the forms of representation used to make events meaningful in specific interpretive communities. Because communication takes place within an environment of plural and partial publics, it cannot be considered solely in terms of its ability to produce a shared commitment to a singular vision of the good, or to some "rational" consensus; it must also be evaluated in terms of its ability to keep a conversation going, and to protect the possibility of opening up this dialogue to new narratives and to new points of difference. This is most likely to happen, as I have argued throughout the pages of this book, if there is a differentiated and diverse set of communication media – both large and small, universalistic and particularistic.

There is little question that the African-American public sphere has been an important part of the communicative geography of civil society, and that the African-American press has been one of its central communicative institutions. Historically, African-Americans have turned to the black press in order to develop alternative interpretations of public events; to develop arguments that might prove more effective in engaging those in the hegemonic public spheres; and to monitor the mainstream media in order to counter negative racial stereotypes and interpretations. The black press has consistently refused to label rioters as irrational, or to dehumanize them as "thugs" or "animals." Its journalists and sources have demonstrated a much stronger willingness to cast African-Americans into heroic character positions, encouraging collective mobilization around black leaders. In terms of the plot in the narrative, black newspapers have tended to link racial crises into more ongoing, continuous, and historically-far-reaching stories of racial crisis and racial oppression. All of these representational features of the black press encourage a monitoring of, and an engagement with, the more dominant public spheres.

While the black press has introduced new narratives and new points of difference to the interpretation and discussion of public events, and while it has encouraged engagement with mainstream publics and the mainstream press, there are three factors which have prevented it from having a more significant impact on American civil society: (1) the place-bound nature of news media; (2) the racial stratification of the public sphere; and (3) the rise of tragic discourse as the dominant cultural form for discussing race and racial crisis. Each of these factors has prevented a more open and diverse engagement across different publics about matters of racial concern. The place-bound nature of news media pushes reports about racial crisis into a metropolitan framework that is more likely to offer comparative evaluations of different cities than a real engagement with racial issues. The racial stratification of the public sphere prevents real engagement across points of racial difference, and reinforces feelings of distrust and suspicion on the part of African-Americans toward mainstream civil society. Finally, the rise of tragic discourse encourages an attitude of alienation and resignation, deflating the belief that discussion about matters of common concern might be able to expand the substantive content of social solidarity, or to produce progressive social change.

News media and the home territory

Despite the fact that media communication occurs in a less localized space than interpersonal communication, news narratives about racial crisis are still affected by considerations of territory and place. On average, the *Los Angeles Times* wrote 5.2 times as many articles about the Watts and Rodney King crises as the other daily newspapers; the *Los Angeles Sentinel* wrote an average of 9.7 times as many as the other African-American newspapers. There are a whole host of reasons why this would be the case, including journalistic routines, audience expectations, and the central role newspapers play in the "political economy of place".[1] Regardless of the reasons, however, the relationship between place and news density has the potential to influence the ability of media communication to encourage narrative diversity, openness, and tolerance.

By allowing space for more voices, more perspectives, and more plots about the descriptions, causes, and solutions to a crisis, news density increases the potential that there will be greater narrative diversity in the way matters of racial concern are discussed. I am not suggesting that there is a simple relationship between the number of news articles and the diversity of news narratives. Los Angeles press coverage of the Watts and Rodney King crises was not "better" simply because its newspapers wrote more articles. Indeed, it would be difficult to argue that the Watts coverage of the *Los Angeles Times* was more open to African-American concerns than the *New York Times*. Still, to the extent that the plot is an important structural component of public communication, the inclusion of a larger number of events offers at least the possibility for twists in the plot and narrative variations to develop during the course of a crisis. News density offers the possibility for more flexible news narratives, which allow *events* to have a potentially significant force in changing understandings about racial crisis. Thus, for instance, while the Watts narratives of the *Los Angeles Times* and *Chicago Tribune* were initially very similar to one another, the greater news density of the *Los Angeles Times* coverage allowed it the opportunity to incorporate the McCone Commission hearings into its reports, resulting in a plot development that was more open to discussions of underlying causes and possible solutions.

In addition to influencing the intensity of public attention surrounding a given chain of events, place also shapes public sphere constructions of racial crisis hermeneutically, through a comparison of distant events with more local experiences. Just as Weber's Protestants must sooner or later have asked, "Am I one of the elect?" those living in Chicago and New York must sooner or later have asked, "What do these events in Los Angeles tell me about where I live?" In answering this question, there was a tendency to localize the events as being specific to Los Angeles. This was by no means the only, or even the dominant, form of social construction in the non-Los Angeles press, but it was part of the cultural repertoires of the non-Los Angeles news organizations. For the *New York Times* and *Chicago Tribune*, the comparison between distant events and local experience tended to result in representations of Los Angeles as a city without community. For the *New York Amsterdam News*, comparisons between Los Angeles and New York led to reports claiming that Harlem had learned enough from its own uprisings in 1964 so that Watts could not have happened there, and that the 1992 uprisings in Los Angeles could not have happened in New York because Mayor David Dinkins was willing to listen to the African-American community. In all of these comparisons, the effect was to regionalize the sense of crisis, to the benefit of the home city. By emphasizing the ways in which Los Angeles was different than the metropolitan home territory, all of these news reports served to shift attention toward a comparative evaluation of different cities and, as a consequence, away from matters of racial concern.

In mainstream publics, place considerations also deflected attention away from matters of racial concern through regional conflict and distinction making. This was most evident during the 1965 Watts crisis, when there was a serious division within the mainstream press. The *Chicago Tribune* and *Los Angeles Times* both explained the cause of the Watts uprisings as being the breakdown in law and order, the introduction of "extremist discourse," and the need for more force by police to quell civil disobedience. By contrast, the *New York Times* explained the causes of the uprisings through reports and editorials about the incomplete extension of social rights, and the breakdown of the African-American family. The sense of a culture war over the future direction of the country was palpable in these comparative representations, and news coverage in all three papers took the form of an epic struggle between the forces of good and the forces of evil. In the *Chicago Tribune* and *Los Angeles Times*, this meant resolute support for the police in their battle to maintain order and civility. In the *New York Times*, it meant support for the federal government as it attempted simultaneously to extend social rights and to encourage civility in "disorganized" urban communities. For all three papers, the sense of regional division encouraged an orientation to, and an engagement with, other mainstream spheres; the *New York Times* criticized Chicago and Los Angeles, while the *Chicago Tribune* and *Los Angeles Times* criticized New York and Washington. As a result, representational struggles over the meaning of racial crisis were mostly carried on without regard for African-American issues or African-American voices.

By the 1990s, the *Los Angeles Times* and *Chicago Tribune* had nationalized considerably in their journalistic orientation, the differences between the three daily newspapers were less noticeable than they had been during the 1960s, and, as a result, mainstream media narratives of racial crisis were more engaged with African-American concerns. All three newspapers represented the Los Angeles police as threats to civil society during the 1991 social drama of the Rodney King beating, and all three represented the trial of the officers as a condition of successful resolution for the 1991 crisis. After the Los Angeles uprisings of 1992, all three newspapers pointed to the failure to solve the problems of race and the urban underclass in the 1960s; the failure of politicians to move beyond the cynical rhetoric of fear and blame; and the inability of American society to rid itself of racism, even toward middle-class blacks. With less of an orientation to regional differences and regional conflicts, the possibility was more open for a real engagement about matters of racial concern. Unfortunately, this possibility was undercut by the racial stratification of the public sphere, and by the prevalence of deflationary and tragic discourse.

The racial stratification of the public sphere

In a civil society consisting of multiple publics, the possibility of inter-public communication is absolutely essential for the expansion of solidarity. The problem is that communication, like much else in public life, is racially stratified. Considering the infrastructure of the public sphere, for example, only the largest news publics actually have the resources for regular intercommunication. Those writing in and for the largest daily newspapers, such as the *New York Times*, *Los Angeles Times*, and *Chicago Tribune*, share the same wire services, enjoy large and growing circulations, and, because they are major daily newspapers, they operate regularly as a public forum for intellectuals and politicians to discuss matters of common concern. Additionally, all three papers run their own polling operations, a fact that increases public sphere intercommunication in two important ways: first, because the release of an opinion poll is a newsworthy event, and is likely to be reported by other news organizations, including television; and second, because the activity and publication of opinion polls add additional incentives for political actors to read the newspaper. Intercommunication also operates between the major daily papers and television news: through the concentration of ownership, the use of mainstream newspapers by television journalists, and the use of the same stock of speakers and sources.

By comparison, those writing in and for major African-American newspapers such as the *Chicago Defender*, *Los Angeles Sentinel*, and *New York Amsterdam News* do not share wire services, and they suffer ever-shrinking circulations. From 1965–1992, the *New York Amsterdam News* lost 49.7 percent of its circulation, and the *Chicago Defender* lost 17.1 percent. The *Los Angeles Sentinel* actually gained 7.6 percent in circulation, but this gain is due to the increased attention of the Rodney King crises. Between 1965 and 1990, before Rodney King, the *Sentinel* had actually lost 26.6 percent of its circulation. Furthermore, with the notable exception of the *Chicago Defender*, which has both a daily and a weekly edition, almost all black newspapers are published weekly, limiting their ability to support a daily public forum for discussing matters of common concern. These infrastructural imbalances make the *practice* of intercommunication between African-American and mainstream public spheres ever more difficult.

The infrastructure of the public sphere is also stratified through archiving practices and new communication technologies. The existence of more complete archiving records makes the mainstream press an easier resource for journalists researching new stories, and also, I might add, for academics doing research on media and the public sphere. By contrast, archiving of the African-American press is erratic and incomplete, even for histori-cally important papers. This racial stratification is being reproduced as the archiving of news moves online, to full-text database services such as Lexis-Nexis or Ethnic Newswatch. Lexis-Nexis maintains records for more than 2,300 different news sources, but no African-American papers. Ethnic Newswatch maintains records for African-American papers such as the *Los Angeles Sentinel* and *New York Amsterdam News*, but not the *Chicago Defender*, which is arguably the most historically important of all black newspapers. News from Black Entertainment Television is not archived by Lexis-Nexis or Ethnic Newswatch. And while journalists have access to Lexis-Nexis, they do not generally have access to Ethnic Newswatch.[2] These factors, together with the ubiquity of mainstream newspaper web-sites and the invisibility of African-American ones, make the African-American press and public spheres ever more difficult to access, particularly in relative terms.

In addition to the infrastructural stratification, there are other imbal-ances of perception which hinder the possibilities of inter-public engage-ment. In the pages of the mainstream press, African-Americans were virtually invisible until the 1960s; African-American *newspapers* are still mostly invisible. By contrast, one of the primary functions of the black press historically has been to monitor the mainstream media. The effect of this rather one-sided intercommunication between the African-American and mainstream press is a reinforcement, in the black public sphere, of the sense of white indifference, a reinforcement which suggests a more tragic genre for understanding racial crisis, and which decreases the likelihood of building trust and solidarity across racial lines.

Tragedy and the present crisis of race in civil society

In Chapter 5, I argued that tragedy was the main cultural form adopted by the news media to interpret racial crisis and racial polarization during the 1992 Rodney King crisis, and that the theme of tragedy has dominated sub-sequent events colored by race, such as the Reginald Denny and O. J. Simpson trials. In order to see more fully how tragedy dominated public narratives about race after the 1992 Rodney King uprisings, it is worth pausing for a moment to consider the discursive environment that sur-rounded the 1965 Watts uprisings. In 1965, racial crisis was represented as an epic struggle between the forces of good and evil. Who was the hero and who was the villain depended on the specific public sphere; in all of them, however, the struggle encouraged a collective mobilization in support of the particular vision of resolution. The sense of engagement and urgency surrounding the 1960s racial crises served as a point of contrast, in fact, for the public sense of resignation in the 1990s. If racial crisis was not resolved adequately then, how could people ever hope to do better in the cynical and apathetic 1990s?

Interpretations which suggested an attitude of tragic resignation could be found during all three racial crises, of course. In the African-American press, the tragedy of white racism and indifference was a persistent theme in virtually all news coverage of racial crisis, acting as a warning against too much hope. In the *Los Angeles Times*, the factionalization of city politics was understood tragically, while the *Chicago Tribune* often viewed the entire city of Los Angeles through a tragic lens, as a mass society unable to generate any feeling of solidarity among its residents. But before 1992, the tragic interpretation of events was counterposed against a competing interpretation, through which the challenges of fragmentation and anomie could be romantically overcome. White indifference could be overcome through African-American empowerment. Political factions could be overcome through political leadership. Mass society could be overcome through grassroots community organizing. In these instances, the tension between romance and tragedy only served to heighten the sense of social drama surrounding the crises.

After the 1992 Los Angeles uprisings, most romantic elements of racial discourse disappeared, and the sense of social drama was replaced by resignation and the loss of hope. Accompanying this cultural shift, the linear time of progressive history was replaced with the cyclical time of inevitable return, thereby deflating the hopes and pretensions of progressive politics as well as social movements. For African-Americans, the verdict reinforced what had been feared all along: namely, that white institutions could not be trusted to produce racial justice. For white Americans, the verdict destroyed faith in the ability of political and legal institutions. For both, the aftermath of the verdicts brought a sense that there was an unbridgeable gap between the races, and that talk about matters of racial concern was a hopeless waste of time.

It is curious that tragedy prevailed in mainstream public discourse about racial crisis at the precise time that real engagement across lines of racial difference was most likely. By 1992, the writing staffs of daily newspapers were composed of more women and more minorities, came from more regionally diverse origins, and were more likely than ever before to incorporate African-American voices and viewpoints into their narratives about American civil society. The Rodney King beating and ensuing crisis of 1991 had vindicated longstanding African-American complaints of excessive force by police, reinforcing the authority of those complaints through the official seal of the Christopher Commission report. The return of the not-guilty verdicts showed in a public and dramatic way that African-American complaints of legal injustices, also longstanding, were still valid. All of these factors influenced early mainstream news coverage of the 1992 Los Angeles uprisings, which were indeed open and sympathetic to African-American voices, histories, and interpretations. But any increase in open-ness was quickly overwhelmed by the tragic sense that nothing could be done to overcome the racial divide between American citizens. That the shift to tragedy occurred precisely at the moment of greatest openness to African-American voices and concerns can only be understood in ideologi-cal terms – not in the way that propaganda models explain ideology, where military and corporate interests actively filter the news production process, but in a more subtle, cultural way, where ideology works "behind the scenes" of conscious intent, in the cognitive ordering of events into mean-ingful sequences of significance.[3] This is the type of ideological analysis that Graeme Turner suggests for film studies: "Often the formal problems we might discern within a film are traceable to the intransigence of the ideo-logical opposition; an unsatisfactory ending in a film may emerge from the failure to unite the ideological alternatives convincingly."[4]

In *The Birth of Tragedy*, Friedrich Nietzsche argues that tragedy delivers us from our thirst for earthly satisfaction, reminding us of another existence and a higher delight. Removing the burden of the world from us, the tragic hero allows us to delight in ugliness and disharmony, convincing us "that even the ugly and discordant are merely an esthetic game which the will, in its utter exuberance, plays with itself."[5] For Nietzsche, tragedy was the polar opposite of the ceaselessly optimistic drive toward knowledge and science, forcing people to gaze into the horror of existence, and momentarily lifting them above the phenomenal world.[6] Tragedy, in other words, was the best way to bring myth back to an utterly mundane and empiricist society.

But is tragedy the only way to activate myth? Durkheim, in *The Elementary Forms of the Religious Life*, suggests that it is not, and insists instead that society requires the periodic activation of myth in order to hold its members together in a sense of shared identity and solidarity: "There can be no society which does not feel the need of upholding and reaffirming at regular intervals the collective sentiments and the collective ideas which make its unity and its personality."[7] Whereas Nietzsche linked the activation of myth to a particular kind of cultural form (tragedy), Durkheim linked it to a particular kind of cultural practice, which he defined (broadly) as ritual. According to Durkheim, ritual activated myth by opposing the ideal society to the real society, and by dramatizing the tension between these two antagonists in a social drama linking past, present, and future. This social drama could be narrated through a number of different forms; tragedy was certainly one of these forms, but it was by no means the only one.

In fact, that which makes tragedy such a powerful dramatic force in the theatre is exactly what makes it so dangerous, disempowering, and, ultimately, ideological in the public sphere. What is normatively desirable about the idea of the public sphere, after all, is the belief that engagement with others is a valuable thing: either because it can help to identify shared interests, hopes, and values; or because it can aid in understanding, tolerance, trust, and solidarity. The public sphere encourages an active conception of democratic legitimacy, demanding that the world be ordered according to some coherent notion of the good society. The opposite of such active notions of legitimacy, as Weber argued in his religious sociology, is a more static understanding of legitimacy achieved through a contemplative "flight from the world."[8] If legitimacy is to be achieved solely through contemplation, then it will fail to impact the practical activity of the everyday world. This is precisely the problem tragedy poses for democratic legitimacy generated in the public sphere: namely, that it encourages a flight from the world, privileging the act of private contemplation over that of public interaction or public engagement.

By pointing to the dangers of tragic discourse, I do not mean to suggest that all public events should be understood in purely romantic and heroic terms. After all, the sense of epic struggle crafted in the Watts narratives of the *Los Angeles Times* and *Chicago Tribune* evinced strong affinities with racist projects designed to silence black voices through violence. At the very least, neither paper in 1965 was committed in the slightest bit to the goal of racial engagement, and neither paper took seriously the arguments and worldviews of African-Americans. Both papers, in fact, used the Watts crisis as a springboard for criticizing the civil rights movement, whose leaders they criticized as being the dependent dupes of Communists. While more progressive than the daily papers of Chicago or Los Angeles, the Watts narratives of the *New York Times* were generally paternalistic toward African-Americans, seeing them as utterly dependent on Lyndon Johnson's Great Society programs. In general, the everyday lives of African-Americans were ignored completely by the mainstream press in the 1960s, a fact which was listed by the Kerner Commission as one of the main causes of the 1960s urban uprisings. This fact was not mitigated by being enveloped within a romantic and heroic narrative; indeed, there is good reason to believe that romantic discourse is particularly ill-suited to the task of promoting real engagement with difference.

As I have argued elsewhere, romantic discourse presents significant challenges to the civic ideal of expanding the substantive content of social solidarity.[9] Overpowering romantic discourses tie individuals too closely to collective agendas, providing little room for critical thought, little space for acknowledging contingency and difference within the nation, and no opportunity for constructing a solidarity in common with those excluded from the rights of citizenship. Confronted with a discursive environment dominated by romance, marginalized groups with a concern for maintaining their own cultural autonomy are forced to choose a path of either "exit" or "loyalty," where the latter implies assimilation and the loss of distinctive identity. Furthermore, romantic narratives suffer from an "excess of plot," in which the teleological power of mythically validated past origins and future destinations precludes reflexivity and the interrogation either of present or of possible destinations.

Just as the excesses of romantic narratives must be held in check by a competing genre of interpretation, so too must the excesses of tragic narratives be held in check. Tragedy encourages a mechanistic ordering of events that tends to discredit agency and contingency in favor of structural determinism. While Hayden White maintains that the tragic structure of a plot bears an affinity with radical historiography, Ricoeur reminds us that, as a dramatic form, tragedy encourages in the reader an attitude of resigned acceptance, pointing to an evil "already there and already evil."[10] By emphasizing the inevitability of fate, the acceptance of evil in the world, and the necessity of achieving transcendence or redemption through a contemplative and mythic "flight from the world," unchecked tragic discourse discourages collective mobilization, public engagement, and motivation to work through difficult public problems. It is for this reason that a preponderance of tragic discourse is a significant contributing factor to the present crisis of race in American civil society.

Increasing racial engagement in civil society

The most pressing questions for race, media, and American civil society concern the degree to which discussion, deliberation, and engagement about matters of racial concern can expand the substantive content of social solidarity. Above all else, as Parsons recognized, the promise of civil society rests with its ability to create and to reinforce feelings of inclusion, belonging, and participation.[11] Those who are or would be included in civil society engage in cooperative and conflictual symbolic "conversations" about who deserves membership and just how far the obligations of membership extend. In principle, crisis is among the most important social processes for expanding social solidarity in civil society, because it pushes these symbolic conversations to consider the gulf between who is included and who ought to be included. In practice, however, the consequences of crisis are more open and contingent. If the symbolic conversations driven by crisis are to expand social solidarity, they require an infrastructure which supports inter-public engagement, as well as forms of cultural representation which are open to new voices and new interpretations of past, present, and future. For race, media, and the present crisis of civil society, this infrastructural and cultural environment has tended to be short-circuited by the place-bound nature of news media, the racial stratification of the public sphere, and the growing preponderance of tragic discourse.

In order to create a media infrastructure more supportive of inter-public engagement between African-American and mainstream publics, mechanisms need to be established whereby mainstream journalists monitor the African-American press in the same way that African-American journalists monitor the mainstream press. A more reciprocal monitoring would serve two purposes. First, it would open up the mainstream media more fully to a consideration of African-American issues and narratives. Second, to the extent that it changed the current situation of decidedly one-sided monitoring, it would help to alleviate African-American suspicions of white indifference and racism.

In order to increase reciprocal monitoring practices, mainstream journalists and the audience for mainstream news need to have easier access to African-American news sources. In the current situation, the ubiquity of mainstream news media is increasing at the expense of the African-American press. Twenty-four-hour television news stations are increasing in their number and power. Every major newspaper and news magazine has a website, which journalists and everyday readers can access for no charge. Many of these websites provide hyperlinks to previous stories written about an ongoing event, providing a sense of temporal continuity and thematic coherence to major stories. By contrast, major African-American newspapers are still largely invisible on the newsstands, and still largely invisible on the Internet. Given the practical constraints of news work and the time bind facing most Americans, it is not surprising that the mainstream press continues to increase its relative power over the African-American press.

Mainstream news media, if they are to recognize their public role in supporting civil society, must respond to the crisis of the black press by taking active steps to increase inter-public engagement. Mainstream journalists could insist that Lexis-Nexis add African-American newspapers to its otherwise comprehensive archiving of news; alternatively, they could encourage their management to subscribe to the archiving service offered by Ethnic Newswatch. Once they have better access to African-American news files, these journalists would be in a better position to monitor the black press when writing stories about racial matters, and to try to use those stories to diversify the voices and perspectives they present in their news stories. The Internet divisions of major news organizations could take active steps to help African-American papers to set up websites, and could provide links to stories in the African-American press during times of racial crisis. These practices would not only encourage more of a dialogue between African-American and mainstream publics, but they would also help African-American newspapers with their present circulation crisis. For example, in the weeks leading up to the O. J. Simpson verdict, the *Los Angeles Sentinel* reported that national news attention to the paper's trial coverage had resulted in more than 500 new requests for subscriptions to the paper.[12]

I am not arguing that monitoring of the African-American press should become the central activity of mainstream news media; nevertheless, there should be infrastructure in place enabling these journalists to monitor the black press more effectively during times of racial crisis. This would encourage more dialogical reporting, and would serve to open up mainstream news narratives about race to ever new points of difference. It would encourage a diversification in the genres of crisis reporting, and would signal to African-Americans a more solid commitment to engage openly about matters of racial concern. In short, it would provide the resources necessary for news organization to better fulfill their civic function as the central communicative institutions of civil society.

Notes

Introduction

1 The author of *The Wonderful Wizard of Oz*, Frank Baum, moved from Chicago to Los Angeles in 1910, two years after the first movie company arrived, and many have argued that Southern California was in fact the Emerald City. Furthermore, Southern California had been a land of fantasy and dreams for at least fifty years before the film industry settled there in the 1920s, and the choice of Hollywood was influenced in large part by the dream of Southern Californian life. See Ian Maltby and Richard Craven, *Hollywood Cinema* (Cambridge, MA: Blackwell Press, 1995), p. 15; Kevin Starr, *Inventing the Dream: California Through the Progressive Era* (New York: Oxford University Press, 1985), pp. 283–308.

2 See, for example, the *New York Times*, May 3, 1992: D1.

3 This definition of civil society comes from Jean Cohen and Andrew Arato, *Civil Society and Political Theory* (Cambridge, MA: MIT Press, 1992), p. 23.

4 The understanding that civil society fulfills both defensive and progressive social functions is common to the writings of many theorists whose arguments are otherwise quite different, e.g., Ernest Gellner, "The Importance of Being Modular," in *Civil Society: Theory, History, Comparison*, ed. J. Hall (Cambridge: Polity Press, 1995), pp. 32–55, esp. p. 32; Philip Oxhorn, "From Controlled Inclusion to Coerced Marginalization: The Struggle for Civil Society in Latin America," in *Civil Society: Theory, History, Comparison*, p. 252; and Jeffrey Alexander, "Civil Society I, II, III: Constructing an Empirical Concept from Normative Controversies and Historical Transformations," in *Real Civil Societies: Dilemmas of Institutionalization*, ed. J. Alexander (London: Sage, 1998), p. 10.

5 This shift in the norms and practice of politics can be seen in two historical changes that occurred in England. The first occurred during the early 1700s, when Bolingbroke developed a new theory and practice of political opposition, whereby the opposition sought to influence policy from outside of

government, by mobilizing public opinion through political journalism. The second came to pass during the early 1800s, when journalists were provided an official place in the Houses of Parliament. See Jurgen Habermas, *The Structural Transformation of the Public Sphere* (Cambridge, MA: MIT Press, 1989), pp. 60–64; Cohen and Arato, *Civil Society and Political Theory*, p. 658.

6 Some of the most important arguments in favor of multiple publics include Geoff Eley, "Nations, Publics, and Political Cultures: Placing Habermas in the Nineteenth Century," in *Habermas and the Public Sphere*, ed. C. Calhoun (Cambridge, MA: MIT Press, 1992), pp. 289–339; Nancy Fraser, "Rethinking the Public Sphere: A Contribution to the Critique of Actually Existing Democracy," in *Habermas and the Public Sphere*, pp. 109–142; and Craig Calhoun, "Civil Society and the Public Sphere," *Public Culture* 5 (1993): 267–280.

7 See Calhoun, "Indirect Relationships and Imagined Communities: Large-Scale Social Integration and the Transformation of Everyday Life," in *Social Theory for a Changing Society*, ed. P. Bourdieu and J. S. Coleman (Boulder, CO: Westview Press, 1991), esp. pp. 108–111.

8 The idea of multiple publics which are nested within a larger national or even supra-national public can be found in the writings of Charles Taylor, "Liberal Politics and the Public Sphere," in *New Communitarian Thinking: Persons, Virtues, Institutions, and Communities*, ed. A. Etzioni (Charlottesville, VA: University Press of Virginia, 1995), pp. 207–215; Victor Perez-Diaz, "The Possibility of Civil Society: Traditions, Character and Challenges," in *Civil Society: Theory, History, Comparison*, p. 81.

9 The relationship between media and the public sphere has been taken up most forcefully by John Keane, *The Media and Democracy* (Cambridge: Polity Press, 1991); Keane, "Structural Transformations of the Public Sphere," *The Communication Review*, 1,1 (1995): 1–22; and John Thompson, *The Media and Modernity* (Stanford University Press, 1995).

10 Leo Bogart, *Press and Public*, 2nd ed. (Hillsdale, NJ: Lawrence Ehrlbaum Associates, 1989), p. 237.

11 *Ibid.*, p. 79.

12 Habermas (*Structural Transformation of the Public Sphere*, pp. 248–250) had serious reservations about the ability of modern mass media to support a viable public sphere, arguing that in the world of mass culture (1) far fewer people express opinions than receive them; and (2) people are unable to generate collective opinions independently of mass media institutions. Today, however, a wealth of media theory and research has pointed to the active nature of audiences. Much as eighteenth-century journals provided an infrastructure for discussion in the salons and coffeehouses cited so approvingly by Habermas, today's media do much the same. Some of the exemplary theory and research on active audiences includes Tamar Liebes and Elihu Katz, *The Export of Meaning* (New York: Oxford University Press, 1990); David Morley, *The Nationwide Audience: Structure and Decoding* (London: British Film

Institute, 1980); Morley, *Family Television: Cultural Power and Domestic Leisure* (London: Comedia, 1986); Andrea Press, *Women Watching Television: Gender, Class, and Generation in the American Television Experience* (Philadelphia, PA: University of Pennsylvania Press, 1991); Peter Dahlgren, "What's the Meaning of This? Viewers Plural Sense Making of TV News," *Media, Culture & Society* 10 (1988): 285–307; Stuart Hall, "Encoding/Decoding," in *Culture, Media, Language* (London: Hutchinson, 1980); Klaus Jensen, "Reception Analysis: Media Communication as the Social Production of Meaning," in *A Handbook of Qualitative Methodologies for Mass Communication Research*, ed. K. Jensen and N. Jankowski (London: Routledge, 1991), pp. 135–148; Justin Lewis, "The Meaning of Things: Audiences, Ambiguity, and Power," in *Viewing, Reading, Listening: Audiences and Cultural Reception*, ed. J. Cruz and J. Lewis (Boulder, CO: Westview Press, 1994), pp. 19–32; and Elizabeth Long, "Textual Interpretation as Collective Action," in *Viewing, Reading, Listening*.

13 During the 1989 events in Tiananmen Square, Chinese protesters carried signs quoting Abraham Lincoln and other American democratic heroes, which were translated into English for the audiences of CNN; so long as international media cameras were there, it was believed, Chinese authorities would not turn violent. See Keane, "Structural Transformations of the Public Sphere," 14.

14 Quoted in Armistead Pride and Clint Wilson, *A History of the Black Press* (Washington, D. C.: Howard University Press, 1997), p. 156.

15 Paula Johnson, David Sears and John McConahay, "Black Invisibility, the Press, and the Los Angeles Riot," *American Journal of Sociology* 76 (1971): 698–721; Carolyn Martindale, *The White Press and Black America* (New York: Greenwood Press, 1986); N. P. Gist, "The Negro in the Daily Press," *Social Forces* 10 (1932): 405–411

16 Roland Wolseley, *The Black Press, U. S. A.* (Ames, IA: Iowa State University Press, 1990), p. 392.

17 The *Atlanta Daily World*, which calls itself a daily paper, only publishes four issues per week, and relies heavily on wire service stories. The *New York Daily Challenge*, the only daily newspaper in New York, was not founded until 1972. See Wolseley, *The Black Press, U. S. A.*, pp. 99–102.

18 Todd Gitlin, *The Whole World is Watching: Mass Media in the Making and Unmaking of the New Left* (Berkeley, CA: University of California Press, 1980), pp. 296–305.

19 The influence of the *New York Times* has been noted by Leon Sigal, *Reporters and Officials: The Organization and Politics of Newsmaking* (Lexington, MA: D. C. Heath, 1973), p. 47; Charles Kadushin, *The American Intellectual Elite* (Boston, MA: Little Brown & Co., 1974), pp. 140–141; and David Weaver and G. Cleveland Wilhoit, *The American Journalist in the 1990s* (Matwah, NJ: Lawrence Ehrlbaum Associates, 1996), pp. 20–22. Its continued influence was noted recently in a *US News & World Report* article (July 13, 1998), which

claimed that "Even in today's media-soaked age, the *New York Times* gets to decide what's news . . . The *Times* remains the hometown paper of the network bosses, there on the doorstep each morning to shape and validate top executives' news judgment. Network reporters often say they can't sell a story internally until it has made Page 1 of the *Times*."

20 Andrew Abbott, "From Causes to Events: Notes on Narrative Positivism," *Sociological Methods and Research* 20,4 (1992): 428–455; William Sewell, "Introduction: Narratives and Social Identities," *Sociol Science History* 16,3 (1992): 479–489.

21 Jeffrey Alexander and Philip Smith, "The Discourse of American Civil Society: A New Proposal for Cultural Studies," *Theory and Society*, 22 (1993): 156.

22 Studies of narrative and class formation include Margaret Somers, "Narrativity, Narrative Identity, and Social Action: Rethinking English Working-Class Formation," *Social Science History* 16,4 (1992): 591–630; and George Steinmetz, "Reflections on the Role of Social Narratives in Working-Class Formation: Narrative Theories in the Social Sciences," *Social Science History* 16,3 (1992): 489–516. Studies of narrative and collective action include Janet Hart, "Cracking the Code: Narrative and Political Mobilization in the Greek Resistance," *Social Science History* 16,4 (1992): 631–668; Anne Kane, "Culture and Social Change: Symbolic Construction, Ideology, and Political Alliance During the Irish Land War" (unpublished doctoral dissertation, 1994); and Francesca Polletta, "'It was Like a Fever . . .' Narrative and Identity in Social Protest," *Social Problems*, 2 (1998): 137–159. Studies of narrative and mass communication include Robert Darnton, "Writing News and Telling Stories," *Daedalus*, 104,2 (1975): 175–193; Michael Schudson, "The Politics of Narrative Form: The Emergence of News Conventions in Print and Television," *Daedalus* (1982): 97–112; and Ronald Jacobs, "Producing the News, Producing the Crisis: Narrativity, Television, and News Work," *Media, Culture and Society* 18, 3 (1996): 373–397.

23 The idea of imagined communities is borrowed from Benedict Anderson, *Imagined Communities: Reflections on the Origin and Spread of Nationalism* (London: Verso, 1983).

24 Steinmetz, "Reflections on the Role of Social Narratives," p. 505.

25 See Somers, "Narrating and Naturalizing Civil Society and Citizenship Theory: The Place of Political Culture and the Public Sphere," *Sociological Theory* 13 (1995): 127.

26 Kane, Culture and Social Change, 504–506; Sewell, "Introduction: Narratives," 438–439.

27 Talcott Parsons, *The System of Modern Societies* (Englewood Cliffs, NJ: Prentice-Hall, Inc., 1971), p. 12.

28 Emile Durkheim, *The Elementary Forms of the Religious Life* (New York: The Free Press, 1965), pp. 474–475.

29 The notion of "narrating the social" is borrowed from Steven Sherwood,

whose influence on my thinking about narrative and cultural theory is immeasurable. See Steven Sherwood, "Narrating the Social," *Journal of Narratives and Life Histories* 4,1–2 (1994): 69–88. The idea of narrative lingering is borrowed from Umberto Eco, *Six Walks in the Fictional Woods* (Cambridge, MA: Harvard University Press, 1994).

30 See Victor Turner, *Dramas, Fields, and Metaphors* (New York: Cornell University Press, 1974), p. 39.

31 The most comprehensive theory and description of media events can be found in Daniel Dayan and Elihu Katz, *Media Events* (Cambridge, MA: Harvard University Press, 1992). While Dayan and Katz excluded crisis from their typology of media events, recent theoretical and empirical studies have challenged this exclusion, arguing that crisis is one of the most important types of media events. See Paddy Scannell, "Media Events," *Media, Culture and Society* 17 (1995): 151–157; and Jacobs, "Producing the News."

32 In my thinking about the temporality of crisis, I have been aided immeasurably by conversations with Robin Wagner-Pacifici, and also by frequent reference to her empirical works on the topic. See Robin Wagner-Pacifici, *Discourse and Destruction: The City of Philadelphia versus MOVE* (Chicago, IL: University of Chicago Press, 1994); Robin Wagner-Pacifici, *Standoff: Contingency in a Situation of Paralysis* (Cambridge University Press, 1999).

33 Eco, *Six Walks.*

34 Andrew Abbott, "Transcending General Linear Reality," *Sociological Theory* 6 (1988): 169–186.

35 The relationship between narrators and nonfictional plots is discussed by Steinmetz, "Reflections on the Role of Social Narratives," 500.

36 See Alexander, "Citizen and Enemy as Symbolic Classification: On the Polarizing Discourse of Civil Society," in *Where Culture Talks: Exclusion and the Making of Society,* ed. Marcel Fournier and Michele Lamont (Chicago, IL: University of Chicago Press, 1992), pp. 289–308; Alexander and Smith, "The Discourse of American Civil Society."

37 Hirschman argues that these oppositions regulate reactionary and progressive political rhetoric. See Albert Hirschman, *The Rhetoric of Reaction* (Cambridge, MA: Harvard University Press, 1991).

38 Northrup Frye, *Anatomy of Criticism* (Princeton, NJ: Princeton University Press, 1957), esp. pp. 158–239.

39 *Ibid.*, p. 211.

40 See Ronald Jacobs and Philip Smith, "Romance, Irony, and Solidarity," *Sociological Theory* 15,1 (1997): 60–80.

41 Rogers Brubaker makes much the same argument about cultural idioms of nationhood and citizenship. See Brubaker, *Citizenship and Nationhood in France and Germany* (Cambridge, MA: Harvard University Press, 1992), p. 16.

42 Edward Soja, "Los Angeles 1965–1992: From Crisis-Generated Restructuring to Restructuring-Generated Crisis," in *The City: Los Angeles and Urban Theory at the End of the Twentieth Century*, ed. Allen Scott and Edward Soja (Berkeley, CA: University of California Press, 1996), p. 459.

43 Seymour Spilerman, "The Causes of Racial Disturbances: A Comparison of Alternative Explanations," *American Sociological Review* 35,4 (1970): 631.

44 Population data for Los Angeles in 1870 are drawn from Soja and Scott, "Introduction to Los Angeles: City and Region," in *The City: Los Angeles and Urban Theory*, p. 3. All other population data are drawn from the U. S. Bureau of the Census.

45 Soja, "Los Angeles 1965–1992," p. 441.

46 See Maltby and Craven, *Hollywood Cinema*, pp. 59–106.

47 See Robert Fogelson, *The Fragmented Metropolis: Los Angeles, 1850–1930* (Berkeley and Los Angeles: University of California Press, 1967), pp. 43–62.

48 For good discussions of the early migrants to Los Angeles, see Fogelson, *Fragmented Metropolis*, p. 191; Raphael Sonenshein, *Politics in Black and White: Race and Power in Los Angeles* (Princeton, NJ: Princeton University Press, 1993), p. 26.

49 For good discussions of early transportation history in Los Angeles, see Fogelson, *Fragmented Metropolis*, pp. 164–185; Martin Wachs, "The Evolution of Transportation Policy in Los Angeles: Images of Past Policies and Future Prospects," in *The City: Los Angeles and Urban Theory*, pp. 106–159.

50 Soja, "Los Angeles 1965–1992," pp. 433–434.

51 See Fogelson, *The Fragmented Metropolis*, pp. 109–115.

52 *Ibid.*, pp. 127–128.

53 *Ibid.*, pp. 149–150.

54 For a good discussion of the industrial geography of Los Angeles, see Allen Scott, *Technopolis: High Technology Industry and Regional Development in Southern California* (Berkeley, CA: University of California Press, 1993).

55 Measurement and analysis of racial segregation in Los Angeles, Chicago, and New York can be found in Karl Taeuber and Alma Taeuber, *Negroes in Cities: Residential Segregation and Neighborhood Change* (Chicago: Aldine, 1965); Douglas Massey and Nancy Denton, *American Apartheid: Segregation and the Making of the Underclass* (Cambridge, MA: Harvard University Press, 1993).

56 For a discussion of the history of race and housing policy in Los Angeles, see Susan Anderson, "A City Called Heaven: Black Enchantment and Despair in Los Angeles," in *The City: Los Angeles and Urban Theory*, esp. pp. 344–345.

57 Soja, "Los Angeles 1965–1992," p. 437.

58 The development of the black urban "underclass" has been most famously described and analyzed in two books by William Julius Wilson: *The Declining Significance of Race: Blacks and American Institutions* (Chicago, IL: University of Chicago Press, 1978); and *The Truly Disadvantaged: The Inner City, The Underclass, and Public Policy* (Chicago, IL: University of Chicago Press, 1987).

59 Soja, "Los Angeles 1965–1992," p. 430.

60 Soja and Scott, "Introduction to Los Angeles," p. 10; Anderson, "A City Called Heaven," p. 353.

61 More detailed descriptions of the events surrounding the Watts uprisings can be found in John McCone, "Violence in the City – An End or a Beginning? A Report by the Governor's Commission on the Los Angeles Riots" (Los Angeles, 1965); and Fogelson, "White on Black: A Critique of the McCone Commission Report," in *Mass Violence in America: The Los Angeles Riots*, ed. R. Fogelson (New York: Arno Press and the *New York Times*, 1969), pp. 111–145.

62 King was booed off the stage when he went to speak at the Westminster Neighborhood Center, according to Anderson, "A City Called Heaven," p. 357.

63 The theme of the difficulty Americans seem to have in talking about race is a central theme of Cornel West, *Race Matters* (Boston: Beacon Press, 1994).

64 Data on the damage caused during the 1992 Los Angeles uprising are drawn from Melvin Oliver, James Johnson, and Walter Farrell, "Anatomy of a Rebellion: A Political-Economic Analysis," in *Reading Rodney King, Reading Urban Uprising*, ed. R. Gooding-Williams (New York: Routledge, 1993) p. 119.

Chapter 1. Race, media, and multiple publics

1 On the fractured quality of contemporary civil society, see Keane, "Structural Transformations of the Public Sphere," p. 8.

2 Jurgen Habermas, "Further Reflections on the Public Sphere," in *Habermas and the Public Sphere*, ed. C. Calhoun (Cambridge, MA: MIT Press, 1992), p. 425.

3 For historical accounts of the plebian public sphere, see Eley, "Nations, Publics, and Political Cultures," pp. 325–331; Kenneth Tucker, *French Revolutionary Syndicalism and the Public Sphere* (Cambridge University Press, 1996), pp. 71–103. For historical accounts of women's publics, see Mary Ryan, "Gender and Public Access: Women's Politics in Nineteenth-Century America," in *Habermas and the Public Sphere*, pp. 259–288; Keith Baker, "Defining the Public Sphere in Eighteenth-Century France: Variations on a Theme by Habermas," in *Habermas and the Public Sphere*, pp. 181–211; Joan Landes, *Women and the Public Sphere in the Age of the French Revolution* (Ithaca, NY: Cornell University Press, 1988). On festive communication and the public sphere, see Keane, *Public Life and Late Capitalism: Toward a Socialist Theory of Democracy* (Cambridge University Press, 1984); Tucker, "Harmony and Transgression: Aesthetic Imagery and the Public Sphere in Habermas and Post-structuralism," *Current Perspectives in Social Theory* 16 (1996): 101–120.

4 On the early history of the women's suffrage press, see Linda Steiner, "Nineteenth-Century Suffrage Periodicals: Conceptions of Womanhood and the Press," in *Ruthless Criticism: New Perspectives in U. S. Communication History*, ed. W. Solomon and R. McChesney (Minneapolis, MN: University of Minnesota Press, 1993), pp. 38–65.

5 On the early history of the working class press, see Jon Bekken, "The Working-Class Press at the Turn of the Century," in *Ruthless Criticism*, pp.151–175.

6 Eley, "Nations, Publics, and Political Cultures," p. 307.

7 On the relationship between white abolitionists and the African-American press, see Pride and Wilson, *A History of the Black Press*, pp. 26–30.

8 Alexis de Tocqueville, *Democracy in America* (New York: Doubleday, 1969), vol. 2, p. 120.

9 Bogart, *Press and Public*, p. 23.

10 This definition of news is drawn from Mitchell Stevens, *A History of News* (New York: Viking Press, 1988), p. 9.

11 For critical theory and research on the inequality of media access, see Nicholas Garnham, *Capitalism and Communication: Global Culture and the Economics of Information* (London: Sage Publications, 1990); Keane, *The Media and Democracy*; Monroe Price, *Television, the Public Sphere, and National Identity* (Oxford: Clarendon Press, 1995).

12 Newspaper editors, for example, regard the number of letters to the editor as one of the most important measures of editorial quality. See Bogart, *Press and Public*, pp. 260–261.

13 See Diana Crane, "Reconceptualizing the Public Sphere: The Electronic Media and the Public," in *Gessellschaften im Umbau*, ed. C. Honegger, J. Gabriel, R. Hirsig, J. Pfaff-Czarnacka, and E. Poglia (Berne: Seismo, 1995), pp. 175–195.

14 See Joshua Gamson, *Freaks Talk Back: Tabloid Talk Shows and Sexual Nonconformity* (Chicago, IL: University of Chicago Press, 1998).

15 As Thompson has noted in this regard, "the inability to control the phenomenon of visibility [in the media] completely is a constant source of trouble for political leaders." Thompson, *The Media and Modernity*, p. 141.

16 On the porous and contingent qualities of "newsworthiness," see Jacobs, "Producing the News, Producing the Crisis," pp. 377–381.

17 On news media and the possibility of trans-spatial intersubjectivity, see Calhoun, "Indirect Relationships and Imagined Communities," pp. 106–112; Thompson, *The Media and Modernity*; Scannell, "Public Service Broadcasting and Modern Public Life," *Media, Culture and Society*, 1 (1989): 135–166

18 Bogart, *Press and Public*, p. 237.

19 *Ibid.*, p. 79.

20 As Habermas wrote, the articles "were not only made the objects of discussion by the public of the coffee houses but were viewed as integral parts of this discussion; this was demonstrated by the flood of letters from which the editor each week published a selection. When the *Spectator* separated from the *Guardian* the letters to the editor were provided with a special institution: on the west side of Burton's Coffee House a lion's head was attached through whose jaws the reader threw his letter." Habermas, *Structural Transformation of the Public Sphere*, p. 42.

21 See William Gamson, *Talking Politics* (Cambridge University Press, 1992), pp. 178–181.

22 See Elihu Katz and Paul Lazarsfeld, *Personal Influence* (Glencoe, IL: The Free Press, 1955); Liebes and Katz, *The Export of Meaning*; and Morley, *The Nationwide Audience*.

23 For exemplary studies regarding the agenda-setting effects of news media, see Maxwell McCombs and Donald Shaw, "The Agenda-Setting Function of the Press," *Public Opinion Quarterly* 36 (1972): 176–187; McCombs and Shaw, *The Emergence of American Political Issues: The Agenda-Setting Function of the Mass Media* (St. Paul, MN: West Publishing, 1977); Shanto Iyengar and Donald Kinder, *News That Matters: Agenda-Setting and Priming in a Television Age* (Chicago, IL: University of Chicago Press, 1987).

24 On the relationship between the media agenda and the polling agenda, see James Dearing, "Setting the Polling Agenda for the Issue of AIDS," *Public Opinion Quarterly* 53 (1989): 309–329.

25 On the power of agenda-setting for new issues or issues which have not been widely discussed, see Michael MacKuen and Steven Coombs, *More Than News: Media Power in Public Affairs* (Beverly Hills, CA: Sage Publications, 1981).

26 On the size of the television news audience, see Stephen Ansolabehere, Roy Behr, and Shanto Iyengar, *The Media Game: American Politics in the Media Age* (New York: Macmillan, 1993), pp. 12–15.

27 In a 1990 study of news in Chicago, Graber found that 22.1 percent of available news space was devoted to political news in the *Chicago Tribune*, 47 percent for *ABC News*, and 34.7 percent for the local news of ABC's Chicago affiliate. See Doris Graber, *Mass Media and American Politics*, 4th ed. (Washington, DC: Congressional Quarterly, Inc., 1993), pp. 122–123.

28 *Ibid.*, pp. 288–321.

29 This was a problem in the early days of the feminist movement. As Gaye Tuchman described matters, "many members of the women's movement have jobs outside the home, just as these feminist reporters do. Consequently, the movement tends to schedule evening meetings, after work when baby-sitters are available. Conferences . . . are held on weekends. Those who go to cover women's weekend activities must have their stories filed by Saturday afternoon. The activities themselves may have barely started by that time." Tuchman, *Making News: A Study in the Construction of Reality* (New York: Free Press, 1978), pp. 144–145.

30 On the relationship between a journalist's sources and her status, see Tuchman, *Making News*, pp. 68–81

31 On the narrative organization of the news world, see Jacobs, "Producing the News, Producing the Crisis"; Darnton, "Writing News and Telling Stories."

32 Price, *Television, the Public Sphere*, p. 209.

33 On the exclusionary nature of civil society discourse, see Eley, "Nations, Publics, and Political Cultures," pp. 289–300; Jacobs, "The Racial Discourse

of Civil Society: The Rodney King Affair and the City of Los Angeles," in *Real Civil Societies: Dilemmas of Institutionalization*, ed. J. Alexander (London and Thousand Oaks, CA: Sage Publications, 1998), pp. 138–161.

34 Alexander, "Modern, Anti, Post, Neo: How Social Theories Have Tried to Understand the 'New World' of 'Our Time'," *Zeitschrift fur Soziologie* 23,3 (1994): 165–197.

35 In arguing that the binary discourse of civil society operates as an open and informal system of social closure, I am relying on the excellent discussion of social closure by Brubaker, *Citizenship and Nationhood*, esp. pp. 29–31.

36 Fraser, "Rethinking the Public Sphere," p. 114.

37 Alexander, "Civil Society I, II, III," pp. 6–8

38 Fraser, "Rethinking the Public Sphere," p. 123.

39 Tocqueville, *Democracy in America*, vol. 1, p. 203.

40 See Pride and Wilson, *A History of the Black Press*, p. 153.

41 Seyla Benhabib, "In the Shadow of Aristotle and Hegel: Communicative Ethics and Current Controversies in Practical Philosophy," in *Situating the Self: Gender, Community and Postmodernism in Contemporary Ethics* (New York: Routledge, 1992), p. 38.

42 On civil society and the ideal of universalistic solidarity, see Alexander, "Bringing Democracy Back In: Universalistic Solidarity and the Civil Sphere," in *Intellectuals and Politics: Social Theory in a Changing World*, ed. C. Lemert (Newbury Park, CA: Sage, 1991), pp. 157–176.

43 Quoted in *Chicago Sun-Times*, January 19, 1998: A55.

Chapter 2. Historicizing the public spheres: New York, Los Angeles, Chicago

1 The influence of the penny press on modern journalism is discussed in Michael Schudson, *Discovering the News* (New York: Basic Books, 1978), pp. 14–31.

2 Circulation data was neither regularly nor reliably collected until well into the twentieth century, with the development of the Audit Bureau of Circulation. See Charles Bennett, *Facts Without Opinion: First Fifty Years of the Audit Bureau of Circulation* (Chicago, IL: Audit Bureau of Circulations, 1965). Circulation figures regarding the penny press in the 1830s and 1840s are drawn here from Schudson, *Discovering the News*, pp. 13–14.

3 James Lee, *History of American Journalism* (Garden City, NY: Garden City Publishing, 1923), pp. 206–229.

4 Martin Walker, *Powers of the Press: the World's Great Newspapers* (London: Quartet Books, 1982), p. 213.

5 Alexander, *Action and its Environments* (New York: Columbia University Press, 1988), pp. 136–137.

6 Schudson, *Discovering the News*, p. 60.

7 Walker, *Powers of the Press*, p. 213.

8 Schudson, *Discovering the News*, pp. 65–66.
9 Lee, *History of American Journalism*, p. 272.
10 Schudson, *Discovering the News*, p. 108.
11 *Ibid.*, pp. 98–99, 206–207.
12 Theses circulation figures are drawn from Walker, *Powers of the Press*, p. 217.
13 Lee has described the impact of the Civil War on American journalism in the following way: "During the war the people demanded the latest news, and in their efforts to supply this demand the newspapers had put forth every energy, regardless of the cost. After the war the press realized that the reading public which had been accustomed to startling events would be no longer willing to go back to the newspapers of slavery days, and it continued the custom of seeking the news which interested the people. The chief contribution of the War of the States to American journalism . . . was the willingness of news-papers to spend money for news-gathering." Lee, *History of American Journalism*, p. 318.
14 The reliance of journalists on official sources has been documented in research by Richard Ericson, Patricia Baranek and Janet Chan, *Negotiating Control: A Study of News Sources* (University of Toronto Press, 1989), pp. 186–188; Mark Fishman, *Manufacturing the News* (Austin, TX: University of Texas Press, 1980); Herbert Gans, *Deciding What's News* (New York: Vintage, 1979); David Miller, "Official Sources and 'Primary Definition': the Case of Northern Ireland," *Media, Culture and Society* 15 (1993): 385–406; and Tuchman, *Making News*.
15 Lee, *A History of American Journalism*, p. 279.
16 Sales figures for *Narrative of the Life of Frederick Douglass* are drawn from Henry Louis Gates (ed.), *The Classic Slave Narratives* (New York: Penguin, 1987), p. xi.
17 See Pride and Wilson, *A History of the Black Press*, p. 31.
18 John Hope Franklin, *From Slavery to Freedom: A History of American Negroes* (New York: Alfred A. Knopf, 1948), pp. 186–189. This does not mean that community was absent from the antebellum south. An interpretive community of resistance was institutionalized in the songs and folk-tales passed down from generation to generation, the hidden places of prayer, the secret meetings used for planning escape or insurrection, and the covert communications which found their way south from the Caribbean and the free north (see V. P. Franklin, *Black Self-Determination* (Westport, CT: Lawrence Hill & Co., 1984), pp. 77–83; Lawrence Levine, *Black Culture and Black Consciousness: Afro-American Folk Thought From Slavery to Freedom* (New York: Oxford University Press, 1977), pp. 102–135; Vincent Harding, *There is a River: The Black Struggle for Freedom in America* (New York: Harcourt Brace Jovanovich, 1981)). These were by definition secret acts, and as a result their immediate influence in forming a strong public sphere was muted, although they were ultimately of signal importance in shaping what Harding (p. 75) has called the "core values of the Afro-American cultural system." A further com-

plicating fact was that escape was one of the most successful and popular forms of resistance. Herbert Aptheker, in his study of slave revolts, concluded that "flight was a major factor in the battle against bondage," and that "it is probable that hundreds of thousands in the course of slavery *succeeded* in gaining liberty by flight" (quoted in Harding, p. 76); for a more detailed analysis of slave revolts, see Marion D. Kilson, "Towards Freedom: An Analysis of Slave Revolts in the United States," in *The Making of Black America*, ed. A. Meier (New York: Athenum, 1969), pp. 165–178.

19 John Franklin, *From Slavery to Freedom*, pp. 79–81.
20 Of the 319,000 free blacks in 1830, for example, 57.2 percent resided in the urban areas of four states: New York, Maryland, Pennsylvania, and Virginia. It is worth remembering, however, that approximately ninety percent of blacks lived in the unfree southern states. In 1790, there were some 697,000 slaves as opposed to 59,000 freedmen; by 1860, the number of slaves had reached nearly four million, while the free black population was approximately 488,000. See E. Franklin Frazier, *The Negro in the United States* (New York: MacMillan, 1949), pp. 63–65.
21 Quoted in Harding, *There is a River*, p. 85.
22 On the location of black churches in nineteenth-century New York City, see Gilbert Osofsky, *Harlem: The Making of a Ghetto* (New York: Harper & Row, 1963), pp. 36–38; Harding, *There is a River*, pp. 75–76.
23 In New York City, the Bethel A. M. E. Church established the Bethel Charity School in 1816; the African Free School Number 2, which educated Henry Highland Garnet and Alexander Crummell, among others, was established in 1820. See Osofsky, *Harlem*, pp. 34–36; John Franklin, *From Slavery to Freedom*, p. 226
24 Pride and Wilson, *A History of the Black Press*, pp. 8–11.
25 On the early history of the African-American press, and its concentration in New York City, see Wolseley, *The Black Press, U. S. A.*, p. 19.
26 On the relationship between white abolitionists and the black press, see Pride and Wilson, *A History of the Black Press*, pp. 26–27.
27 On the black convention movement, see John Bracey, August Meier and Elliot Rudwick (eds.), *Black Nationalism in America* (New York: Bobbs-Merill, 1970), p. 51.
28 Frederick Douglass, *The Liberator*, July 28, 1843. Quoted in Howard Bell, "National Negro Conventions of the Middle 1840s," in *The Making of Black America*, pp. 316–317.
29 John Russworm, "Too Long Have Others Spoken For Us," in *Black Nationalism in America*, p. 24.
30 On the economic troubles of the early black press, see Pride and Wilson, *A History of the Black Press*, pp. 237–238.
31 See Wolseley, *The Black Press, U. S. A.*, pp. 33–35.
32 Frazier, *The Negro in the United States*, pp. 174–175
33 On racial segregation during the first half of the twentieth century, see Stanley

Lieberson, *A Piece of the Pie: Blacks and White Immigrants Since 1880* (Berkeley, CA: University of California Press, 1980); Taeuber and Taeuber, *Negroes in Cities*; Massey and Denton, *American Apartheid*.

34 On the shift from regional segregation to neighborhood level segregation, see Douglas Massey and Zoltan Hajnal, "The Changing Geographic Structure of Black-White Segregation in the United States," *Social Science Quarterly* 76,3 (1995): 527–542.

35 See Lieberson, *A Piece of the Pie*, pp. 266–268.

36 On 1940 segregation levels, see Taeuber and Taeuber, *Negroes in Cities*, pp. 39–40.

37 John Logan and Harvey Molotch, *Urban Fortunes: The Political Economy of Place* (Berkeley and Los Angeles: University of California Press, 1987), p. 127.

38 William Wilson, *The Declining Significance*, p. 72.

39 William Wilson, *The Truly Disadvantaged: The Inner City, The Underclass, and Public Policy*, p. 3.

40 Lonnie Bunch, "A Past Not Necessarily Prologue: The Afro-American in Los Angeles," in *20th Century Los Angeles: Power, Promotion, and Social Conflict*, ed. N. Klein and M. Schiesl (Claremont, CA: Regina Books, 1990), p. 123.

41 On the early history of African-American settlement in New York City, see Osofsky, *Harlem*, pp. 9–12.

42 *Ibid.*, p. 93.

43 W. E. B. DuBois, *The Philadelphia Negro* (Philadelphia, PA: University of Pennsylvania Press, 1996 [1899]), pp. 44–45

44 Alain Locke, *The New Negro* (New York: Johnson, 1968), p. 7.

45 On the composition of the New York audience for Harlem Renaissance cultural production, see David Levering Lewis, ed., *Harlem Renaissance Reader* (New York: Viking, 1994), p. xv.

46 This reaction was naturalized in part by the spatial organization of Harlem itself, because the residences in the neighborhood had been designed for middle-class and upper-middle-class lifestyles. Harlem was simply too expensive and too inadequate for the lifestyles of poor blacks, who could only live in Harlem by taking in boarders or having "rent parties." The result was a population density in Harlem of 336 persons per acre – fifty percent higher than the city of Manhattan, and 500 percent higher than Chicago. See Osofsky, *Harlem*, pp. 137–140.

47 Marcus Garvey, *Philosophy and Opinions of Marcus Garvey*, vol. 2., ed. A. Jacques-Garvey (New York: Universal Publishing House, 1923), p. 60.

48 *Ibid.*, p. 42.

49 David Lewis, *Harlem Renaissance Reader*, p. svi.

50 Tony Martin, *Literary Garveyism: Garvey, Black Arts, and the Harlem Renaissance* (Dover, MA: The Majority Press, 1983), pp. 27–156. Wolseley places the average circulation figures for *Negro World* closer to 50,000. See Wolseley, *The Black Press, U. S. A.*, p. 67.

51 On the participation of Harlem Renaissance artists in Garvey's *Negro World* newspaper, see Martin, *Literary Garveyism*, pp. 27, 156.

52 On the early history of the *New York Amsterdam News*, see Wolseley, *The Black Press, U. S. A.*, pp. 72–73.
53 See Clint Wilson, *Black Journalists in Paradox: Historical Perspectives and Current Dilemmas* (New York: Greenwood Press, 1991), pp. 66–68.
54 For evidence that Chicago is the most racially segregated city in the nation, see Massey and Denton, *American Apartheid*, p. 71.
55 On the early settlement of African-Americans in Chicago, see Allan Spear, *Black Chicago: The Making of a Negro Ghetto* (Chicago, IL: University of Chicago Press, 1967), pp. 5–17.
56 *Ibid.*, p. 7.
57 *Ibid.*, p. 22.
58 *Ibid.*, p. 36.
59 *Ibid.*, pp. 208–211.
60 St. Clair Drake and Horace Cayton, *Black Metropolis: A Study of Negro Life in a Northern City* (Chicago, IL: University of Chicago Press, 1993).
61 Spear, *Black Chicago*, pp. 140–146.
62 See Gunnar Myrdal, *An American Dilemma: The Negro Problem and Modern Democracy* (New York: Harper and Row, 1944), p. 935.
63 The following description of the *Chicago Defender* is drawn from Spear, *Black Chicago*, pp. 81–185; Drake and Cayton, *Black Metropolis*, pp. 398–411.
64 This circulation figure is drawn from Wolseley, *The Black Press, U. S. A.*, p. 54.
65 *Ibid.*, p. 185.
66 Drake and Cayton, *Black Metropolis*, p. 398.
67 On the *Chicago Defender*'s role in the "Bronzeville" celebrations, see Wolseley, *The Black Press, U. S. A.*, p. 363.
68 *Ibid.*, p. 55.
69 Fogelson, *The Fragmented Metropolis*, p. 78.
70 quoted in Bunch, "A Past Not Necessarily Prologue," p. 103.
71 *Ibid.*, p. 101.
72 *Ibid.*, pp. 103–104.
73 On the cultural and institutional life of the Central Avenue district, see Bunch, "A Past Not Necessarily Prologue," pp. 110–114.
74 On the presence of the Garvey movement in Los Angeles, see Emory Tolbert, *The UNIA and Black Los Angeles: Ideology and Community in the American Garvey Movement* (Los Angeles, CA: Centre for Afro-American Studies, 1980).
75 Quoted in Bunch, "A Past Not Necessarily Prologue," p. 104.
76 Fogelson, *The Fragmented Metropolis*, p. 191; Sonenshein, *Politics in Black and White*, p. 26. Of course Los Angeles, and California more generally, did not have to import racist attitudes, as its citizens had demonstrated a strong hostility against the "other" time and time again. In 1871 a Los Angeles mob, which included prominent citizens, tortured and hanged seventeen Chinese men. In 1906 the state of California banned marriages between whites and "Mongolians," and in 1919 President Wilson dispatched William Jennings Bryan to try to persuade (unsuccessfully) the California legislature from

passing anti-immigrant legislation. The decade of the 1930s witnessed massive deportations of Mexican immigrants in Los Angeles.

77 Sonenshein, *Politics in Black and White*, p. 27.

78 Quoted in Fogelson, *The Fragmented Metropolis*, p. 200.

79 Taeuber and Taeuber, *Negroes in Cities*, pp. 35–40; Massey and Denton, *American Apartheid*, p. 64.

80 Quoted in Bunch, "A Past Not Necessarily Prologue," p. 107.

81 *Ibid.*, pp. 107–108.

82 See Wolseley, *The Black Press, U. S. A.*, pp. 126–127.

83 Pride and Wilson, *A History of the Black Press*, p. 153. The African-American press was not alone in its growth; the first half of the twentieth century was a great period of newspaper growth, and particularly so for the leading metropolitan dailies. The ratio of circulation to households reached an all-time high during the 1920s and, after declining during the Depression years, rebounded by the mid-1940s to near-record levels. See Bogart, *Press and Public*, p. 16.

84 Pride and Wilson, *A History of the Black Press*, pp. 185–192.

85 Quoted in Pride and Wilson, *A History of the Black Press*, p. 56.

86 On race news as a percentage of total mainstream news space, see Johnson, Sears and McConahay, "Black Invisibility," pp. 708–715; Martindale, *The White Press*, pp. 66–68.

87 On the participation of journalists in wartime propaganda, see Schudson, *Discovering the News*, pp. 141–142.

88 Myrdal, *An American Dilemma*, p. 914.

89 Pride and Wilson, *A History of the Black Press*, pp. 219–220. Certainly, there were some important differences between the daily newspapers, in terms of the intensity with which they applied the wartime interpretive filter to their stories and the effect these filters had on their subsequent editorial tone. For the *Los Angeles Times* and *Chicago Tribune*, the wartime filter reinforced an already aggressively pro-growth, anti-Communist, and anti-union attitude; after the war, their anti-Communist and anti-union attitude combined with an anti-eastern establishment attitude, resulting in consistent criticisms of Franklin Roosevelt and his New Deal. While the *New York Times* also contributed to the war propaganda campaign, and participated in the criticisms of the African-American press, it did not link these editorial positions so strongly to anti-Communist or anti-union stances. In comparison to the *Chicago Tribune* and *Los Angeles Times*, the *New York Times* was much more pro-Moscow in its reporting – so much so that it was nicknamed "the uptown *Daily Worker*" in the 1930s – much more sympathetic to labor issues, and much more pro-Roosevelt and pro-New Deal. See Robert Gottlieb and Irene Wolt, *Thinking Big: The Story of the Los Angeles Times* (New York: Putnam, 1977), pp. 185–201; Lee, *A History of American Journalism*, pp. 419–246; Walker, *Powers of the Press*, pp. 218–225.

90 Wolseley, *The Black Press, U. S. A.*, p. 81.

91 Bogart, *Press and Public*, p. 234.

92 Weaver and Wilhoit, *The American Journalist in the 1990s*, pp. 38–39.

93 *Ibid.*, p. 22.

94 Schudson, *The Power of News* (Cambridge, MA: Harvard University Press, 1995), p. 176.

95 *Ibid.*, p. 174.

96 Jack Hart, *The Information Age: The Rise of the Los Angeles Times and the Times Mirror Corporation* (Washington, D. C.: University Press of America, 1981), p. 174.

97 Bogart, "The State of the Industry," in *The Future of News*, ed. P. Cook, D. Gomery and L. Lichty (Baltimore, MD: Johns Hopkins University Press, 1992), p. 91; Jean Folkerts, "From the Heartland," in *The Future of News*, p. 128.

98 See William Wilson, *The Declining Significance of Race*, pp. 92–93.

99 Loic Wacquant, "The Ghetto, the State, and the New Capitalist Economy," in *Metropolis: Center and Symbol of Our Times*, ed. P. Kasinitz (New York University Press, 1995), p. 424.

100 The proportion of metropolitan blacks living inside central cities increased from fifty-two percent in 1960 to sixty percent in 1963, while the proportion of metropolitan whites residing in central cities has decreased from thirty-one percent to twenty-six percent. In general, the geographic concentration of poverty-based segregation remains at least two to three times higher for blacks than for whites, and is increasing at an accelerated rate. See William Wilson, *The Declining Significance of Race*, pp. 111–112; Massey and Denton, *American Apartheid*, p. 129. The irony is that African-Americans have begun to gain political control of urban areas precisely at the time when those areas have become politically dependent: "The relative decline of the central-city tax base has made urban politicians increasingly dependent on state and federal sources of funding in order to maintain properly the services that are vital for community health and stability . . . Thus America's metropolises are increasingly controlled by politicians whose constituencies do not necessarily live in those cities. It is this *politics of dependency* that changes the meaning and reduces the significance of the greater black participation in urban political processes." William Wilson, *The Declining Significance of Race*, p. 139.

101 William Wilson, *The Truly Disadvantaged*, p. 57.

102 Wacquant, "The Ghetto, the State," p. 432.

103 As one resident of Los Angeles commented, "there was something exciting about buying from the white stores." Quoted in Bunch, "A Past Not Necessarily Prologue," p. 123.

104 Gottlieb and Wolt, *Thinking Big*, pp. 376–380.

105 Pride and Wilson, *A History of the Black Press*, p. 229.

106 Quoted in Clint Wilson, *Black Journalists in Paradox*, p. 87.

107 Quoted in Wolseley, *The Black Press, U. S. A.*, p. 393.

108 Weaver and Wilhoit, *The American Journalist*, p. 11.

Chapter 3: The Watts uprisings of 1965

1 See, for example, McCone, *Violence in the City*; Fogelson, "White on Black," pp. 111–145; Bayard Rustin, "The Watts 'Manifesto' and the McCone Report," in *Mass Violence in America: The Los Angeles Riots*, ed. R. Fogelson (New York: Arno Press and the New York Times, 1969), pp. 145–164; Robert Blauner, "Whitewash Over Watts: The Failure of the McCone Commission Report," in *Mass Violence in America*, pp. 165–188; David Sears and John McConahay, *The Politics of Violence: The New Urban Blacks and the Watts Riot* (Boston, MA: Houghton Mifflin, 1973).

2 Sonenshein, *Politics in Black and White*, pp. 81–85.

3 *Ibid.*, p. 69.

4 J. David Greenstone and Paul Peterson, *Race and Authority in Urban Politics* (New York: Russell Sage, 1973), p. 276.

5 Sonenshein, *Politics in Black and White*, p. 70.

6 More detailed descriptions of the events surrounding the Watts uprisings can be found in McCone, *Violence in the City*; Fogelson, "White on Black," pp. 111–121.

7 Quoted in Fogelson, "White on Black," p. 114.

8 *Los Angeles Times*, August 14, 1965: A1, A8

9 *Ibid.*, August 15, 1965: A1

10 *Ibid.*, August 13, 1965: A1.

11 See *Ibid.*, August 13, 1965: A3; August 14, 1965: A1

12 *Ibid.*, August 15, 1965: A4

13 *Ibid.*, August 15, 1965: A2

14 See Richard Morris and Vincent Jeffries, "The White Reaction Study," in *The Los Angeles Riots: A Socio-Psychological Study*, ed. N. Cohen (New York: Praeger Publishers, 1970), pp. 480–501; Sears and McConahay, *The Politics of Violence*.

15 See T. M. Tomlinson and David Sears, "Negro Attitudes Toward the Riot," in *The Los Angeles Riots*, pp. 288–325

16 *Los Angeles Sentinel*, August 19, 1965: A1.

17 *Los Angeles Times*, August 29, 1965: G6.

18 For an excellent history of the *Los Angeles Times*, see Gottlieb and Wolt, *Thinking Big*. A similarly comprehensive history of the *Chicago Tribune* does not exist, although some very good historical material can be found in a special 150th anniversary edition of the *Chicago Tribune* (June 8, 1997). I thank Michele Katz for bringing this issue to my attention.

19 *Chicago Tribune*, August 15, 1965: A2.

20 *Ibid.*, August 18, 1965: A2.

21 *Ibid.*, August 21, 1965: A10.

22 *Ibid.*, August 14, 1965: A1.

23 *Ibid.*, August 15, 1965: A2.

24 *Ibid.*, August 17, 1965: A1.

25 *Ibid.*, August 15, 1965: A3.
26 *Chicago Defender*, September 4, 1965: A2.
27 Houston Baker, "Critical Memory and the Public Sphere," *Public Culture*, 7 (1994): 3–33
28 *Chicago Defender*, August 28, 1965: A1.
29 *Ibid.*, August 21, 1965: A5.
30 *Ibid.*, September 4, 1965, A10.
31 *Ibid.*, August 21, 1965: A1.
32 E.g., *New York Times*, August 15, 1965: A1; August 18, 1965: A20.
33 *New York Times*, August 24, 1965: A1.
34 *Ibid.*, August 17, 1991: A32.
35 *New York Amsterdam News*, August 21, 1965: A14.
36 *Ibid.*, A2.
37 News routines have been studied extensively in sociological literature. Exemplary studies include Fishman, *Manufacturing the News*, pp. 35–75; Miller, "Official Sources and 'Primary Definition'," pp. 385–406; Harvey Molotch and Marilyn Lester, "News as Purposive Behavior: On the Strategic Use of Routine Events, Accidents, and Scandals," *American Sociological Review* 39 (1974): 101–112; Tuchman, *Making News*, pp. 28–50; Jacobs, "Producing the News, Producing the Crisis," pp. 377–385
38 *Chicago Defender*, December 18, 1965: A10.
39 *New York Times*, December 7, 1965: A26; December 8, 1965: A46.
40 *Los Angeles Times*, September 17, 1965: B1.
41 *Ibid.*, September 21, 1965: A24.
42 *Ibid.*, September 29, 1965: A26.
43 *Ibid.*, November 2, 1965: B1.
44 *Ibid.*, December 1, 1965: B4.
45 *Ibid.*, December 7, 1965: B4.
46 *Ibid.*, December 10, 1965: B4.
47 Tomlinson and Sears, "Negro Attitudes Toward the Riot."
48 Howard Omi and Michael Winant, *Racial Formation in the United States* (New York: Routledge, 1994), p. 91.
49 *Ibid.*, p. 201.

Chapter 4: The Rodney King beating

1 Sonenshein, *Politics in Black and White*, pp. 210–212.
2 See Jewelle Taylor Gibbs, *Race and Justice: Rodney King and O. J. Simpson in a House Divided* (San Francisco, CA: Jossey-Bass Publishers, 1996), pp. 18–21.
3 "Report of the Independent Commission on the Los Angeles Police Department," 1991.
4 *Los Angeles Times*, March 6, 1991: A22.
5 *Ibid.*, March 9, 1991: B7.
6 While there was not an explicit connection, the implication here was that

Chicago represented the community form of spatial organization, as compared to Los Angeles's mass society form. In fact, an August 1991 opinion poll conducted by the *Tribune* during that same year had reported that Chicago was a city of tightly-knit communities, where most residents were very satisfied and content with the communities in which they lived.

7 *Chicago Tribune*, March 24, 1991: A1.

8 *New York Times*, March 18, 1991: B7.

9 *Ibid.*, March 16, 1991: A22.

10 *Chicago Tribune*, March 23, 1991: A14.

11 *New York Times*, March 26, 1991: A14.

12 *Los Angeles Sentinel*, March 7, 1991: A8.

13 Frye, *Anatomy of Criticism*, pp. 36–37, 282–287.

14 On civil society and the "drama of democracy," see Sherwood, "Narrating the Social."

15 *Los Angeles Times*, March 14, 1991: B5

16 Paul Ricoeur, *The Symbolism of Evil* (Boston, MA: Beacon Press, 1967), p. 313.

17 *Los Angeles Sentinel*, March 7, 1991: A1

18 *Ibid.*, March 14, 1991: A5.

19 E.g., *Chicago Defender*, May 18, 1991: A16.

20 *New York Amsterdam News*, March 30, 1991: A28.

21 Victor Turner, *Dramas, Fields and Metaphors*, pp. 39–41.

22 The role of blocking characters in comedy is discussed by Frye, who notes that "the blocking characters are more often reconciled or converted than simply repudiated. Comedy often includes a scapegoat ritual of expulsion which gets rid of some irreconcilable character, but exposure and disgrace makes for pathos, or even tragedy." Frye, *Anatomy of Criticism*, p. 165.

23 See, for example, articles in the *Los Angeles Times*, March 26, 1991: A1, A19; April 3, 1991: A10.

24 *New York Times*, March 16, 1991: A8.

25 *Los Angeles Times*, April 3, 1991: A1.

26 *Ibid.*, A10.

27 *Ibid.*, April 6, 1991: A1.

28 *Ibid.*, April 5, 1991: A23.

29 Melanie Lomax, quoted in *Los Angeles Times*, April 5, 1991: A1.

30 *Los Angeles Times*, April 6, 1991: A1.

31 *Ibid.*, April 1, 1991: A13.

32 *Ibid.*, March 29, 1991: B6.

33 Frye, *Anatomy of Criticism*, p. 235.

34 *Los Angeles Sentinel*, April 4, 1991: A1; April 11, 1991: A6; May 16, 1991: A6.

35 *Ibid.*, April 11, 1991: A7; April 18, 1991: A1,A7; April 25, 1991: A1,A16; May 2, 1991: A1,A14; May 9, 1991: A1; May 16, 1991: A1; May 23, 1991: A1; June 13, 1991: A1.

36 *Los Angeles Sentinel*, April 11, 1991: A6.

37 Sonenshein, *Politics in Black and White*, p. 213.

38 *Chicago Tribune*, April 5, 1991: A26.
39 *New York Times*, April 11, 1991: A20.
40 *New York Amsterdam News*, April 20, 1991: A13.
41 *Los Angeles Times*, April 11, 1991: A10.
42 "Report of the Independent Commission on the Los Angeles Police Department."
43 See Victor Turner, *The Ritual Process* (Chicago: Aldine, 1969).
44 *Los Angeles Sentinel*, July 11, 1991:A6.
45 *Ibid.*
46 *Ibid.*, A15.
47 *Ibid.*, July 18, 1991:A1.
48 *Chicago Tribune*, July 13, 1991: A20.
49 *Ibid.*, July 23, 1991: A9.
50 *New York Times*, July 12, 1991: A6.
51 *Ibid.*, September 10, 1991: A1; *ABC News*, September 20, 1991.
52 *New York Times*, July 11, 1991: A21.

Chapter 5: Rodney King 1992

1 Omi and Winant, "The Los Angeles 'Race Riot' and Contemporary U.S. Politics," in *Reading Rodney King, Reading Urban Uprising*, ed. R. Gooding-Williams (New York: Routledge, 1993), pp. 97–116.
2 Jerry Watts, "Reflections on the Rodney King Verdict and the Paradoxes of the Black Response," in *Reading Rodney King*, pp. 236–248.
3 West, *Race Matters*, p. 4.
4 See Wacquant, "The Ghetto, The State, and the New Capitalist Economy," p. 437.
5 Officers Briseno, Koon, and Wind were found not guilty on all counts; Officer Powell was found guilty on one count of excessive force.
6 This point was brought to my attention by Susan Douglas.
7 *Los Angeles Times*, May 5, 1992: A9.
8 See Lawrence Bobo, Camille Zubrinski, James Johnson, Jr. and Melvin Oliver, "Public Opinion Before and After a Spring of Discontent," in *The Los Angeles Riots: Lessons for the Urban Future*, ed. M. Baldassare (Boulder, CO: Westview Press, 1994), p. 111.
9 *New York Times*, May 3, 1992: A26.
10 *Los Angeles Times*, April 30, 1992: A1; *New York Times*, April 30, 1992: A1.
11 *Los Angeles Times*, April 30, 1992: A23.
12 *New York Times*, May 1, 1992: A23.
13 See *Los Angeles Times*, May 6, 1992: A1; *New York Times*, May 3, 1992: A6.
14 E.g., *New York Times*, May 8, 1992: A30; *Los Angeles Times*, April 30, 1992: A22.
15 E.g., *Los Angeles Times*, April 30, 1992: A1; *Chicago Tribune*, April 30, 1992: A20; *ABC News*, April 29, 1992.
16 E.g., *Los Angeles Times*, April 30, 1992: A23; May 6, 1992: A1; *Chicago*

Tribune, May 3, 1992: A1; *New York Times*, May 1, 1992: A23; May 2, 1992: A10; *ABC News*, April 30, 1992.

17 E.g., *Los Angeles Times*, May 3, 1992: M5; *New York Times*, May 8, 1992: A30.

18 E.g., *Chicago Defender*, May 2, 1992: A3; May 23, 1992: A12; *Los Angeles Sentinel*, May 21, 1992: A6; *New York Amsterdam News*, May 9, 1992: A6; May 16, 1992: A13; May 23, 1992: A13.

19 *New York Amsterdam News*, April 4, 1992: A4; April 25, 1992: A4; *Los Angeles Sentinel*, April 2, 1992: A6.

20 *ABC News*, May 7, 1992.

21 *New York Amsterdam News*, May 9, 1992: A6.

22 Oliver, Johnson and Farrell, "Anatomy of a Rebellion," p. 119.

23 *Chicago Defender*, May 2, 1992: A13.

24 *Los Angeles Sentinel*, April 30, 1992: A7.

25 On moral panics and the deployment of deviance, see Kai Erikson, *Wayward Puritans: A Study in the Sociology of Deviance* (New York: Wiley, 1966), pp. 27–29; Eric Goode and Nachmen Ben-Yehuda, "Moral Panics: Culture, Politics, and Social Construction," *Annual Review of Sociology* 20 (1994): 149–171.

26 *Los Angeles Times*, May 1, 1992: A1; *Chicago Tribune*, May 1, 1992: A10.

27 *New York Times*, May 1, 1992: A20.

28 *ABC News*, May 3, 1992.

29 *Chicago Tribune*, May 11, 1992: A11; *Los Angeles Times*, May 6, 1992: B8; *New York Times*, May 8, 1992: A19.

30 *New York Times*, May 6, 1992: A23; *Los Angeles Times*, May 2, 1992: A10.

31 *Los Angeles Times*, May 1, 1992: B7; May 6, 1992: B9; *ABC News*, May 4, 1992.

32 Frye wrote that "in tragedy the *cognitio* is normally the recognition of the inevitability of a causal sequence of time, and the forebodings and ironic anticipations surrounding it are based on a sense of cyclical return . . . The extraordinary treatment of the tragic vision of time by Nietzsche's Zarathustra, in which the heroic acceptance of cyclical return becomes a glumly cheerful acceptance of a cosmology of identical recurrence, marks the influence of an age of irony." Frye, *Anatomy of Criticism*, p. 214.

33 See *Chicago Defender*, May 9, 1992: A47; *New York Amsterdam News*, May 9, 1992: A26; *Los Angeles Sentinel*, June 11, 1992: A6.

34 *New York Amsterdam News*, June 27, 1992: A5.

35 *New York Times*, May 2, 1992: A9; *Los Angeles Times*, May 2, 1992: A4; *Chicago Tribune*, May 1, 1992: A1.

36 *Los Angeles Times*, May 5, 1992: A9.

37 *New York Times*, May 11, 1992: B7.

38 *New York Times*, May 7, 1992: A1.

39 *Chicago Defender*, May 14, 1992: A14.

40 *Chicago Defender*, May 16, 1992: A18.

41 *ABC News*, May 4, 1992.

42 *Chicago Tribune*, May 1, 1992: A5.

43 E.g., *Ibid.*, May 6, 1992: A29; May 10, 1992: D3.

44 *Ibid.*, May 31, 1992: D1.

45 *Ibid.*, May 17, 1992: D4.

46 *Ibid.*, May 17, 1992: D4; May 31, 1992: D1; June 21, 1992: C1.

47 See Darnell Hunt, *Screening the Los Angeles 'Riots': Race, Resistance, and Seeing* (Cambridge University Press, 1997), pp. 53–123.

48 *Chicago Tribune*, August 12, 1992: A12.

49 *Ibid.*, August 10, 1992: A5.

50 *Los Angeles Times*, August 29, 1992: B7.

51 This theme about an unbridgeable racial gap continued after the release of verdicts in both trials. According to Gibbs, the split verdicts in the federal trial against the Los Angeles police officers reinforced "yet again, the lingering suspicion that factors beyond the evidence and outside the law had influenced the jury's deliberations – factors of race, of riots, of reconciliation." Likewise, "the visceral responses to the verdicts in the Denny assault trial again revealed the deep schisms among blacks and whites in their views of the American criminal justice system." Gibbs, *Race and Justice*, pp. 91, 106.

52 *Los Angeles Sentinel*, June 4, 1992: A6.

53 *Ibid.*, May 7, 1992: A6.

54 *Ibid.*, May 14, 1992: A1; May 21, 1992: A1. Mainstream press coverage of the gang truce, which never emphasized the theme of African-American unity or empowerment, grew increasingly negative as memories of the Simi Valley jury grew more distant. During the same *ABC News* program in which Ted Koppel interviewed Los Angeles gang members, calling them "impressive" and "likeable," he described the cause of the gang truce as being a "common enemy" (*ABC News*, April 30, 1992). Early reports in the *Chicago Tribune* (May 8, 1992: A15) reported that the Los Angeles gangs had used the uprisings to steal guns and police uniforms, and that the truce was motivated by a desire to kill police officers. Twelve weeks later, with the gang truce still in effect, *ABC News* reported that "the fragile peace has lasted longer than almost everyone, including the gangs, thought possible"; the report ended with the conclusion that the truce was probably "too good to be true" and that residents in inner-city neighborhoods "can only hope the gangsters do not become bored with peace" (*ABC News*, July 29, 1992). By October 21, *ABC News* was reporting that the gang truce had not really been a success, because the drop in gang-related murders corresponded with a rise in gang-related robberies and assaults, and with an increase in violence between black and Latino gangs.

55 *Los Angeles Sentinel*, June 4, 1992: A7. The *New York Amsterdam News* also made a similar complaint about media coverage of black-Korean relations.

56 See, for example, *Los Angeles Sentinel*, May 21, 1992: A7.

57 *Ibid.*, May 28, 1992: B6.

58 *Los Angeles Times*, September 10, 1992: B1.

59 Quoted in *Los Angeles Times*, October 22, 1992: A1.
60 See, for example, *New York Times*, October 18, 1992: A32; *Los Angeles Times*, October 22, 1992: A1; *Los Angeles Sentinel*, November 12, 1992: A17.
61 *New York Times*, June 27, 1992: A6; *Los Angeles Times*, July 1, 1992: B2; October 18, 1992: M3; *Los Angeles Sentinel*, August 13, 1992: A3; October 8, 1992: A3.
62 For a more detailed account of the events leading up to the O. J. Simpson trial, see Gibbs, *Race and Justice*, pp. 140–148.
63 *Ibid.*, 143–145.
64 *Los Angeles Sentinel*, June 23, 1994: A1.
65 Gibbs, *Race and Justice*, pp. 200–201.
66 *New York Times*, October 5, 1995: B18.
67 Gibbs, *Race and Justice*, pp. 209–216.
68 *Ibid.*, p. 216.
69 *Los Angeles Sentinel*, November 1, 1995: A7.
70 *Ibid.*, October 18, 1995: A12; *New York Amsterdam News*, October 7, 1995: A12.
71 *New York Times*, October 6, 1995: A31.

Conclusion

1 On the interests that newspapers have in urban growth, see Logan and Molotch, *Urban Fortunes*, pp. 70–73.
2 Personal correspondence with Michele Katz, February 1997.
3 On the propaganda model of ideology, see Edward Herman and Noam Chomsky, *Manufacturing Consent* (New York: Pantheon, 1988), pp. 1–35.
4 Graeme Turner, *Film as Social Practice* (New York: Routledge, 1993), p. 147.
5 Friedrich Nietzsche, "The Birth of Tragedy," in *The Birth of Tragedy and The Geneology of Morals*, trans. F. Golffing (New York: Anchor Books, 1956), p. 143.
6 *Ibid.*, esp. pp. 102–104.
7 Durkheim, *The Elementary Forms of the Religious Life*, pp. 474–475.
8 See Max Weber, "The Social Psychology of World Religions," in *From Max Weber: Essays in Sociology*, ed. H. H. Gerth and C. W. Mills (New York: Oxford University Press, 1946), esp. pp. 285–290.
9 On the problems with romantic discourse, see Jacobs and Smith, "Romance, Irony and Solidarity," pp. 68–70
10 Hayden White, *Tropics of Discourse* (Baltimore, MD: Johns Hopkins University Press, 1978), pp. 128–129; Ricoeur, *The Symbolism of Evil*, p. 313.
11 Parsons, *The System of Modern Societies*, p. 12.
12 *Los Angeles Sentinel*, September 27, 1995: A1.

Bibliography

Abbott, Andrew. "From Causes to Events: Notes on Narrative Positivism," *Sociological Methods and Research* 20, 4 1992: 428–455.

"Transcending General Linear Reality," *Sociological Theory* 6 1988: 169–186.

Alexander, Jeffrey C. "Civil Society I, II, III: Constructing an Empirical Concept from Normative Controversies and Historical Transformations," in *Real Civil Societies: Dilemmas of Institutionalization.* London: Sage, 1998, pp. 1–19.

"Modern, Anti, Post, Neo: How Social Theories Have Tried to Understand the 'New World' of 'Our Time'," *Zeitschrift fur Soziologie*, 23, 3 (1994): 165–197.

"Citizen and Enemy as Symbolic Classification: On the Polarizing Discourse of Civil Society," in *Where Culture Talks: Exclusion and the Making of Society,* ed. Marcel Fournier and Michele Lamont. Chicago, IL: University of Chicago Press, 1992, pp. 289–308.

"Bringing Democracy Back In: Universalistic Solidarity and the Civil Sphere," in *Intellectuals and Politics: Social Theory in a Changing World*, ed. C. Lemert. Newbury Park, CA: Sage, 1991, pp. 157–176.

Action and its Environments. New York: Columbia University Press, 1988.

Alexander, Jeffrey C. and Philip Smith. "The Discourse of American Civil Society: A New Proposal for Cultural Studies." *Theory and Society*, 22 (1993): 151–207.

Anderson, Benedict. *Imagined Communities: Reflections on the Origin and Spread of Nationalism.* London: Verso, 1983.

Anderson, Susan. "A City Called Heaven: Black Enchantment and Despair in Los Angeles," in *The City: Los Angeles and Urban Theory at the End of the Twentieth Century*, ed. Allen Scott and Edward Soja. Berkeley, CA: University of California Press, 1996, pp. 336–364.

Ansolabehere, Stephen, Roy Behr and Shanto Iyengar. *The Media Game: American Politics in the Media Age*. New York: Macmillan, 1993.

Baker, Houston A., Jr. "Critical Memory and the Public Sphere," *Public Culture*, 7 (1994): 3–33.

Baker, Keith. "Defining the Public Sphere in Eighteenth-Century France: Variations on a Theme by Habermas," in *Habermas and the Public Sphere*, ed. C. Calhoun. Cambridge, MA: MIT Press, 1992, pp. 181–211.

Bekken, Jon. "The Working-Class Press at the Turn of the Century," in *Ruthless Criticism: New Perspectives in U. S. Communication History*, ed. W. Solomon and R. McChesney. Minneapolis, MN: University of Minnesota Press, 1993, pp.151–175.

Bell, Howard. "National Negro Conventions of the Middle 1840s," in *The Making of Black America*, ed. A. Meier. New York: Athenum, 1969.

Benhabib, Seyla. "In the Shadow of Aristotle and Hegel: Communicative Ethics and Current Controversies in Practical Philosophy," in *Situating the Self: Gender, Community and Postmodernism in Contemporary Ethics*. New York: Routledge, 1992, pp. 23–67.

Bennett, Charles O. *Facts Without Opinion: First Fifty Years of the Audit Bureau of Circulation*. Chicago, IL: Audit Bureau of Circulations, 1965.

Berger, Meyer. *The Story of the New York Times, 1851–1951*. New York: Simon & Schuster, 1951.

Blauner, Robert. "Whitewash Over Watts: The Failure of the McCone Commission Report," in *Mass Violence in America: The Los Angeles Riots*, ed. R. Fogelson. New York: Arno Press and the New York Times, 1969 (1966), pp. 165–188.

Bobo, Lawrence, Camille Zubrinski, James Johnson, Jr., and Melvin Oliver. "Public Opinion Before and After a Spring of Discontent," in *The Los Angeles Riots: Lessons for the Urban Future*, ed. M. Baldassare. Boulder, CO: Westview Press, 1994, pp. 103–134.

Bogart, Leo. *Press and Public*, 2nd ed. Hillsdale, NJ: Lawrence Ehrlbaum Associates, 1989.

"The State of the Industry," in *The Future of News*, ed. P. Cook, D. Gomery and L. Lichty. Baltimore, MD: Johns Hopkins University Press, 1992.

Bracey, John H., Jr., August Meier and Elliot Rudwick, eds. *Black Nationalism in America*. New York: Bobbs-Merill, 1970.

Brubaker, Rogers. *Citizenship and Nationhood in France and Germany*. Cambridge, MA: Harvard University Press, 1992.

Bunch, Lonnie. "A Past Not Necessarily Prologue: The Afro-American in Los Angeles," in *20th Century Los Angeles: Power, Promotion, and Social Conflict*, N. Klein and M. Schiesl, eds., Claremont, CA: Regina Books, 1990, pp. 101–130.

Calhoun, Craig. "Civil Society and the Public Sphere," *Public Culture* 5 (1993): 267–280.

"Indirect Relationships and Imagined Communities: Large-Scale Social Integration and the Transformation of Everyday Life," in *Social Theory for a Changing Society*, ed. P. Bourdieu and J. S. Coleman, Boulder, CO: Westview Press, 1991, pp. 95–121.

Cohen, Jean and Andrew Arato. *Civil Society and Political Theory*. Cambridge, MA: MIT Press, 1992.

Crane, Diana. "Reconceptualizing the Public Sphere: The Electronic Media and the Public," in *Gessellschaften im Umbau*, ed. C. Honegger, J. Gabriel, R. Hirsig, J. Pfaff-Czarnacka, and E. Poglia. Berne: Seismo, 1995, pp. 175–195.

Dahlgren, Peter. "What's the Meaning of This? Viewers Plural Sense Making of TV News," *Media, Culture & Society* 10 (1988): 285–307.

Darnton, Robert. "Writing News and Telling Stories," *Daedalus*, 104, 2 (1975):175–193.

Dayan, Daniel and Elihu Katz. *Media Events*. Cambridge, MA: Harvard University Press, 1992.

Dearing, James. "Setting the Polling Agenda for the Issue of AIDS," *Public Opinion Quarterly*, 53 (1989): 309–329.

Drake, St. Clair and Horace R. Cayton. *Black Metropolis: A Study of Negro Life in a Northern City*. Chicago, IL: University of Chicago Press, 1993 (1945).

Durkheim, Emile. *The Elementary Forms of the Religious Life*. New York: The Free Press, 1965.

Eco, Umberto. *Six Walks in the Fictional Woods*. Cambridge, MA: Harvard University Press, 1994.

Eley, Geoff. "Nations, Publics, and Political Cultures: Placing Habermas in the Nineteenth Century," in *Habermas and the Public Sphere*, ed. C. Calhoun. Cambridge, MA: MIT Press, 1992, pp. 289–339

Ericson, Richard, Patricia Baranek and Janet Chan, *Negotiating Control: A Study of News Sources*. Toronto: University of Toronto Press.

Erikson, Kai. *Wayward Puritans: A Study in the Sociology of Deviance*. New York: Wiley, 1966.

Fishman, Mark. *Manufacturing the News*. Austin, TX: University of Texas Press, 1980.

Fogelson, Robert. "White on Black: A Critique of the McCone Commission Report on the Los Angeles Riots," in *Mass Violence in America: The Los Angeles Riots*, ed. R. Fogelson. New York: Arno Press and the *New York Times*, 1969 [1967], pp. 111–145.

   The Fragmented Metropolis: Los Angeles, 1850–1930. Berkeley and Los Angeles: University of California Press, 1967.

Folkerts, Jean. "From the Heartland," in *The Future of News*, ed. P. Cook, D. Gomery, and L. Lichty. Baltimore, MD: Johns Hopkins University Press, 1992.

Franklin, John Hope. *From Slavery to Freedom: A History of American Negroes*. New York: Alfred A. Knopf, 1948.

Franklin, V. P. *Black Self-Determination*. Westport, CT: Lawrence Hill & Co., 1984.

Fraser, Nancy. "Rethinking the Public Sphere: A Contribution to the Critique of Actually Existing Democracy," in *Habermas and the Public Sphere*, ed. C. Calhoun, Cambridge, MA: MIT Press, 1992, pp. 109–142.

Frazier, E. Franklin. *The Negro in the United States*. New York: MacMillan, 1949.

Frye, Northrup. *Anatomy of Criticism*. Princeton, NJ: Princeton University Press, 1957.

Gamson, Joshua. *Freaks Talk Back: Tabloid Talk Shows and Sexual Nonconformity*. Chicago, IL: University of Chicago Press, 1998.

Gamson, William. *Talking Politics*. Cambridge University Press, 1992.

Gans, Herbert. *Deciding What's News*. New York: Vintage, 1979.

Garnham, Nicholas. *Capitalism and Communication: Global Culture and the Economics of Information*. London: Sage Publications, 1990.

Garvey, Marcus. *Philosophy and Opinions of Marcus Garvey*, vol. 2., ed. A. Jacques-Garvey. New York: Universal Publishing House, 1923.

Gates, Henry Louis, Jr., ed. *The Classic Slave Narratives*, New York: Penguin, 1987.

Gellner, Ernest. "The Importance of Being Modular," in *Civil Society: Theory, History, Comparison*, ed. J. Hall. Cambridge: Polity Press, 1995, pp. 32–55.

Gibbs, Jewelle Taylor. *Race and Justice: Rodney King and O. J. Simpson in a House Divided*. San Francisco, CA: Jossey-Bass Publishers, 1996.

Gist, N. P. "The Negro in the Daily Press," *Social Forces*, 10 (1932): 405–411.

Gitlin, Todd. *The Whole World is Watching: Mass Media in the Making and*

Unmaking of the New Left. Berkeley, CA: University of California Press, 1980.

Goode, Eric and Nachmen Ben-Yehuda. "Moral Panics: Culture, Politics, and Social Construction," *Annual Review of Sociology* 20 (1994): 149–171.

Gottlieb, Robert and Irene Wolt. *Thinking Big: The Story of the Los Angeles Times*. New York: Putnam, 1977.

Graber, Doris A. *Mass Media and American Politics*, 4th ed. Washington, DC: Congressional Quarterly, Inc., 1993.

Greenstone, J. David and Paul Peterson. *Race and Authority in Urban Politics*. New York: Russell Sage, 1973.

Habermas, Jurgen. "Further Reflections on the Public Sphere," in *Habermas and the Public Sphere*, ed. C. Calhoun. Cambridge, MA: MIT Press, 1992, pp. 421–461.

   The Structural Transformation of the Public Sphere, transl. Thomas Burger. Cambridge, MA: MIT Press, 1989 (1962).

Hall, Stuart. "Encoding/Decoding," in *Culture, Media, Language*. London: Hutchinson, 1980.

Harding, Vincent. *There is a River: The Black Struggle for Freedom in America*. New York: Harcourt Brace Jovanovich, 1981.

Hart, Jack. *The Information Age: The Rise of the Los Angeles Times and the Times Mirror Corporation*. Washington, DC: University Press of America, 1981.

Hart, Janet. "Cracking the Code: Narrative and Political Mobilization in the Greek Resistance," *Social Science History* 16, 4 (1992): 631–668.

Herman, Edward and Noam Chomsky. *Manufacturing Consent*. New York: Pantheon, 1988.

Hirschman, Albert O. *The Rhetoric of Reaction*. Cambridge, MA: Harvard University Press, 1991.

Hunt, Darnell. *Screening the Los Angeles 'riots': Race, Resistance, and Seeing*. Cambridge University Press, 1997.

Iyengar, Shanto and Donald Kinder. *News That Matters: Agenda-Setting and Priming in a Television Age*. Chicago, IL: University of Chicago Press, 1987.

Jacobs, Ronald N. "Producing the News, Producing the Crisis: Narrativity, Television, and News Work," *Media, Culture and Society*, 18, 3 (1996): 373–397.

   "The Racial Discourse of Civil Society: The Rodney King Affair and the City of Los Angeles," in *Real Civil Societies: Dilemmas of Institutionalization*, ed. J. Alexander. London and Thousand Oaks, CA: Sage Publications, 1998, pp. 138–161.

Jacobs, Ronald and Philip Smith. "Romance, Irony, and Solidarity," *Sociological Theory* 15, 1 (1997): 60–80.

Jensen, Klaus B.. "Reception Analysis: Media Communication as the Social Production of Meaning," in *A Handbook of Qualitative Methodologies for Mass Communication Research*, ed. K. Jensen and N. Jankowski. London: Routledge, 1991, pp. 135–148.

Johnson, Paula, David Sears and John McConahay. "Black Invisibility, the Press, and the Los Angeles Riot," *American Journal of Sociology* 76 (1971): 698–721

Kadushin, Charles. *The American Intellectual Elite*. Boston, MA: Little Brown & Co., 1974.

Kane, Anne. "Culture and Social Change: Symbolic Construction, Ideology, and Political Alliance During the Irish Land War, 1879–1881." Unpublished doctoral dissertation, 1994.

Katz, Elihu and Paul Lazarsfeld. *Personal Influence*. Glencoe, IL: The Free Press, 1955.

Keane, John. *Public Life and Late Capitalism: Toward a Socialist Theory of Democracy*. Cambridge: Cambridge University Press, 1984.

  The Media and Democracy. Cambridge: Polity Press, 1991.

  "Structural Transformations of the Public Sphere," *The Communication Review*, 1, 1 (1995): 1–22.

Kilson, Marion D. "Towards Freedom: An Analysis of Slave Revolts in the United States," in *The Making of Black America*, ed. A. Meier. New York: Athenum, 1969, pp. 165–178.

Landes, Joan. *Women and the Public Sphere in the Age of the French Revolution*, Ithaca, NY: Cornell University Press, 1988.

Lee, James M. *History of American Journalism*. Garden City, NY: Garden City Publishing, 1923.

Levine, Lawrence. *Black Culture and Black Consciousness: Afro-American Folk Thought From Slavery to Freedom*. New York: Oxford University Press, 1977.

Lewis, David Levering, ed. *Harlem Renaissance Reader*. New York: Viking, 1994.

Lewis, Justin. "The Meaning of Things: Audiences, Ambiguity, and Power," in *Viewing, Reading, Listening: Audiences and Cultural Reception*, ed. J. Cruz and J. Lewis. Boulder, CO: Westview Press, 1994, pp. 19–32.

Lieberson, Stanley. *A Piece of the Pie: Blacks and White Immigrants Since 1880*. Berkeley, CA: University of California Press, 1980.

Liebes, Tamar and Elihu Katz. *The Export of Meaning: Cross-Cultural Readings of Dallas*. New York: Oxford University Press, 1990.

Locke, Alain. *The New Negro*. New York: Johnson, 1968 (1925).

Logan, John and Harvey Molotch. *Urban Fortunes: The Political Economy of Place*. Berkeley and Los Angeles: University of California Press, 1987.

Long, Elizabeth. "Textual Interpretation as Collective Action," in *Viewing, Reading, Listening: Audiences and Cultural Reception*, ed. J. Cruz and J. Lewis. Boulder, CO: Westview Press, 1994.

MacKuen, Michael B. and Steven L. Coombs. *More Than News: Media Power in Public Affairs*. Beverly Hills, CA: Sage Publications, 1981.

Maltby, Ian and Richard Craven. *Hollywood Cinema*. Cambridge, MA: Blackwell Press, 1995.

Martin, Tony. *Literary Garveyism: Garvey, Black Arts and the Harlem Renaissance*. Dover, MA: The Majority Press, 1983.

Martindale, Carolyn. *The White Press and Black America*. New York: Greenwood Press, 1986.

Massey, Douglas and Nancy A. Denton. *American Apartheid: Segregation and the Making of the Underclass*. Cambridge, MA: Harvard University Press, 1993.

Massey, Douglas and Zoltan Hajnal. "The Changing Geographic Structure of Black-White Segregation in the United States," *Social Science Quarterly*, 76, 3 (1993): 527–542.

McCombs, Maxwell and Donald Shaw. "The Agenda-Setting Function of the Press," *Public Opinion Quarterly*, 36 (1972): 176–187.

The Emergence of American Political Issues: The Agenda-Setting Function of the Mass Media. St. Paul, MN: West Publishing, 1977.

McCone, John. "Violence in the City – An End or a Beginning? A Report by the Governor's Commission on the Los Angeles Riots." Los Angeles, 1965.

Miller, David. "Official Sources and 'primary definition': the case of Northern Ireland," *Media, Culture and Society*, 15 (1993): 385–406.

Molotch, Harvey and Marilyn Lester. "News as Purposive Behavior: On the Strategic Use of Routine Events, Accidents, and Scandals," *American Sociological Review*, 39 (1974): 101–112.

Morley, David. *The Nationwide Audience: Structure and Decoding*. London: British Film Institute, 1980.

Family Television: Cultural Power and Domestic Leisure. London: Comedia, 1986.

Morris, Richard and Vincent Jeffries. "The White Reaction Study," in *The Los Angeles Riots: A Socio-Psychological Study*, ed. N. Cohen. New York: Praeger Publishers, 1970, pp. 480–501.

Myrdal, Gunnar. *An American Dilemma: The Negro Problem and Modern Democracy*. New York: Harper and Row, 1944.

Nietzsche, Friedrich. "The Birth of Tragedy," in *The Birth of Tragedy and*

The Geneology of Morals, transl. F. Golffing. New York: Anchor Books, 1956, pp. 1–146.

Oliver, Melvin, James Johnson, Jr., and Walter Farrell, Jr. "Anatomy of a Rebellion: A Political-Economic Analysis," in *Reading Rodney King, Reading Urban Uprising*, ed. R. Gooding-Williams. New York: Routledge, 1993, pp. 117–141.

Omi, Michael and Howard Winant. *Racial Formation in the United States*. New York: Routledge, 1994.

"The Los Angeles 'Race Riot' and Contemporary U.S. Politics," in *Reading Rodney King, Reading Urban Uprising*, ed. R. Gooding-Williams. New York: Routledge, 1993, pp. 97–116.

Osofsky, Gilbert. *Harlem: The Making of a Ghetto*. New York: Harper & Row, 1963.

Oxhorn, Philip. "From Controlled Inclusion to Coerced Marginalization: The Struggle for Civil Society in Latin America," in *Civil Society: Theory, History, Comparison*, ed. J. Hall. Cambridge: Polity Press, 1995, pp. 250–277.

Parsons, Talcott. *The System of Modern Societies*. Englewood Cliffs, NJ: Prentice-Hall, Inc., 1971.

Perez-Diaz, Victor. "The Possibility of Civil Society: Traditions, Character and Challenges," in *Civil Society: Theory, History, Comparison*, ed. J. Hall. Cambridge: Polity Press, 1995, pp. 80–109.

Polletta, Francesca. "'It was Like a Fever . . .' Narrative and Identity in Social Protest," *Social Problems*, 2 (1998): 137–159.

Press, Andrea. *Women Watching Television: Gender, Class, and Generation in the American Television Experience*. Philadelphia, PA: University of Pennsylvania Press, 1991.

Price, Monroe E. *Television, the Public Sphere, and National Identity*. Oxford: Clarendon Press, 1995.

Pride, Armistead S. and Clint C. Wilson. *A History of the Black Press*. Washington, D. C. Howard University Press, 1997.

Ricoeur, Paul. *The Symbolism of Evil*. Boston, MA: Beacon Press, 1967.

Russworm, John. "Too Long Have Others Spoken For Us," in *Black Nationalism in America*, ed. J. Bracey, A. Meier and E. Rudwick. New York: Bobbs-Merrill, 1970 (1827), p. 24.

Rustin, Bayard. "The Watts 'Manifesto' and the McCone Report," in *Mass Violence in America: The Los Angeles Riots*, ed. R. Fogelson. New York: Arno Press and the *New York Times*, 1969 (1966), pp. 145–164.

Ryan, Mary. "Gender and Public Access: Women's Politics in Nineteenth-Century America," in *Habermas and the Public Sphere*, ed. C. Calhoun. Cambridge, MA: MIT Press, 1992, pp. 259–288.

Scannell, Paddy. "Public Service Broadcasting and Modern Public Life," *Media, Culture and Society*, 1 (1989): 135–166.

"Media Events," *Media, Culture and Society* 17 (1995): 151–157.

Scott, Allen. *Technopolis: High Technology Industry and Regional Development in Southern California*. Berkeley, CA: University of California Press, 1993.

Schudson, Michael. *Discovering the News*. New York: Basic Books, 1978.

"The Politics of Narrative Form: The Emergence of News Conventions in Print and Television," *Daedalus*, 1982, pp. 97–112.

The Power of News. Cambridge, MA: Harvard University Press, 1995.

Sears, David and John McConahay. *The Politics of Violence: The New Urban Blacks and the Watts Riot*. Boston, MA: Houghton Mifflin, 1973.

Sewell, William H. Jr. "Introduction: Narratives and Social Identities," *Social Science History* 16, 3 (1992): 479–489.

Sherwood, Steve. "Narrating the Social," *Journal of Narratives and Life Histories*, 4, 1–2 (1994): 69–88.

Sigal, Leon V. *Reporters and Officials: The Organization and Politics of Newsmaking*. Lexington, MA: D. C. Heath, 1973.

Soja, Edward. "Los Angeles 1965–1992: From Crisis-Generated Restructuring to Restructuring-Generated Crisis," in *The City: Los Angeles and Urban Theory at the End of the Twentieth Century*, ed. Allen Scott and Edward Soja. Berkeley, CA: University of California Press, 1996, pp. 426–462.

Soja, Edward and Allen Scott. "Introduction to Los Angeles: City and Region," in *The City: Los Angeles and Urban Theory at the End of the Twentieth Century*, ed. Allen Scott and Edward Soja. Berkeley, CA: University of California Press, 1996, pp. 1–21.

Somers, Margaret. "What's Political or Cultural about Political Culture and the Public Sphere? Toward an Historical Sociology of Concept Formation," *Sociological Theory*, 13, 2 (1995): 113–144.

"Narrating and Naturalizing Civil Society and Citizenship Theory: The Place of Political Culture and the Public Sphere," *Sociological Theory*, 13, 3 (1995): 229–274.

"Narrativity, Narrative Identity, and Social Action: Rethinking English Working-Class Formation," *Social Science History* 16, 4 (1992): 591–630.

Sonenshein, Raphael. *Politics in Black and White: Race and Power in Los Angeles*. Princeton, NJ: Princeton University Press, 1993.

Spear, Allan. *Black Chicago: The Making of a Negro Ghetto*. Chicago, IL: University of Chicago Press, 1967.

Spilerman, Seymour, 1967. "The Causes of Racial Disturbances: A Comparison of Alternative Explanations," *American Sociological Review*, 35, 4 (1970): 627–649.

Starr, Kevin. *Inventing the Dream: California Through the Progressive Era.* New York: Oxford University Press, 1985.

Steiner, Linda. "Nineteenth-Century Suffrage Periodicals: Conceptions of Womanhood and the Press," in *Ruthless Criticism: New Perspectives in U.S. Communication History*, ed. W. Solomon and R. McChesney. Minneapolis, MN: University of Minnesota Press, 1993, pp. 38–65.

Steinmetz, George. "Reflections on the Role of Social Narratives in Working-Class Formation: Narrative Theories in the Social Sciences," *Social Science History* 16, 3 (1992): 489–516.

Stevens, Mitchell. *A History of News.* New York: Viking Press, 1988.

Taeuber, Karl E. and Alma F. Taeuber. *Negroes in Cities: Residential Segregation and Neighborhood Change.* Chicago: Aldine, 1965.

Taylor, Charles. "Liberal Politics and the Public Sphere," in *New Communitarian Thinking: Persons, Virtues, Institutions, and Communities*, ed. A. Etzioni. Charlottesville, VA: University Press of Virginia, 1995, pp. 183–217.

Thompson, John B. *The Media and Modernity.* Stanford, CA: Stanford University Press, 1995.

Tocqueville, Alexis de. *Democracy in America.* 2 vols. New York: Doubleday, 1969.

Tolbert, Emory. *The UNIA and Black Los Angeles: Ideology and Community in the American Garvey Movement.* Los Angeles, CA: Center For Afro-American Studies, 1980.

Tomlinson, T. M. and David Sears. "Negro Attitudes Toward the Riot," in *The Los Angeles Riots: A Socio-Psychological Study*, ed. N. Cohen. New York: Praeger Publishers, 1970, pp. 288–325.

Tuchman, Gaye. *Making News: A Study in the Construction of Reality.* New York: Free Press, 1978.

Tucker, Kenneth H. *French Revolutionary Syndicalism and the Public Sphere.* Cambridge University Press, 1996.

   "Harmony and Transgression: Aesthetic Imagery and the Public Sphere in Habermas and Post-structuralism." *Current Perspectives in Social Theory*, 16 (1996): 101–120.

Turner, Graeme. *Film as Social Practice.* New York: Routledge, 1993.

Turner, Victor. *Dramas, Fields and Metaphors.* New York: Cornell University Press, 1974.

   The Ritual Process. Chicago: Aldine, 1969.

Wachs, Martin. "The Evolution of Transportation Policy in Los Angeles:

Images of Past Policies and Future Prospects," in *The City: Los Angeles and Urban Theory at the End of the Twentieth Century*, ed. Allen Scott and Edward Soja. Berkeley, CA: University of California Press, 1996, pp. 106–159.

Wacquant, Loic. "The Ghetto, the State, and the New Capitalist Economy," in *Metropolis: Center and Symbol of Our Times*, ed. P. Kasinitz. New York University Press, 1995.

Wagner-Pacifici, Robin. *Discourse and Destruction: The City of Philadelphia versus MOVE*. Chicago, IL: University of Chicago Press, 1994.

Standoff: Contingency in a Situation of Paralysis. Cambridge University Press, 1999.

Walker, Martin. *Powers of the Press: the World's Great Newspapers*. London: Quartet Books, 1982.

Watts, Jerry G. "Reflections on the Rodney King Verdict and the Paradoxes of the Black Response," in *Reading Rodney King, Reading Urban Uprising*, ed. R. Gooding-Williams. New York: Routledge, 1993, pp. 236–248.

Weaver, David H. and G. Cleveland Wilhoit. *The American Journalist in the 1990s*. Matwah, NJ: Lawrence Ehrlbaum Associates,1996.

Weber, Max. "The Social Psychology of World Religions," in *From Max Weber: Essays in Sociology*, ed. H. H. Gerth and C. W. Mills. New York: Oxford University Press, 1946, pp. 267–301.

West, Cornel. *Race Matters*. Boston, MA: Beacon Press, 1994.

White, Hayden. *Tropics of Discourse*. Baltimore, MD: Johns Hopkins University Press, 1978.

Wilson, Clint. *Black Journalists in Paradox: Historical Perspectives and Current Dilemmas*. New York: Greenwood Press, 1991.

Wilson, William Julius. *The Declining Significance of Race: Blacks and Changing American Institutions*. Chicago, IL: University of Chicago Press, 1978.

Wilson, William Julius. *The Truly Disadvantaged: The Inner City, The Underclass, and Public Policy*. Chicago, IL: University of Chicago Press, 1987.

Wolseley, Roland. *The Black Press, U.S.A.* Ames, IA: Iowa State University Press, 1990.

Index